D0878713

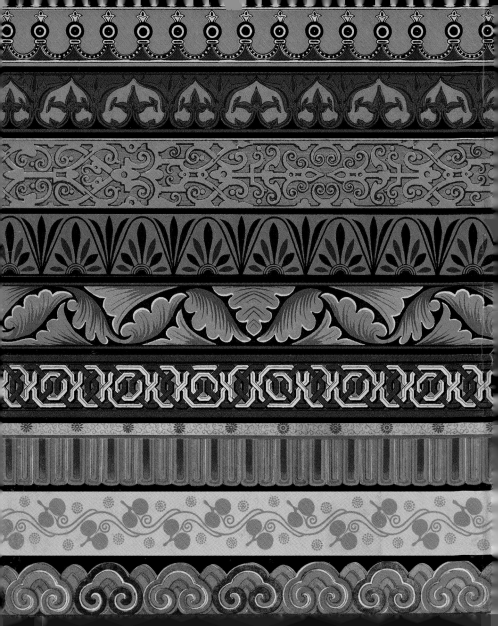

THE GRAMMAR OF
ORNAMENT

OWEN JONES

ILLUSTRATED BY EXAMPLES FROM
VARIOUS STYLES OF ORNAMENT

A Dorling Kindersley Book

LONDON, NEW YORK, SYDNEY, DELHI, PARIS,
MUNICH and JOHANNESBURG

This book was conceived, designed, and produced by
THE IVY PRESS LIMITED
The Old Candlemakers, Lewes, East Sussex BN7 2NZ

Art director: *Peter Bridgewater*
Publisher: *Sophie Collins*
DTP designer: *Ginny Zeal*
Editor: *Mandy Greenfield*

The Grammar of Ornament was first published in 1856 by Day & Son, Lincoln's Inn Fields, London

First American Edition, 2001

01 02 03 04 05 06 10 9 8 7 6 5 4 3 2 1

Published in the United States by DK Publishing, Inc.
95 Madison Avenue, New York, New York 10016

Library of Congress Cataloging-in-Publication Data

Jones, Owen, 1809–1874

The grammar of ornament/Owen Jones; illustrated by examples from various styles of ornament.
p. cm.
Includes index.
ISBN 0-7894-7646-0 (alk. paper)
1. Decoration and ornament — Themes, motives. 2. Decoration and ornament — History. I. Title
NK1510 .J7 2001
745.4—dc21
00–066020

Originated and printed in Hong Kong
by Hong Kong Graphics and Printing Ltd

See our complete
catalog at

www.dk.com

A NOTE ON THIS EDITION

This new edition of *The Grammar of Ornament* keeps Owen Jones's
original Victorian English much as it was written (and with the original English spelling),
although we have redesigned the material into a modern, compact format. It has been
necessary to reposition illustrations and to renumber the captions and cross references
accordingly. Occasionally, for reasons of space, minor deletions in the captions have been
required, but in the main Jones's text differs little from the original version published in
1856 and we have tried to keep the spirit of his classic work.

The contemporary commentaries on the left-hand pages aim to set the period
and the illustrations in context. The index is divided into two parts: references to
the original book and references to the modern commentaries.

Inevitably some place-names have changed with the passage of time. In many
cases this is simply a matter of spelling (Balbeck is now more commonly spelled Baalbek,
Aboo-simbel as Abu Simbel), but in other cases names have altered completely. For ease
of reference, the most common place-name changes are given below:

Asia Minor was the historical name for Anatolia, the Asian part of Turkey

Burma is now officially known as Myanmar

Byzantium/Constantinople = Istanbul

Edfu = Idfu

Etruria was an area roughly equivalent to present-day Tuscany

Friendly Islands = Tonga

Ispahan = Esfahan

The Low Countries = the region of Europe consisting of Belgium,
the Netherlands, and usually Luxembourg

Nineveh = Kuyunjik

Persia = Iran

Sandwich Islands = Hawaii

Savage Island = Niue

Swabia = a region in southwest Germany.

CONTENTS

INTRODUCTION

Owen Jones is a key figure in the history of British design. He was closely involved with one of the finest achievements of the Victorian age, the Great Exhibition of 1851, and was swept along by the tide of enthusiasm and confidence that it helped to generate. At the same time he shared the concerns of many of his fellow countrymen about the quality of British design. With its sumptuous illustrations, its detailed analysis of individual cultures, and its manifesto of "General Principles," *The Grammar of Ornament* was meant to redress this situation, offering guidance for the designers of the future. In this respect, the book was a great success, and it is frequently cited as one of the seminal texts of the Arts and Crafts Movement.

Owen Jones was born in London in 1809 but, as his name might suggest, he had a proud Welsh ancestry. His father—also called Owen—founded the Gwyneddigion Society of London (1770), dedicated to the study of Welsh literature and archeology, and went on to produce a much-acclaimed anthology of Welsh manuscripts. Young Owen evidently inherited his father's energy and versatility, for he would excel in a number of different fields. His first love, however, was for architecture, and he was determined to make this his profession.

At the age of 16, Jones began a six-year apprenticeship with Lewis Vulliamy (1791–1871), an eclectic and highly talented young architect. Vulliamy had recently published an influential survey of *Examples of Ornamental Sculpture in*

Architecture (1818), illustrating it with many details from European and Asian buildings. Jones coupled his architectural studies with classes at the Royal Academy, where his masters confirmed that he was a skilled draftsman, "but did not master the figure."

To supplement his studies, Jones began to travel. In 1830, he journeyed around France and Italy. Three years later he undertook a longer tour of Greece, Egypt, and Turkey. This awakened an interest in Islamic forms of architecture, which would exert a profound influence on his career. In the short term, it prompted Jones to embark upon an exhaustive survey of the Alhambra in Granada, which would become the subject of one of his most important books. The *Plans, Elevations, Sections, and Details of the Alhambra* (1836–45) was a massive undertaking, lavishly illustrated with 101 chromolithographic plates, most of them based on Jones's own drawings.

The *Alhambra* project proved a costly business, and Jones had to sell off some land that he had inherited from his father in order to finance it. On a more positive note, he decided to print the plates himself, gaining invaluable experience in the process. As a result, he became increasingly active as a graphic designer and printer. Some of his work in this field was on specialist architectural publications, but he was also employed by commercial publishers, designing a series of elegant gift books. Needless to say, Jones's intimate knowledge of the printing and publishing world came in very handy when he produced his *Grammar of Ornament.*

At the same time Jones was forging a reputation for himself in other areas of design. In the early 1840s his association with Herbert Minton (1793–1858) led him to design a wide range of tiles and mosaics. He was also busy as an architect and decorator, his most striking creations being two Moorish-style houses in London's Kensington Palace Gardens (1845–47). More importantly, perhaps, he was starting to move in distinguished circles. In particular, he joined the architectural clique that surrounded Sir Henry Cole (1808–82).

A hugely influential figure, Cole was closely involved with Prince Albert's most cherished artistic projects and would eventually become the first director of the South Kensington Museum. It was probably through his recommendation that Jones gained the prestigious appointment of joint architect of the Great

Exhibition. In this capacity, he collaborated with Joseph Paxton (1803–65) on the design of the Crystal Palace. Jones took responsibility for the interior decoration of the building and also assisted in the arrangement of the exhibits.

The Great Exhibition proved an overwhelming success. The splendor of the event was a source of immense national pride, especially since so many of the objects on show came from places under British control. Nevertheless, Cole and his colleagues were swift to admit that the quality of English design was disappointingly poor. In a lecture of 1853, for example, Jones lamented that, "We have no principles, no unity; the architect, the upholsterer, the paper-stainer, the weaver, the calico-printer and the potter, run each their independent course; each struggles fruitlessly, each produces in art novelty without beauty, or beauty without intelligence."

Immediate steps were taken to rectify this situation. Attempts were made to introduce more efficient patent laws, protecting the work of designers, and to improve standards in art colleges. In addition, Cole set up an educational program, which he hoped would demonstrate to the public—and to manufacturers, in particular—the value of an informed approach to design. Together with Jones and A. W. N. Pugin (1812–52), he formed a committee that began acquiring suitable objects for a permanent exhibition of decorative art. This "Museum of Manufactures," initially located in Marlborough House, opened its doors in 1852. In true didactic fashion, it even included a section with "Examples Illustrating False Principles in Decoration," which Charles Dickens satirized as "a House full of Horrors." In later years the Museum of Manufactures went through several name changes, becoming the Museum of Ornamental Art, the South Kensington Museum, and, finally, the Victoria and Albert Museum.

In the meantime, Jones had become involved in another, similar project. In 1852, the Crystal Palace in Hyde Park was dismantled and re-erected on a new site at Sydenham. Jones was appointed director of decorations at the revamped building, which was designed to provide a permanent showcase for the architectural styles of many different cultures. Together with Sir Matthew Digby Wyatt (1820–77) and Gottfried Semper (1803–79), he set about creating a series of "Courts," where the public could marvel at "the history of the civilization of the world . . . examining side by side portions of buildings of every age." This display was officially opened by Queen Victoria in June 1854.

The Grammar of Ornament was to provide a natural accompaniment to this project. Jones had already started to formulate his own ideas about the basic elements of design in 1851. Six of his "General Principles" appeared in a series of articles entitled *Gleanings from the Great Exhibition* (1851), and the list was expanded for lectures at the Society of Arts (1852) and Marlborough House (1852). The full set was published in a pamphlet the same year.

There was nothing radically new about manifestoes of this kind. The campaigning tone had been set in two of Pugin's earliest books, *Contrasts* (1836) and *The True Principles of Pointed or Christian Architecture* (1841), and several of Cole's colleagues produced manuals of ornament, each with its own personal creed about the principles of design. None, however, was as comprehensive or as lavishly illustrated as *The Grammar of Ornament.* In this regard, Jones's book benefited greatly from the impressive range of architectural casts that were available at Sydenham; from the long list of specialist contributors, who assisted him with the project; and from his personal knowledge of the intricacies of color printing.

The *Grammar* was published in 1856 and proved an immediate success. A review in *The Athenaeum* described it mysteriously as "beautiful enough to be the hornbook of angels." In more mundane terms, it was rapidly accepted as the definitive source book for ornamental motifs and was reprinted no fewer than nine times prior to 1910. An American edition appeared in 1880, introducing Jones's ideas to an international readership.

In its day the *Grammar* was hugely influential. William Morris (1834–96) certainly used it, and it is safe to assume that most of the main practitioners of the Arts and Crafts Movement were familiar with it. Its reputation also remained intact into the twentieth century, when Louis Sullivan (1856–1924) and Frank Lloyd Wright (1869–1959, *see page 326*) acknowledged a debt to it. Some of these figures rebelled against the rigid theorizing of Jones and his colleagues, claiming that designers should enjoy the same artistic liberty as painters, but all of them respected the scholarship, the scope, and the sheer physical beauty of one of the greatest publications of the Victorian age.

IAIN ZACZEK.
September, 2000.

PREFACE TO OWEN JONES'S ORIGINAL FOLIO EDITION

I t would be far beyond the limits of the powers of any one individual to attempt to gather together illustrations of the innumerable and ever-varying phases of Ornamental Art. It would be barely possible if undertaken by a Government, and even then it would be too voluminous to be generally useful. All, therefore, that I have proposed to myself in forming the collection which I have ventured to call the *Grammar of Ornament*, has been to select a few of the most prominent types in certain styles closely connected with each other, and in which certain general laws appeared to reign independently of the individual peculiarities of each. I have ventured to hope that, in thus bringing into immediate juxtaposition the many forms of beauty which every style of ornament presents, I might aid in arresting that unfortunate tendency of our time to be content with copying, whilst the fashion lasts, the forms peculiar to any bygone age, without attempting to ascertain, generally completely ignoring, the peculiar circumstances which rendered an ornament beautiful, because it was appropriate, and which, as expressive of other wants when thus transplanted, as entirely fails.

It is more than probable that the first result of sending forth to the world this collection will be seriously to increase this dangerous tendency, and that many will be content to borrow from the past those forms of beauty which have not already been used up *ad nauseam*. It has been my desire to arrest this tendency, and to awaken a higher ambition.

If the student will but endeavour to search out the thoughts which have been expressed in so many different languages, he may assuredly hope to find an ever-gushing fountain in place of a half-filled stagnant reservoir.

In the following chapters I have endeavoured to establish these main facts,—

First. That whenever any style of ornament commands universal admiration, it will always be found to be in accordance with the laws which regulate the distribution of form in nature.

Secondly. That however varied the manifestations in accordance with these laws, the leading ideas on which they are based are very few.

Thirdly. That the modifications and developments which have taken place from one style to another have been caused by a sudden throwing off of some fixed trammel, which set thought free for a time, till the new idea, like the old, became again fixed, to give birth in its turn to fresh inventions.

Lastly. I have endeavoured to show, in the twentieth chapter, that the future progress of Ornamental Art may be best secured by engrafting on the experience of the past the knowledge we may obtain by a return to Nature for fresh inspiration. To attempt to build up theories of art, or to form a style, independently of the past, would be an act of supreme folly. It would be at once to reject the experiences and accumulated knowledge of thousands of years. On the contrary, we should regard as our inheritance all the successful labours of the past, not blindly following them, but employing them simply as guides to find the true path.

In taking leave of the subject, and finally surrendering it to the judgment of the public, I am fully aware that the collection is very far from being complete; there are many gaps which each artist, however, may readily fill up for himself. My chief aim, to place side by side types of such styles as might best serve as landmarks and aids to the student in his onward path, has, I trust, been fulfilled.

It remains for me to offer my acknowledgment to all those friends who have kindly assisted me in the undertaking.

In the formation of the Egyptian Collection I received much valuable assistance from Mr. J. Bonomi, and from Mr. James Wild, who has also contributed the materials for the Arabian Collection, his long residence in Cairo having afforded him the opportunity of forming a very large collection of Cairean Ornament, of which the portion contained in this work can give but an imperfect idea, and which I trust he may some day be encouraged to publish in a complete form.

I am indebted to Mr. T. T. Bury for the plate of Stained Glass. From Mr. C. J. Richardson I obtained the principal portion of the materials of the

Elizabethan Collection; from Mr. J. B. Waring, those of the Byzantine, and I am also indebted to him for the very valuable essays on Byzantine and Elizabethan Ornament. Mr. J. O. Westwood having directed special attention to the Ornament of the Celtic races, has assisted in the Celtic Collection, and written the very remarkable history and exposition of the style.

Mr. C. Dresser, of Marlborough House, has provided the interesting plate No. 8 of the twentieth chapter, exhibiting the geometrical arrangement of natural flowers.

My colleague at the Crystal Palace, M. Digby Wyatt, has enriched the work with his admirable essays on the Ornament of the Renaissance and the Italian periods.

Whenever the material has been gathered from published sources, it has been acknowledged in the body of the work.

The remainder of the drawings have been chiefly executed by my pupils, Mr. Albert Warren and Mr. Charles Aubert, who, with Mr. Stubbs, have reduced the whole of the original drawings, and prepared them for publication.

The drawing upon stone of the whole collection was entrusted to the care of Mr. Francis Bedford, who, with his able assistants, Messrs. H. Fielding, W. R. Tymms, A. Warren, and S. Sedgfield, with occasional help, have executed the One Hundred Plates in less than one year.

My special thanks are due to Mr. Bedford for the care and anxiety which he has evinced, quite regardless of all personal consideration, to render this work as perfect as the advanced stage of chromolithography demanded;

and I feel persuaded that his valuable services will be fully recognised by all in any way acquainted with the difficulties and uncertainties of this process.

Messrs. Day and Son, the enterprising publishers, and at the same time the printers of the work, have put forth all their strength; and notwithstanding the care required, and the vast amount of printing to be performed, the resources of their establishment have enabled them, not only to deliver the work with perfect regularity to the Subscribers, but even to complete it before the appointed time.

OWEN JONES.

9 Argyll Place, December 15, 1856.

GENERAL PRINCIPLES IN THE ARRANGEMENT
OF FORM AND COLOUR, IN ARCHITECTURE AND THE
DECORATIVE ARTS, WHICH ARE ADVOCATED
THROUGHOUT THIS WORK

GENERAL PRINCIPLES

PROPOSITION 1

The Decorative Arts arise from, and should properly be attendant upon, Architecture.

PROPOSITION 2

Architecture is the material expression of the wants, the faculties, and the sentiments, of the age in which it is created.

Style in Architecture is the peculiar form that expression takes under the influence of climate and materials at command.

PROPOSITION 3

As Architecture, so all works of the Decorative Arts, should possess fitness, proportion, harmony, the result of all which is repose.

PROPOSITION 4

True beauty results from that repose which the mind feels when the eye, the intellect, and the affections, are satisfied from the absence of any want.

PROPOSITION 5

Construction should be decorated. Decoration should never be purposely constructed.

That which is beautiful is true; that which is true must be beautiful.

ON GENERAL FORM

PROPOSITION 6

Beauty of form is produced by lines growing out one from the other in gradual undulations: there are no excrescences; nothing could be removed and leave the design equally good or better.

DECORATION OF THE SURFACE

PROPOSITION 7

The general forms being first cared for, these should be subdivided and ornamented by general lines; the interstices may then be filled in with ornament, which may again be subdivided and enriched for closer inspection.

PROPOSITION 8

All ornament should be based upon a geometrical construction.

ON PROPORTION

PROPOSITION 9

As in every perfect work of Architecture a true proportion will be found to reign between all the members which compose it, so throughout the Decorative Arts every assemblage of forms should be provided on certain definite proportions; the whole and each particular member should be a multiple of some simple unit.

Those proportions will be the most beautiful which it will be most difficult for the eye to detect.

Thus the proportion of a double square, or 4 to 8, will be less beautiful than the more subtle ratio of 5 to 8; 3 to 6, than 3 to 7; 3 to 9, than 3 to 8; 3 to 4, than 3 to 5.

ON HARMONY AND CONTRAST

PROPOSITION 10

Harmony of form consists in the proper balancing, and contrast of, the straight, the inclined, and the curved.

DISTRIBUTION. RADIATION. CONTINUITY

PROPOSITION 11

In surface decoration all lines should flow out of a parent stem. Every ornament, however distant, should be traced to its branch and root. *Oriental practice.*

PROPOSITION 12

All junctions of curved lines with curved or of curved lines with straight should be tangential to each other. *Natural law. Oriental practice in accordance with it.*

ON THE CONVENTIONALITY OF NATURAL FORMS

PROPOSITION 13

Flowers or other natural objects should not be used as ornaments, but conventional representations founded upon them sufficiently suggestive to convey the intended image to the mind, without destroying the unity of the object they are employed to decorate. *Universally obeyed in the best periods of Art, equally violated when Art declines.*

ON COLOUR GENERALLY

PROPOSITION 14

Colour is used to assist in the development of form, and to distinguish objects or parts of objects one from another.

PROPOSITION 15

Colour is used to assist light and shade, helping the undulations of form by the proper distribution of the several colours.

PROPOSITION 16

These objects are best attained by the use of the primary colours on small surfaces and in small quantities, balanced and supported by the secondary and tertiary colours on the larger masses.

PROPOSITION 17

The primary colours should be used on the upper portions of objects, the secondary and tertiary on the lower.

ON THE PROPORTIONS BY WHICH HARMONY IN COLOURING IS PRODUCED

PROPOSITION 18

(FIELD'S CHROMATIC EQUIVALENTS)

The primaries of equal intensities will harmonise or neutralise each other, in the proportions of 3 yellow, 5 red, and 8 blue,—integrally as 16. The secondaries in the proportions of 8 orange, 13 purple, 11 green,—integrally as 32. The tertiaries, citrine (compound of orange and green), 19; russet (orange and purple), 21; olive (green and purple), 24;—integrally as 64. It follows that,—Each secondary being a compound of two primaries is neutralised by the remaining primary in the same proportions: thus, 8 of orange by 8 of blue, 11 of green by five of red, 13 of purple by 3 of yellow.

Each tertiary being a binary compound of two secondaries, is neutralised by the remaining secondary: as, 24 of olive by 8 of orange, 21 of russet by 11 of green, 19 of citrine by 13 of purple.

ON THE CONTRASTS AND HARMONIOUS EQUIVALENTS
OF TONES, SHADES, AND HUES

PROPOSITION 19

The above supposes the colours to be used in their prismatic intensities, but each colour has a variety of *tones* when mixed with white, or of *shades* when mixed with grey or black.

When a full colour is contrasted with another of a lower tone, the volume of the latter must be proportionally increased.

PROPOSITION 20

Each colour has a variety of *hues*, obtained by admixture with other colours, in addition to white, grey, or black: thus we have of yellow,—orange-yellow on the one side, and lemon-yellow on the other; so of red,—scarlet-red, and crimson-red; and of each every variety of *tone* and *shade*.

When a primary tinged with another primary is contrasted with a secondary, the secondary must have a hue of the third primary.

ON THE POSITIONS THE SEVERAL COLOURS SHOULD OCCUPY

PROPOSITION 21

In using the primary colours on moulded surfaces, we should place blue, which retires, on the concave surfaces; yellow, which advances, on the convex; and red, the intermediate colour, on the undersides; separating the colours by white on the vertical planes.

When the proportions required by Proposition 18 cannot be obtained, we may procure the balance by a change in the colours themselves: thus, if the surfaces to be coloured should give too much yellow, we should make the red more crimson and the blue more purple,—*i.e.* we should take the yellow out of them; so if the surfaces should give too much blue, we should make the yellow more orange and the red more scarlet.

PROPOSITION 22

The various colours should be so blended that the objects coloured, when viewed at a distance, should present a neutralised bloom.

PROPOSITION 23

No composition can ever be perfect in which any one of the three primary colours is wanting, either in its natural state or in combination.

ON THE LAW OF SIMULTANEOUS CONTRASTS
OF COLOURS, DERIVED FROM MONS. CHEVRUIL

PROPOSITION 24

When two tones of the same colour are juxtaposed, the light colour will appear lighter, and the dark colour darker.

PROPOSITION 25

When two different colours are juxtaposed, they receive a double modification; first, as to their tone (the light colour appearing lighter, and the dark colour appearing darker); secondly, as to their hue, each will become tinged with the complementary colour of the other.

PROPOSITION 26

Colours on white grounds appear darker; on black grounds lighter.

PROPOSITION 27

Black grounds suffer when opposed to colours which give a luminous complementary.

PROPOSITION 28

Colours should never be allowed to impinge upon each other.

ON THE MEANS OF INCREASING THE HARMONIOUS EFFECTS OF JUXTAPOSED COLOURS. OBSERVATIONS DERIVED FROM A CONSIDERATION OF ORIENTAL PRACTICE

PROPOSITION 29

When ornaments in a colour are on a ground of a contrasting colour, the ornament should be separated from the ground by an edging of lighter colour; as a red flower on a green ground should have an edging of lighter red.

PROPOSITION 30

When ornaments in a colour are on a gold ground, the ornaments should be separated from the ground by an edging of a darker colour.

PROPOSITION 31

Gold ornaments on any coloured ground should be outlined with black.

PROPOSITION 32

Ornaments of any colour may be separated from grounds of any other colour by edgings of white, gold, or black.

PROPOSITION 33

Ornaments in any colour, or in gold, may be used on white or black grounds, without outline or edging.

PROPOSITION 34

In "self-tints," tones, or shades of the same colour, a light tint on a dark ground may be used without outline; but a dark ornament on a light ground requires to be outlined with a still darker tint.

ON IMITATIONS

PROPOSITION 35

Imitations, such as the graining of woods, and of the various coloured marbles, allowable only, when the employment of the thing imitated would not have been inconsistent.

PROPOSITION 36

The principles discoverable in the works of the past belong to us; not so the results. It is taking the end for the means.

PROPOSITION 37

No improvement can take place in the Art of the present generation until all classes, Artists, Manufacturers, and the Public, are better educated in Art, and the existence of general principles is more fully recognised.

CHAPTER I

ORNAMENT
OF SAVAGE TRIBES

From the universal testimony of travellers it would appear, that there is scarcely a people, in however early a stage of civilisation, with whom the desire for ornament is not a strong instinct. The desire is absent in none, and it grows and increases with all in the ratio of their progress in civilisation. Man appears everywhere impressed with the beauties of Nature which surround him, and seeks to imitate to the extent of his power the works of the Creator.

Man's earliest ambition is to create. To this feeling must be ascribed the tattooing of the human face and body, resorted to by the savage to increase the expression by which he seeks to strike terror on his enemies or rivals, or to create what appears to him a new beauty.* As we advance higher, from the decoration of the rude tent or. wigwam to the sublime

* The tattooing on the head which we introduce from the Museum at Chester is very remarkable, as showing that in this very barbarous practice the principles of the very highest ornamental art are manifest, every line upon the face is the best adapted to develope the natural features.

works of a Phidias and Praxiteles, the same feeling is everywhere apparent: the highest ambition is still to create, to stamp on this earth the impress of an individual mind.

From time to time a mind stronger than those around will impress itself on a generation, and carry with it a host of others of less power following in the same track, yet never so closely as to destroy the individual ambition to create; hence the cause of styles, and of the modification of styles. The efforts of a people in an early stage of civilisation are like those of children, though presenting a want of power, they possess a grace and *naïveté* rarely found in mid-age, and never in manhood's decline. It is equally so in the infancy of any art. Cimabue and Giotto have not the material charm of Raphael or the manly power of Michael Angelo, but surpass them both in grace and earnest truth. The very command of means leads to their abuse: when Art struggles, it succeeds; when revelling in its own successes, it as signally fails. The pleasure we receive in contemplating the rude attempts at ornament of the most savage tribes arises from our appreciation of a difficulty accomplished; we are at once charmed by the evidence of the intention, and surprised at the simple and ingenious process by which the result is obtained. In fact, what we seek in every work of Art, whether it be humble or pretentious, is the evidence of mind,—the evidence of that desire to create to which we have referred, and which all, feeling a natural instinct within them, are satisfied with when they find it developed in others. It is strange, but so it is, that this evidence of mind will be more readily found in the rude attempts at ornament of a savage tribe than in the innumerable

FEMALE HEAD FROM
NEW ZEALAND, IN THE MUSEUM, CHESTER

productions of a highly-advanced civilisation. Individuality decreases in the ratio of the power of production. When Art is manufactured by combined effort, not originated by individual effort, we fail to recognise those true instincts which constitute its greatest charm.

Plate I. *(pages 40–41)*. The ornaments on this Plate are from portions of clothing made chiefly from the bark of trees. Patterns No. 2 and 11 are from a dress brought by Mr. Oswald Brierly from Tongotabu, the principal of the Friendly Island group. It is made from thin sheets of the inner rind of the bark of a species of hibiscus, beaten out and united together so as to form one long parallelogram of cloth, which being wrapped many times round the body as a petticoat, and leaving the chest, arms, and shoulders bare, forms the only dress of the natives. Nothing, therefore, can be more primitive, and yet the arrangement of the pattern shows the most refined taste and skill. No.11 is the border on the edge of the cloth; with the same limited means of production,

it would be difficult to improve upon it. The patterns are formed by small wooden stamps, and although the work is somewhat rude and irregular in execution, the intention is everywhere apparent; and we are at once struck with the skilful balancing of the masses, and the judicious correction of the tendency of the eye to run in any one direction by opposing to them lines having an opposite tendency.

When Mr. Brierly visited the island one woman was the designer of all the patterns in use there, and for every new pattern she designed she received as a reward a certain number of yards of cloth. The pattern No. 2, from the same place, is equally an admirable lesson in composition which we may derive from an artist of a savage tribe. Nothing can be more judicious than the general arrangement of the four squares and the four red spots. Without the red spots on the yellow ground there would have been a great want of repose in the general arrangement; without the red lines round the red spots to carry the red through the yellow, it would have been still imperfect. Had the small red triangles turned outwards instead of inwards, the repose of the pattern would again have been lost, and the effect produced on the eye would have been that of squinting; as it is, the eye is centred in each square, and centred in each group by the red spots around the centre square. The stamps which form the pattern are very simple, each triangle ▲ and each leaf ◆ being a single stamp: we thus see how readily the possession of a simple tool, even by the most uncultivated, if guided by an

instinctive observation of the forms in which all the works of Nature are arranged, would lead to the creation of all the geometrical arrangements of form with which we are acquainted. On the upper left-hand corner of pattern No. 2, the eight-pointed star is formed by eight applications of the same tool; as also the black flower with sixteen pointing inwards ❢ and sixteen pointing outwards. ▐ The most complicated patterns of the Byzantine, Arabian, and Moresque mosaics would be generated by the same means. The secret of success in all ornament is the production of a broad general effect by the repetition of a few simple elements; variety should rather be sought in the arrangement of the several portions of a design, than in the multiplicity of varied forms.

The stamping of patterns on the coverings of the body, when either of skins of animals or materials such as this, would be the first stage towards ornament after the tattooing of the body by an analogous process. In both

HEAD OF CANOE,
NEW GUINEA

there would remain a greater variety and individuality than in subsequent processes, which would become more mechanical. The first notions of weaving, which would be given by the plaiting of straws or strips of bark, instead of using them as thin sheets, would have equally the same result of gradually forming the mind to an appreciation of a proper disposition of

PLAITED STRAW
FROM THE
SANDWICH ISLANDS

masses: the eye of the savage, accustomed only to look upon Nature's harmonies, would readily enter into the perception of the true balance both of form and colour; in point of fact, we find that it is so, that in savage ornament the true balance of both is always maintained.

After the formation of ornament by stamping and weaving, would naturally follow the desire of forming ornament in relief or carving. The weapons for defence or the chase would first attract attention. The most skilful and the bravest would desire to be distinguished from

HEAD
OF CANOE,
NEW GUINEA

their fellows by the possession of weapons, not only more useful, but more beautiful. The shape best fitted for the purpose having been found by experience, the enriching of the surface by carving would naturally follow; and the eye, already accustomed to the geometrical forms produced by weaving, the hand would seek to imitate them by a similar repetition of cuts of the knife. The ornaments on Plate II. *(pages 42–43)* show this instinct very fully. They are executed with the utmost precision, and exhibit great taste and judgment in the distribution of the masses. Nos. 10 and 12 are interesting, as showing how much this taste and skill may exist in the formation of geometrical patterns, whilst those resulting from curved lines, and the human form more especially, remain in the very first stage.

The ornaments in the woodcuts above and overleaf show a far higher advance in the distribution of curved lines, the twisted rope forming the type as it naturally would be of all curved lines in ornament. The uniting of two strands for additional strength would early accustom the eye to the spiral

FROM THE SIDE OF A
CANOE, NEW ZEALAND

line, and we always find this form side by side with geometrical patterns formed by the interlacing of equal lines in the ornament of every savage tribe, and retained in the more advanced art of every civilised nation.

The ornament of a savage tribe, being the result of a natural instinct, is necessarily always true to its purpose; whilst in much of the ornament of civilised nations, the first impulse which generated received forms being enfeebled by constant repetition, the ornament is oftentimes misapplied, and instead of first seeking the most convenient form and adding beauty, all beauty is destroyed, because all fitness, by superadding ornament to ill-contrived form. If we would return to a more healthy condition, we must even be as little children or as savages; we must get rid of the acquired and artificial, and return to and develope natural instincts.

The beautiful New Zealand paddle, Nos. 2 and 3, on Plate III. *(pages 44–45)*, would rival works of the highest civilisation: there is not a line upon its surface misapplied. The general shape is most elegant, and the decoration everywhere the best adapted to develope the form. A modern manufacturer, with his stripes and plaids, would have continued the bands of rings around the handle across the blade. The New Zealander's instinct taught him

HANDLE OF
A PADDLE—B.M.

better. He desired not only that his paddle should be strong, but should appear so, and his ornament is so disposed as to give an appearance of additional strength to what it would have had if the surface had remained undecorated. The centre band in the length of the blade is continued round on the other side, binding together the border on the edge, which itself fixes all the other bands. Had these bands run out like the centre one, they would have appeared to slip off. The centre one was the only one that could do so without disturbing the repose.

The swelling form of the handle where additional weight was required is most beautifully contrived, and the springing of the swell is well defined by the bolder pattern of the rings.[†]

[†] Captain Cook and other voyagers repeatedly notice the taste and ingenuity of the islanders of the Pacific and South Seas: instancing especially cloths, painted "in such an endless variety of figures that one might suppose they borrowed their patterns from a mercer's shop in which the most elegant productions of China and Europe are collected, besides some original patterns of their own." The "thousand different patterns" of their basket-work, their mats, and the fancy displayed in their rich carvings and inlaid shell-work, are, likewise, constantly mentioned. See *The Three Voyages of Captain Cook*, 2 vols. Lond. 1841–42; DUMONT D'URVILLE'S *Voyage au Pole Sud*, 8vo. Paris, 1841; Ditto, *Atlas d'Histoire*, fol.; PRICHARD'S *Natural History of Man*, Lond. 1855; G. W. EARLE'S *Native Races of Indian Archipelago*, Lond. 1852; KERR'S *General History and Collections of Voyages and Travels*, London, 1811–17.

CLUB, EASTERN
ARCHIPELAGO

SAVAGE TRIBES

The Victorians were fascinated by the natives of Australasia, believing them to be "relic savages." The anthropologist Sir Baldwin Spencer (1860–1929) described them as "human beings that still remain on the cultural level of men of the Stone Age." Ideas of this kind were not seriously challenged until after the publication of Charles Darwin's *On the Origin of Species* in 1859. Jones's own views about the childlike quality of primitive culture were also colored by the romantic notion of the "noble savage," which was popularized by the philosopher Jean-Jacques Rousseau (1712–78).

1

2

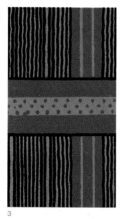

3

4

5

6

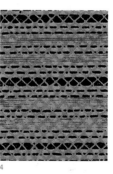

7

8

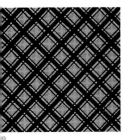

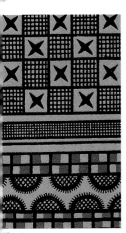

9

10

11

12

13

Initially two main forms of Oceanic art were publicized in the West. There were fabrics, decorated with repetitive, geometrical patterns; carvings, on the other hand, tended to feature flowing, curvilinear designs, which covered every available inch of space. These same, rhythmic patterns were also used for facial tattoos, and sometimes heads of this kind were mummified and preserved as cult objects. A few examples were brought to the West as curios, but, by and large, Europeans received a distorted image of Polynesian culture. Its finest artifacts were the spirited sculptures of ancestral gods, but most of these were destroyed by early Christian missionaries. Faint echoes of them can be seen here, in the stylized figures and heads that featured on ceremonial drums (Nos. 10, 12).

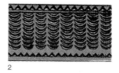

1

2

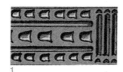

3

5

6

8

9

10

11

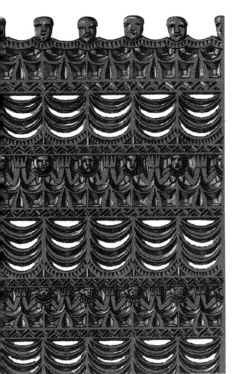

2

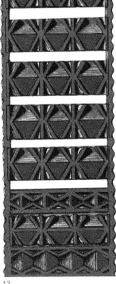

13

PLATE II

1 South America. United
Service Museum.
2 South Sea Islands.
U.S.M.
3 Sandwich Islands. U.S.M.
4, 6 Sandwich Islands.
U.S.M.
5 Owhyhee. U.S.M.
7 Sandwich Islands. U.S.M.
8, 20 Tahiti. Adze. U.S.M.
9 New Hebrides. Inlaid
Shield. U.S.M.
10, 12 Friendly Islands.
Drum. U.S.M.
11, 13 Tahiti. Adze. U.S.M.
14 Sandwich Islands.
U.S.M.
15, 17, 19 Sandwich
Islands. U.S.M.
16, 18 New Zealand.
U.S.M.

4

15

6

17

19

20

Most members of the British public still associated the South Seas with the voyages of Captain Cook (1728–79), even though he had been dead for more than 50 years. As a result, they regarded the war clubs and spears of the islanders with morbid curiosity. Every schoolchild would have known of Cook's account of Savage Island (now Niue), where the explorers were greeted with a hail of stones and spears. They would also have been familiar with the manner of Cook's death in the Sandwich Islands (Hawaii), where he was clubbed by a hostile group of natives.

PLATE III

1 New Zealand. Patoo-Patoo. United Services Museum.
2 Handle, full size of Fig. 3. U.S.M.
3 New Zealand. Paddle. U.S.M.
4 Owhyhee. Club. U.S.M.
5 Sandwich Islands. Club. U.S.M.
6 Tahiti. Adze. U.S.M.
7 South Sea Isles. War Club. U.S.M.
8 Feejee Islands. Club. U.S.M.
9 New Zealand. Pajee, or War Club. U.S.M.

CHAPTER II

EGYPTIAN ORNAMENT

The Architecture of Egypt has this peculiarity over all other styles, that the more ancient the monument the more perfect is the art. All the remains with which we are acquainted exhibit Egyptian Art in a state of decline. Monuments erected two thousand years before the Christian era are formed from the ruins of still more ancient and more perfect buildings. We are thus carried back to a period too remote from our time to enable us to discover any traces of its origin; and whilst we can trace in direct succession the Greek, the Roman, the Byzantine, with its offshoots, the Arabian, the Moresque, and the Gothic, from this great parent, we must believe the architecture of Egypt to be a pure original style, which arose with civilisation in Central Africa,* passed

* In the British Museum may be seen a cast of a bas-relief from Kalabshee in Nubia, representing the conquests of Ramses II. over a black people, supposed to be Ethiopians. It is very remarkable, that amongst the presents which these people are represented as bringing with them as a tribute to the King, besides the leopard-skins and rare animals, ivory, gold, and other products of the country, there are three ivory carved chairs precisely similar to that on which the King sits to receive them; from which it would appear that these highly-elaborated articles of luxury were derived by the Egyptians from the interior of Africa.

through countless ages, to the culminating point of perfection and the state of decline in which we see it. Inferior as this state doubtless is to the unknown perfection of Egyptian Art, it is far beyond all that followed after; the Egyptians are inferior only to themselves. In all other styles we can trace a rapid ascent from infancy, founded on some bygone style, to a culminating point of perfection, when the foreign influence was modified or discarded, to a period of slow, lingering decline, feeding on its own elements. In the Egyptian we have no traces of infancy or of any foreign influence; and we must, therefore, believe that they went for inspiration direct from nature. This view is strengthened when we come to consider more especially the ornament of Egypt; the types are few and natural types, the representation is but slightly removed from the type. The later we descend in art, the more and more do we find original types receded from; till, in much ornament, such as the Arabian and Moresque, it is difficult to discover the original type from which the ornament has been by successive mental efforts developed.

The lotus and papyrus, growing on the banks of their river, symbolising the food for the body and mind; the feathers of rare birds, which were carried before the king as emblems of sovereignty; the palm-branch, with the twisted cord made from its stems; these are the few types which form the basis of that immense variety of ornament with which the Egyptians decorated the temples of their gods, the palaces of their kings, the covering of their persons, their articles of luxury or of more modest daily use, from the wooden spoon which fed them to the boat which carried their similarly adorned embalmed bodies across the Nile to their last home in the valley of the dead. Following these types as they did in a manner so nearly allied to their natural form, they could hardly fail to observe the same laws which the works of nature ever display; and we find, therefore, that Egyptian ornament, however conventionalised, is always true. We are never shocked by any misapplication or violation of a natural principle. On the other hand, they never, by a too servile imitation of the type, destroyed the consistency of the representation. A lotus carved in stone, forming a graceful termination to a column, or painted on the walls as an offering to their gods, was never such a one as might be plucked, but an architectural representation; in either case the best adapted for the purpose it had to fill, sufficiently resembling the type to call forth in the beholder the poetic idea which it was sought to supply, without shocking his feeling of consistency.

Egyptian ornament is of three kinds: that which is constructive, or forming part of the monument itself, of which it is the outward and graceful covering of the skeleton within; that which is representative, but at the same time conventionally rendered; and that which is simply decorative. In all cases it was symbolic, and, as we have observed, formed on some few types, which were but slightly changed during the whole period of Egyptian civilisation.

Of the first kind, viz. constructive ornament, are the decorations of the means of support and the crowning members of the walls. The column only a few feet high, or one forty or sixty feet, as at Luxor and Karnac, was an enlarged papyrus plant: the base representing the root; the shaft, the stalk; and the capital, the full-blown flower, surrounded by a bouquet of smaller plants (No. 6, Plate VI., *pages 60–61*), tied together by bands. Not only did a series of columns represent a grove of papyri, but each column was in itself a grove; and at No. 15 of Plate IV. *(pages 56–57)* we have a representation of a grove of papyri in various stages of growth, which would only have to be assembled as they stand, and be tied round with a string, and we should have the Egyptian shaft and its highly-ornamental capital; and further, we have in Nos. 5, 9, 10, 11, 12, on Plate IV., pointed representations of columns forming parts of temples, in which the original idea is unmistakably portrayed.

We may imagine it the custom of the Egyptians in early times to decorate the wooden posts of their primitive temples with their native flowers tied round them; and this custom, when their art took a more permanent character, became solidified in their monuments of stone. These forms, once sacred, their religious laws forbade a change; but a single glance, however, at Plates VI. and VI*. *(pages 60–63)* will show how little this possession of one leading idea resulted in uniformity. The lotus and papyrus form the type of fifteen of the capitals we have selected for illustration; yet how ingeniously varied, and what a lesson do they teach us! From the Greeks to our own time the world has been content with the acanthus leaf arranged round a bell for the capitals of columns of all architecture called classic, differing only in the more or less perfection of the modelling of the leaves, or the graceful or otherwise proportions of the bell: a modification in plan has but rarely been attempted. And this it was that opened the way to so much development in the Egyptian capital; beginning with the circle, they surrounded it with four, eight, and sixteen other circles. If the same change were attempted with the Corinthian capital, it could not fail to produce an entirely new order of forms whilst still retaining the idea of applying the acanthus leaf to the surface of a bell-shaped vase.

The shaft of the Egyptian column, when circular, was made to retain the idea of the triangular shape of the papyrus stalk, by three raised lines, which divided its circumference into three equal portions; when the column was formed by a union of four or eight shafts bound together, these had each a sharp arris on their outer face with the same intention. The crowning member or cornice of an Egyptian building was decorated with feathers, which appear to have been an emblem of sovereignty; whilst in the centre was the winged globe, emblem of divinity.

The second kind of Egyptian ornament results from the conventional representation of actual things on the walls of the temples and tombs; and here again, in the representations of offerings to the gods or of the various articles of daily use, in the paintings of actual scenes of their domestic life, every flower or other object is portrayed, not as a reality, but as an ideal representation. It is at the same time the record of a fact and an architectural decoration, to which even their hieroglyphical writing, explanatory of the scene, by its symmetrical arrangement added effect. In No. 4, on Plate IV. *(pages 56–57)*, we have an example in the representation of the three papyrus-plants and three lotus-flowers, with two buds, in the hand of a king as an offering to the gods. The arrangement is symmetrical and graceful, and we here see that the Egyptians, in thus conventionally rendering the lotus and papyrus, instinctively obeyed the law which we find everywhere in the leaves of plants, viz. the radiation of the leaves, and all the veins on the leaves, in graceful curves from the parent stem; and not only do they follow this law in the drawing of the individual flower, but also in the grouping of several flowers together, as may be seen, not only in No. 4, but also in their representation of plants growing in the desert, Nos. 13 and 14 of the same plate, and in No. 16. In Nos. 7 and 8 of Plate V. *(pages 58–59)* they learned the same lesson from the feather, another type of ornament (14 and 16, Plate V.): the same instinct is again at work at Nos. 4 and 5, where the type is one of the many forms of palm-trees so common in the country.

The third kind of Egyptian ornament, viz. that which is simply decorative, or which appears so to our eyes, but which has doubtless its own laws and reasons for its application, although they are not so apparent to us. Plates VIII., IX., X., XI. *(pages 66–73)*, are devoted to this class of ornament, and are from paintings on tombs, dresses, utensils, and sarcophagi. They are all distinguished by graceful symmetry and perfect distribution. The variety that can be produced by the few simple types we have referred to is very remarkable.

On Plate IX. *(pages 68–69)* are patterns of ceilings, and appear to be reproductions of woven patterns. Side by side with the conventional rendering of actual things, the first attempts of every people to produce works of ornament take this direction. The early necessity of plaiting together straw or bark of trees, for the formation of articles of clothing, the covering of their rude dwelling, or the ground on which they reposed, induced the employment at first of straws and bark of different natural colours, to be afterwards replaced by artificial dyes, which gave the first idea, not only of ornament, but of geometrical arrangement. Nos. 1–4, Plate IX., are from Egyptian paintings, representing mats whereon the king stands; whilst Nos. 6 and 7 are from the ceilings of tombs, which evidently represent tents covered by mats. No. 9, 10, 12, show how readily the meander or Greek fret was produced by the same means. The universality of this ornament in every style of architecture, and to be found in some shape or other amongst the first attempts of ornament of every savage tribe, is an additional proof of their having had a similar origin.

The formation of patterns by the equal division of similar lines, as by weaving, would give to a rising people the first notions of symmetry, arrangement, disposition, and the distribution of masses. The Egyptians, in their decoration of large surfaces, never appear to have gone beyond a geometrical arrangement. Flowing lines are very rare, comparatively, and never the motive of the composition, though the germ of even this mode of decoration, the volute form, exists in their rope ornament. (No. 10, 13–16, 18–24, on Plate X., *pages 70–71*, and 1, 2, 4, 7, Plate XI., *pages 72–73*) Here the several coils of rope are subjected to a geometrical arrangement; but the unrolling of this cord gives the very form which is the source of so much beauty in many subsequent styles. We venture, therefore, to claim for the Egyptian style, that though the oldest, it is, in all that is requisite to constitute a true style of art, the most perfect. The language in which it reveals itself to us may seem foreign, peculiar, formal and rigid; but the ideas and the teachings it conveys to us are of the soundest. As we proceed with other styles, we shall see that they approach perfection only so far as they followed, in common with the Egyptians, the true principles to be observed in every flower that grows. Like these favourites of Nature, every ornament should have its perfume; *i.e.* the reason of its application. It should endeavour to rival the grace of construction, the harmony of its varied forms, and due proportion and subordination of one part to the other found in the model. When we find any of these characteristics wanting in a work of ornament, we may be sure that it belongs to a borrowed style, where the spirit which animated the original work has been lost in the copy.

The architecture of the Egyptians is thoroughly polychromatic,—they painted everything; therefore we have much to learn from them on this head. They dealt in flat tints, and used neither shade nor shadow, yet found no difficulty in poetically conveying to the mind the identity of the object they desired to represent. They used colour as they did form, conventionally. Compare the representation of the lotus (No. 3, Plate IV., *pages 56–57*) with the natural flower (No. 1); how charmingly are the characteristics of the natural flower reproduced in the representations! See how the outer leaves are distinguished by a darker green, and the inner protected leaves by a lighter green; whilst the purple and yellow tones of the inner flower are represented by red leaves floating in a field of yellow, which most completely recalls the yellow glow of the original. We have here Art added to Nature, and derive an additional pleasure in the perception of the mental effort which has produced it.

The colours used by the Egyptians were principally red, blue, and yellow, with black and white to define and give distinctiveness to the various colours; with green used generally, though not universally, as a local colour, such as the green leaves of the lotus. These were, however, indifferently coloured green or blue; blue in the more ancient times, and green during the Ptolemaic period; at which time, also, were added both purple and brown, but with diminished effect. The red also, which is found on the tombs or mummy-cases of the Greek or Roman period, is lower in tone than that of the ancient times; and it appears to be a universal rule that, in all archaic periods of art, the primary colours, blue, red, and yellow, are the prevailing colours, and these used most harmoniously and successfully. Whilst in periods when art is practised traditionally, and not instinctively, there is a tendency to employ the secondary colours and hues, and shades of every variety, though rarely with equal success. We shall have many opportunities of pointing this out in subsequent chapters.

Lotus buds and papyrus plants were extremely common motifs in Egyptian temples, being the emblems of Upper and Lower Egypt respectively. Many European architects borrowed these images, without being aware of their symbolic nature. The papyrus was linked with creation and the Sun; on many pillars its flowers were shown either open or closed, to represent the path of the Sun god. Similarly the lotus was a type of water lily that symbolized the primeval ocean of creation. The Sun god Re was often depicted reclining on a lotus flower, while the sky goddess Hathor held one in her hand.

PLATE IV

1 The Lotus, drawn from Nature.
2 Egyptian representation of the Lotus.
3 Another, in a different stage of growth.
4 Three Papyrus Plants, and three full-blown Lotus Flowers with two Buds, held in the hand of a King as an offering to a God.

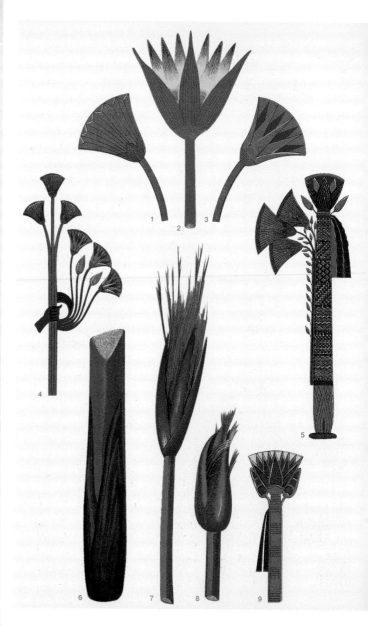

PLATE IV

5 The Lotus and Buds in the form of a Column, bound round with Matting, from a Painting representing the Portico of a Temple.

6 The Base of the Stem of the Papyrus, drawn from Nature; the type of the Bases and Shafts of Egyptian Columns.

7 Expanding Bud of the Papyrus, drawn from Nature.

8 Another, in a less advanced stage of growth.

9 A full-blown Lotus and two Buds, bound together with Ribbons, the type of the Capitals of Egyptian Columns.

10 Egyptian representation of the Papyrus Plant; the complete type of the Capital, Shaft, and Base of the Egyptian Columns.

11 A combination of the Lotus and Papyrus, representing a Column bound with Matting and Ribbons.

12 As Fig. 10, in combination with Lotus Buds, Grapes, and Ivy.

13 Representation of Plants growing in the Desert.

14 Another variety of Desert Plants.

15 Representation of the Lotus and Papyrus growing in the Nile.

16 Egyptian representation of the Lotus and Buds.

17, 18 Representations of the Papyrus, from an Egyptian Painting.

Jones recorded several images that related to Egyptian ritual practices. Everyday the Sun god journeyed over the celestial ocean in a boat (hence the solar disks in No. 18), which returned east by night via the underworld. Model boats were also buried with the dead, to assist them in their passage to the afterlife. The eyes painted on the rudder (No. 13) were designed to enable the deceased to see on their final journey. The markings around them were linked with Horus, the sky god. His eyes represented the Sun (bright) and the Moon (in shadow). Eyes were also painted on many other funerary objects to act as protective talismans.

PLATE V

1 Feathers from the Headdress of the Horses of the Royal Chariots.
2 Another variety, from Aboo-Simbel.
3 Fan made of Feathers, inserted into a wooden Stem in the form of a Lotus.
4 Fans made of dried Leaves.
5 Ditto.
6 Fan.
7 Representation of a species of Lotus.
8 The true Lotus.
9 Royal Head-dress.
10 Ditto.
11, 12, 15 Gold and enamelled Vases in the form of the Lotus.
13 A Rudder Oar decorated with the Lotus and the Eye, representing the Divinity.
14, 16 Insignia borne by certain Officers of the time of the Pharaohs.
17 Another variety of Rudder Oar.
18, 19 Boats made of Papyrus Plants bound together.

The remains at Luxor and Philae were highly picturesque, and illustrations of them appeared in many contemporary travel books. The most celebrated examples were by the Scottish artist David Roberts (1796–1864), who had toured extensively around the Middle East in 1838–39. He produced detailed oils, watercolors, and prints of Egyptian temples, most notably in *Egypt and Nubia*, a huge series of lithographs that was published in 21 monthly parts (1846–49). Roberts's drawings confirm that many sites were still almost submerged in sand, enabling the capitals of the pillars to be studied at close quarters.

PLATE VI

1 Capital from the unfinished hypæthral Temple, Philæ. Composed of three tiers of the Papyrus Plant in three stages of growth. The stem of each plant is distinguished by its size and colour, and continued down to the horizontal bands or fasciæ.
2 Capital from the unfinished hypæthral Temple, Philæ. Roman period, B.C. 140.

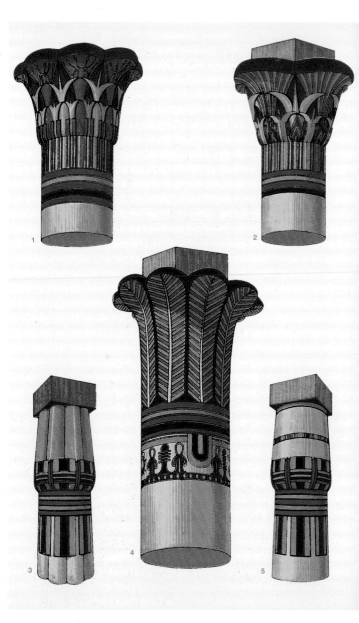

PLATE VI

3 Capital of the smaller Columns of the Temple of Luxor, B.C. 1250. Representing eight Buds of the Papyrus bound together, and adorned with pendent and coloured Fasciæ.

4 Capital from the Portico of Edfu, B.C. 145. Represents the Palm-tree, with nine branches, or faces. The horizontal fasciæ of the Palm-tree Capital differ from the fasciæ of all the other capitals, inasmuch as there is always a pendent loop.

5 Capital of the smaller columns of the Memnonium, Thebes, B.C. 1200. Represents a single Bud of the Papyrus decorated with the coloured pendent Fasciæ that are seen in the painted representations of Columns of Plate IV. Nos. 5, 9, 11.

6 Capital of the large Columns of the Temple of Luxor, Thebes, of the time of Amunoph III., 1250 B.C., according to Sharpe. It represents the full-blown Papyrus, and around it Papyri and Lotus Buds alternating.

7 Capital from the principal Temple, Philæ. Representing two tiers of the Papyrus, in three stages of growth. In this capital the circular form is not disturbed, as in No. 2.

8 Capital from the Temple at Koom-Ombos. The full-grown Papyrus surrounded by various flowers.

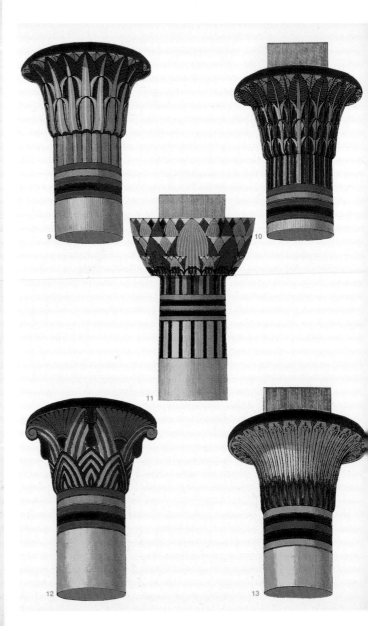

EGYPTIAN

The pillars in Egyptian temples were decorated with a variety of natural motifs, which may have had their origins in prehistoric harvest rites. The most common elements were papyrus plants, palms, and lotus flowers. Pillars with these nature symbols were meant to represent the pharaoh's earthly domains, while also supporting the canopy of heaven (temple roofs were usually decorated with stars and birds). During the New Kingdom period (1567–1085 BC) the pillar became a traditional symbol of the fertility god, Osiris. This made the plant motifs particularly appropriate, since Osiris was credited with the introduction of agriculture to Egypt.

PLATE VI*

9 Capital from a Temple in the Oasis of Thebes. Representing a collection of Aquatic Plants, with triangular Stalks tied round a single full-blown Papyrus.
10 Capital from the Portico of Edfu, B.C. 145, of similar structure to No. 9.

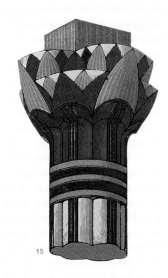

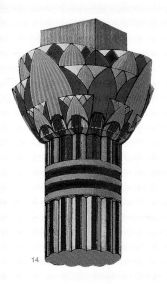

14

15

16

17

PLATE VI*

11 Capital from the Colonnade of the Island of Philæ. Representing sixteen Lotus Flowers bound together in three tiers. Shown in elevation.

12 Capital from a Temple in the Oasis of Thebes.

13 Capital from the principal Temple in the Island of Philæ, B.C. 106. The full-blown Papyrus surrounded by the same flower in various stages of growth.

14 The Capital No. 11 seen in Perspective.

15 Capital from a Temple in the Oasis of Thebes. Representing eight Lotus Flowers bound together in two tiers.

16 Capital from the unfinished hypæthral Temple, Philæ. Composed of the Papyrus in two stages of growth, arranged in three tiers. The first composed of four full-blown and four expanding flowers; the second tier, of eight smaller, full-blown; and the third tier, of sixteen, still smaller.

17 Capital of the Græco-Egyptian form, but of the Roman period. Very remarkable, as showing the Egyptian and Greek elements combined, viz. the Papyrus in two stages of growth, with the Acanthus leaf and the tendrils of the Honeysuckle.

EGYPTIAN

Jones produced the illustrations in this Egyptian section in collaboration with Joseph Bonomi (1796–1878), who was both an architect and an Egyptologist. Bonomi had accompanied the Scottish antiquarian Robert Hay (1799–1863) on his tour of Egypt, helping him to make detailed records of its ancient monuments. Jones and Bonomi became lifelong friends, working together on a number of projects. The most notable was the spectacular Egyptian Court at the Crystal Palace exhibition in 1854. Bonomi also designed buildings in the Egyptian revival style, the most famous being a flax mill in Leeds, which resembled a Nile temple.

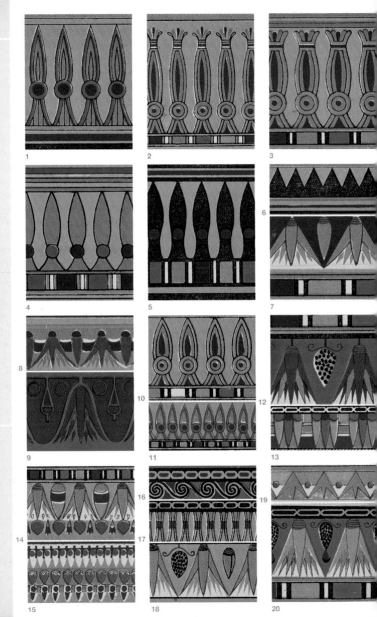

1

22

23

4

25

26

7

28

29

30

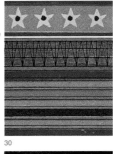

1

32

33

34

PLATE VII

7, 8, 9 From a wooden Sarcophagus.
10 From the Tombs, El Kab.
11 From the Tombs, Benihassan.
12, 13, 14 From the Tombs, Gourna.
15 From a Necklace.
16 From the Wall of a Tomb, Gourna, immediately under the Ceiling.
17, 18, 19 Portions of a Necklace.
20 From the Wall of a Tomb.
21 From a Necklace.
22 From the upper part of the Wall of a Tomb, Sakhara.
23 Ditto, at Thebes.
24 From a Necklace.
25 From the Wall of a Tomb, Gourna.
26 From a Sarcophagus.
27 From the Wall of a Tomb.
28 From a Sarcophagus.
29 From the upper part of a Picture.
30 Arrangement of Lines from dados.
31 From a Sarcophagus in the Louvre.
32 From the Wall of a Tomb, Gourna, representing the Lotus, in plan as well as in elevation.
33 From a Ceiling at Medinet Haboo.
34 Arrangement of Lines from dados, in Tombs.

Nos. 1–5, 10, 11, always occur on vertical surfaces, and on the upper part of the walls of tombs and temples. Nos. 7–9, 12, 14, 18, 20, are all derived from the Lotus in a pendent position, with a bunch of grapes intervening. Nos. 13, 15, 24, 32, are derived from the separated leaves of the Lotus.

Above all else, most Victorians associated ancient Egypt with mummies. Many examples had been transported to Europe over the centuries, partly as historical curiosities, but also as medical specimens. The bitumen used in the embalming process was believed to have health-giving properties, and *mumia* was a common sight in apothecary shops; it was still used in some nineteenth-century medicines. With advances in archeological techniques came a greater interest in other funerary objects, but mummies themselves were treated with scant respect. While looking for artifacts in the burial pits, one noted archeologist reported that "with every step I took, I crushed a mummy in some part or other."

1

2

3

4

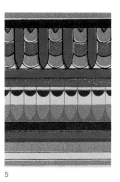

5

6

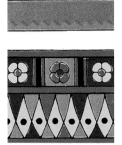

7

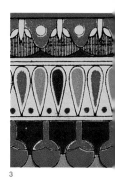

8

9

0

11

12

3

14

15

6

17

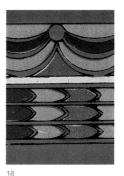

18

PLATE VIII

The whole of the Ornaments on this plate are from Mummy-cases in the British Museum and the Louvre, and, like those of the last Plate, are mostly composed of the Lotus-flower and single leaves of the same plant. In No. 2, above the Lotus-leaves, is a white ornament on a black ground, very common in the tombs, suggested by the interwoven strands of a rope; and in No. 7 we have the chequered pattern, one of the earliest ornaments, evidently derived from the weaving together of different-coloured strands. In the lower part of No. 18 we have another very common ornament, derived from feathers.

By the mid-nineteenth century the study of Egyptology had entered one of its most exciting phases. Europeans had long been fascinated by the exotic remnants of this ancient civilization, and wealthy collectors competed to acquire them, even though they had very little understanding of the objects they were purchasing. With the discovery of the Rosetta Stone in 1799, however, archeologists finally gained the key to hieroglyphics. These were fully deciphered by Jean Champollion (1790–1832), who published his initial findings in 1824. A welter of historical studies ensued, enabling Jones to give accurate descriptions of the date, dynasty, and function of his Egyptian motifs.

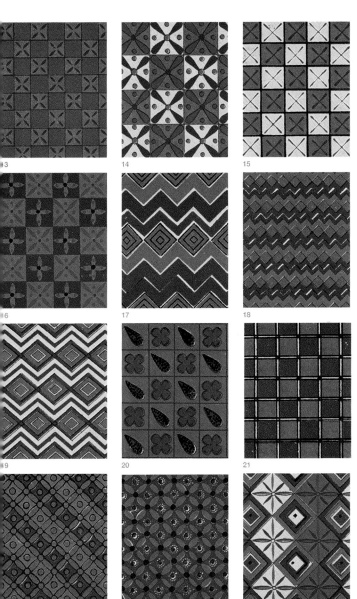

PLATE IX

The Ornaments on this Plate are taken from Paintings on Tombs in various parts of Egypt, from original Drawings. They are chiefly patterns that could be produced by the loom, and a single glance will show that this is doubtless the origin of most of them. **1–8** are representations of Mats on which the kings stand. They were evidently formed of interwoven straws of different colours. The transition from this state to the formation of patterns, such as 9–12, 17–19, 21, would be very rapid, and they are most probably only reproductions of woven articles of daily use. Nos. 9 and 10 may have suggested the fret to the Greeks, unless they arrived at it themselves by a similar process. **20** is from a Ceiling of a Tomb at Gourna. It represents the Trellis-work of a Garden Walk, covered with a Vine. It is by no means an uncommon ornament for the curved ceilings of small tombs, and usually occupies the whole ceiling of each excavation at the period of the nineteenth dynasty. **21–23** are derived from Mummy-cases in the Louvre, of a late period.

EGYPTIAN

🐾 Egyptian motifs were a familiar feature in nineteenth-century design. The trend was sparked off by Napoleon's invasion of Egypt in 1798. As a result, Egyptian ornament became a key element in the nineteenth-century Empire style, which was intially linked with the Napoleonic regime, but also affected other European countries. It impacted on the design of French furniture and interior decoration, and also stimulated the Egyptian revival in architecture. In England the most famous example of this was the Egyptian Hall (1811–12), a popular exhibition venue in London. Here, in 1821–22, Giovanni Belzoni (1778–1823) displayed the findings from his recent excavations at Thebes. The show proved a phenomenal success, prefiguring the Tutankhamun exhibitions of the twentieth century.

13

14

15

16

17

18

19

20

21

22

23

24

PLATE X

1–5 From Mummy-cases in the Louvre, at a late period. Geometrical arrangements of the single Lotus-leaf.

6 From a Tomb at Thebes. Each circle is formed of four Lotus-flowers and four Buds, the intermediate star probably intended for four Lotus-leaves.

7 From a Tomb at Thebes.

8, 9 From a Mummy-case.

10–24 are from Ceilings of Tombs in various parts of Egypt. In Nos. 10, 13–16, 18–23, are various examples of an ornament representing the unwinding of a pile of rope, which may have given the first suggestion of the volute. In No. 24 the continuous blue line is evidently from the same type.

🕮 Jones's casual reference to Dr. Lepsius (No. 24) relates to the most famous Egyptologist of the day. Through the patronage of the king of Prussia, Karl Richard Lepsius (1810–84) undertook an exhaustive survey of Egypt's monuments. During his main expedition (1842–45) he excavated the mortuary temple of Amenemhat III at Hawara and the labyrinth at Fayoum. He also cleared the sand drifts from Abu Simbel (No. 21). The fruits of his labors were recorded in a huge, 12-volume study, *The Monuments of Egypt and Ethiopia* (1849–60), which remains to this day one of the largest archeological treatises ever produced.

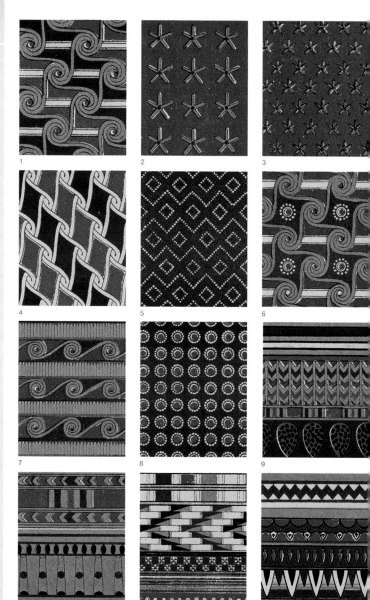

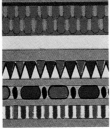

14

15

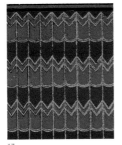

17

18

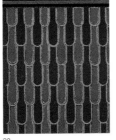

20

21

23

24

PLATE XI

1, 4, 6, 7, are from Tombs at Thebes, and are further examples of the Rope Ornament given in the last Plate. Nos. 2 and 3 are varieties of arrangements of Stars, very common on the ceilings both of tombs and temples. No. 2 is formed on squares, No. 3 on equilateral triangles.

9 From a Mummy-case.

10 From the Embroidery on a King's Robe.

11–16 are varieties of Borders from Paintings in Tombs.

17 From the Dress of a figure in one of the Royal Tombs of Biban el Moluk. It represents the Scales of the Armour worn by the Heroes and Gods of Egypt.

18–20 are similar, and most probably were suggested by the feathers of birds.

21 Ornament on the Dress of the god Amun, from Aboo-simbel.

22 From a Fragment in the Louvre.

23 Dado from the Tomb of Ramses, Biban el Moluk, probably representing, in diagram, a Papyrus-grove, as it occupies a similar position to those dados of a later period which were formed of buds and flowers of the papyrus.

24 From a very ancient tomb at Giza, opened by Dr. Lepsius. The upper part represents the usual Egyptian torus; the lower portion is from the dado of the same tomb, and shows that the practice of imitating grained woods in painting is of the highest antiquity.

CHAPTER III

ASSYRIAN AND
PERSIAN ORNAMENT

R ich as has been the harvest gathered by Mons. Botta and Mr. Layard from the ruins of Assyrian Palaces, the monuments which they have made known to us do not appear to carry us back to any remote period of Assyrian Art. Like the monuments of Egypt, those hitherto discovered belong to a period of decline, and of a decline much further removed from a culminating point of perfection. The Assyrian must have either been a borrowed style, or the remains of a more perfect form of art have yet to be discovered. We are strongly inclined to believe that the Assyrian is not an original style, but was borrowed from the Egyptian, modified by the difference of the religion and habits of the Assyrian people.

On comparing the bas-reliefs of Nineveh with those of Egypt we cannot but be struck with the many points of resemblance in the two styles; not only is the same mode of representation adopted, but the objects represented are oftentimes so similar, that it is difficult to believe that the

EGYPTIAN

ASSYRIAN

same style could have been arrived at by two people independently of each other.

The mode of representing a river, a tree, a besieged city, a group of prisoners, a battle, a king in his chariot, are almost identical,—the differences which exist are only those which would result from the representation of the habits of two different people; the art appears to us to be the same. Assyrian sculpture seems to be a development of the Egyptian, but, instead of being carried forward, descending in the scale of perfection, bearing the same relation to the Egyptian as the Roman does to the Greek. Egyptian sculpture gradually declined from the time of the Pharaohs to that of the Greeks and Romans; the forms, which were at first flowing and graceful, became coarse and abrupt; the swelling of the limbs, which was at first rather indicated than expressed, became at last exaggerated; the conventional was abandoned for an imperfect attempt at the natural. In

Assyrian sculpture this attempt was carried still farther, and while the general arrangement of the subject and the *pose* of the single figure were still conventional, an attempt was made to express the muscles of the limbs and the rotundity of the flesh; in all art this is a symptom of decline, Nature should be idealised not copied. Many modern statues differ in the same way from the Venus de Milo, as do the bas-reliefs of the Ptolemies from those of the Pharaohs.

Assyrian Ornament, we think, presents also the same aspect of a borrowed style and one in a state of decline. It is true that, as yet, we are but imperfectly acquainted with it; the portions of the Palaces which would contain the most ornament, the upper portions of the walls and the ceilings, having been, from the nature of the construction of Assyrian edifices, destroyed. There can be little doubt, however, that there was as much ornament employed in the Assyrian monuments as in the Egyptian: in both styles there is a total absence of plain surfaces on the walls, which are either covered with subjects or with writing, and in situations where these would have been inapplicable, pure ornament must have been employed to sustain the general effect. What we possess is gathered from the dresses on the figures of the bas-reliefs, some few fragments of painted bricks, some objects of bronze, and the representations of the

EGYPTIAN

ASSYRIAN

sacred trees in the bas-reliefs. As yet we have had no remains of their constructive ornament, the columns and other means of support, which would have been so decorated, being everywhere destroyed; the constructive ornaments which we have given in Plate XIV. *(pages 86–87)*, from Persepolis, being evidently of a much later date, and subject to the other influences, would be very unsafe guides in any attempt to restore the constructive ornament of the Assyrian Palaces.

Assyrian Ornament, though not based on the same types as the Egyptian, is represented in the same way. In both styles the ornaments in relief, as well as those painted, are in the nature of diagrams. There is but little surface-modelling, which was the peculiar invention of the Greeks, who retained it within its true limits, but the Romans carried it to great excess, till at last all breadth of effect was destroyed. The Byzantines returned again to moderate relief, the Arabs reduced the relief still farther, while with the Moors a modelled surface became extremely rare. In the other direction, the Romanesque is distinguished in the same way from the Early Gothic, which is itself much broader in effect than the later Gothic, where the surface at last became so laboured that all repose was destroyed.

With the exception of the pine-apple on the sacred trees, Plate XII. *(pages 82–83)*, and in the painted ornaments, and a species of lotus, Nos. 1 and 6, the ornaments do not appear to be formed on any natural type, which still farther strengthens the idea that the Assyrian is not an original style. The natural laws of radiation and tangential curvature, which we find in Egyptian ornament, are equally observed here, but much less truly,—rather, as it were,

SASSANIAN CAPITAL FROM BI SUTOUN
—FLANDIN & COSTE

traditionally than instinctively. Nature is not followed so closely as by the Egyptians, nor so exquisitely conventionalised as by the Greeks. Nos. 2 and 3, Plate XIII. *(pages 84–85)*, are supposed to be the types from which the Greeks derived some of their painted ornaments, but how inferior they are to the Greek in purity of form and in the distribution of the masses!

The colours in use by the Assyrians appear to have been blue, red, white, and black, on their painted ornaments; blue, red, and gold, on their sculptured ornaments; and green, orange, buff, white, and black, on their enamelled bricks.

The ornaments of Persepolis, represented on Plate XIV. *(pages 86–87)*, appear to be modifications of Roman details. Nos. 3, 4, 6, 7, 8, are from bases of fluted columns, which evidently betray a Roman influence. The ornaments from Tak I Bostan,—17, 20, 21, 22, 24,—are all constructed on the same principle as Roman ornament, presenting only a similar modification of the modelled surface, such as we find in Byzantine ornament, and which they resemble in a most remarkable manner.

The ornaments, 12 and 16, from Sassanian capitals, Byzantine in their general outline, at Bi Sutoun, contain the germs of all the ornamentation of the Arabs and Moors. It is the earliest example we meet with of lozenge-shaped diapers. The Egyptians and the Assyrians appear to have covered large spaces with patterns formed by geometrical arrangement of lines; but this is the first instance of the repetition of curved lines forming a general pattern enclosing a secondary form. By the principle contained in No. 16 would be generated all those exquisite forms of diaper which covered the domes of the mosques of Cairo and the walls of the Alhambra.

ASSYRIAN

Austen Layard (1817–94) was the leading light of Mesopotamian archeology. Born in Paris, he settled in London, before embarking on his lengthy expeditions to the East (1845–47 and 1849–51). His greatest finds came from Nimrud and Nineveh (now Kuyunjik). In particular, the sculptures of human-headed bulls caused a great stir when they were shipped by raft down the Tigris. Layard's book, *Nineveh and its Remains* (1849), stirred the public imagination and became a huge best-seller, but he subsequently abandoned archeology in favor of politics. Jones has included here several examples of the Sacred Tree (Nos. 8, 13, 14), one of the most popular Assyrian motifs. It was revered as a manifestation of the goddess Ishtar, and was usually represented by a stylized combination of date palms, pine cones, vines, and pomegranates.

1

2

3

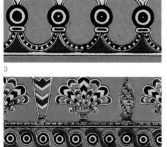

4

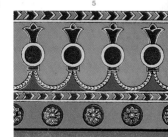

5

6

7

9

10

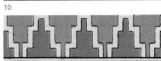

11

12

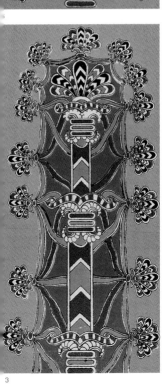

3

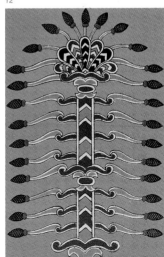

14

PLATE XII

1, 2 Sculptured Pavement, Kouyunjik.
3–7, 9–12 Painted Ornaments from Nimroud.
8, 13, 14 Sacred Trees from Nimroud.

The whole of the ornaments on this Plate are taken from Mr. Layard's great work, *The Monuments of Nineveh.* Nos. 3, 4, 5, 6, 7, 9, 11, 12, are coloured as published in his work. Nos. 1, 2, and the three Sacred Trees, Nos. 8, 13, 14, are in relief, and only in outline. We have treated them here as painted ornaments, supplying the colours in accordance with the principles indicated by those above, of which the colours are known.

ASSYRIAN

🪶 It was the impressive finds at Khorsabad (in present-day Iraq) that sparked off European interest in Mesopotamia. In 1843, the Frenchman Paul-Emile Botta (1802–70) uncovered the remains of an Assyrian palace that had once belonged to King Sargon II (ruled 721–705 BC). This contained a series of richly decorated alabaster wall reliefs, together with monumental carvings of winged bulls. The discoveries caused great excitement in Paris and prompted the British to mount rival expeditions to Nimrud and Nineveh. These gained the initiative, after Botta's efforts were disrupted by the 1848 revolution in France.

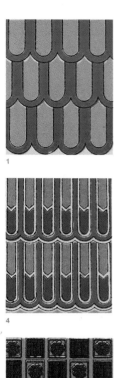

1

2

3

4

5

6

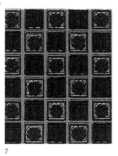

7

8

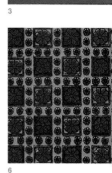

9

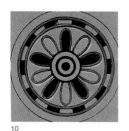

10

11

12

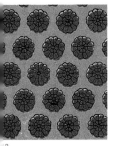

3

14

15

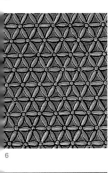

6

17

18

9

20

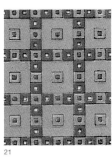

21

2

23

24

PLATE XIII

1–4 Enamelled Bricks, from Khorsabad.— FLANDIN & COSTE.

5 Ornament on King's Dress, from Khorsabad.— F.&C.

6, 7 Ornaments on a King's Dress, Ditto. F.&C.

8, 9 Ornaments from a Bronze Vessel, Nimroud.— LAYARD.

10 Enamelled Brick, from Bashikhah.— LAYARD.

11 Enamelled Brick, from Nimroud.— LAYARD.

12, 17, 18, 19, 20, 24 Enamelled Bricks, from Khorsabad.— F.&C.

13 Ornament on a King's Dress, from Khorsabad.— F.&C.

14 Enamelled Brick, from Khorsabad. F.&C.

15 Ornament on a Battering Ram, Khorsabad.— F.&C.

16 Ornament from a Bronze Vessel, Nimroud.— LAYARD.

21 Enamelled Brick, from Khorsabad.— F.&C.

22, 23 Ornaments on a Bronze Shield, from Khorsabad.—F.&C.

The ornaments Nos. 5, 6, 7, 13, are very common on the royal robes, and represent embroidery. We have restored the colouring in a way which we consider best adapted for developing the various patterns. The remainder of the ornaments on this Plate are coloured as they have been published by Mr. Layard and Messrs. Flandin and Coste.

🦜 The Sassanians were an important Persian dynasty, who held sway from AD 224 until the arrival of Islam (651). Persepolis itself was much older, having been founded by Darius I (ruled 521–486 BC), the most powerful member of the Achaemenid dynasty. Darius created a series of palaces at Persepolis, making it the capital of his empire. These great mansions were notable for their columned reception halls *(apadana)*, which are the source of many of Jones's illustrations. The earliest British excavations at Persepolis were conducted by James Morier in the 1810s, and the site was also visited by Claudius Rich in 1821.

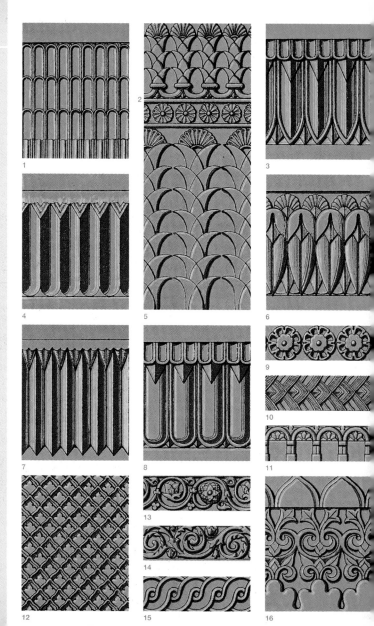

PLATE XIV

1 Feathered Ornament in the Curvetto of the Cornice, Palace No. 8, Persepolis.—FLANDIN & COSTE.

2 Base of Column from Ruin No. 13, Persepolis.—F.&C.

3 Base of Column of Colonnade No. 2, Persepolis—F.&C.

5 Ornament on the Side of the Staircase of Palace No. 2, Persepolis—F.&C.

6 Base of Column, Palace No. 2, Persepolis. F.&C.

7 Base of Column, Portico No. 1, Persepolis. F.&C.

8 Base of Column at Istakhr. F.&C.

9–12 From Sassanian Capitals, Bi Sutoun. F.&C.

13–15 From Sassanian Capitals, at Ispahan.—F.&C.

16 From a Sassanian Moulding, Bi Sutoun. F.&C.

17 Capital of Pilaster, Tak I Bostan. F.&C.

18, 19 Sassanian Ornaments from Ispahan. F.&C.

20 Upper part of Pilaster, Tak I Bostan. F.&C.

21 Archivolt from Tak I Bostan. F.&C.

22 Ornament from Tak I Bostan. F.&C.

23 Sassanian Capital, Ispahan. F.&C.

24 Pilaster, Tak I Bostan. F.&C.

25 Sassanian Capital, Ispahan. F.&C.

CHAPTER IV

GREEK ORNAMENT

We have seen that Egyptian Ornament was derived direct from natural inspiration, that it was founded on a few types, and that it remained unchanged during the whole course of Egyptian civilization, except in the more or less perfection of the execution, the more ancient monuments being the most perfect. We have further expressed our belief that the Assyrian was a borrowed style, possessing none of the characteristics of original inspiration, but rather appearing to have been suggested by the Art of Egypt, already in its decline, which decline was carried still farther. Greek Art, on the contrary, though borrowed partly from the Egyptian and partly from the Assyrian, was the development of an old idea in a new direction; and, unrestrained by religious laws, as would appear to have been both the Assyrian and the Egyptian, Greek Art rose rapidly to a high state of perfection, from which it was itself able to give forth the elements of future greatness to other styles. It carried the perfection of pure form to a point

TERMINATION OF THE MARBLE
TILES OF THE PARTHENON—L. VULLIAMY

which has never since been reached; and from the very abundant remains we have of Greek ornament, we must believe the presence of refined taste was almost universal, and that the land was overflowing with artists, whose hands and minds were so trained as to enable them to execute these beautiful ornaments with unerring truth.

Greek ornament was wanting, however, in one of the great charms which should always accompany ornament,—viz. Symbolism. It was meaningless, purely decorative, never representative, and can hardly be said to be constructive; for the various members of a Greek monument

UPPER PART OF
A STELE—L. VULLIAMY

rather present surfaces exquisitely designed to receive ornament, which they did, at first, painted, and in later times both carved and painted. The ornament was no part of the construction, as with the Egyptian: it could be removed, and the structure remained unchanged. On the Corinthian capital the ornament is applied, not constructed: it is not so on the Egyptian capital; there we feel the whole capital is the ornament,—to remove any portion of it would destroy it.

However much we admire the extreme and almost divine perfection of the Greek monumental sculpture, in its application the Greeks frequently went beyond the legitimate bounds of ornament. The frieze of the Parthenon was placed so far from the eye that it became a diagram: the beauties which so astonish us when seen near the eye could only have been valuable so far as they evidenced the artist-worship which cared not that the eye saw the perfection of the work if conscious that it was to be found there; but we are bound to consider this an abuse of means, and that the Greeks were in this respect inferior to the Egyptians, whose system of incavo relievo for monumental sculpture appears to us the more perfect.

THE UPPER PART OF
A STELE—L. VULLIAMY

The examples of representative ornament are very few, with the exception of the wave ornament and the fret used to distinguish water from land in their pictures, and some conventional renderings of trees, as at No. 14, Plate XXI. *(pages 110–11)*, we have little that can deserve this appellation; but of decorative ornament the Greek and Etruscan vases supply us with abundant materials; and as the painted ornaments of the Temples which have as yet been discovered in no way differ from them, we have little doubt that we are acquainted with Greek ornament in all its phases. Like the Egyptian the types are few, but the conventional rendering is much further removed from the types. In the well-known honeysuckle ornament it is difficult to recognise any attempt at imitation, but rather an appreciation of the principle on which the flower grows; and, indeed, on examining the paintings on the vases, we are rather tempted to believe that the various forms of the leaves of a Greek flower have been generated by the brush of the painter, according as the hand is turned upwards or downwards in the formation of the leaf would the character be given, and it is more likely that the slight resemblance to the honeysuckle may have been an after recognition than that the natural flower should have ever served as the model. In Plate XCIX. *(page 488)* will be found a representation of the honeysuckle; and how faint indeed is the resemblance! What is evident is, that the Greeks in their ornament were close observers of nature, and although they did not copy, or attempt to imitate, they worked on the same principles. The three great laws which we find everywhere in nature— radiation from the parent stem, proportionate distribution of the areas, and the tangential curvature of the lines—are always obeyed, and it is the unerring perfection with which they are, in the most humble works as in the highest, which excites our astonishment, and which is only

fully realised on attempting to reproduce Greek ornament, so rarely done with success. A very characteristic feature of Greek ornament, continued by the Romans, but abandoned during the Byzantine period, is, that the various parts of a scroll grow out of each other in a continuous line, as the ornament from the Choragic Monument of Lysicrates.

In the Byzantine, the Arabian Moresque, and Early English styles, the flowers flow off on either side from a continuous line. We have here an instance how slight a change in any generally received principle is sufficient to generate an entirely new order of forms and ideas. Roman ornament is constantly struggling against this apparently fixed law. At the head of the Roman chapter is a fine example, which may be taken as a type of all other Roman ornament, which scarcely ever got beyond the arrangement of a

FROM THE CHORAGIC MONUMENT
OF LYSICRATES, ATHENS—L. VULLIAMY

volute springing from a stem fitting into another stem, encircling a flower. The change which took place during the Byzantine period in getting rid of this fixed law was as important in its results to the development of ornament as was the substitution of the arch by the Romans for the straight architrave, or the introduction of the pointed arch in Gothic architecture. These changes have the same influence in the development of a new style of ornament as the sudden discovery of a general law in science, or the lucky patented idea which in any work of industry suddenly lets loose thousands of minds to examine and improve upon the first crude thought.

Plate XXII. *(pages 112–13)* is devoted to the remains of coloured ornaments on the Greek monuments. It will be seen that there is no difference whatever in the character of the drawing to those found on the vases. It is now almost universally recognised, that the white marble temples of the Greeks were entirely covered with painted ornament. Whatever doubts may exist as to the more or less colouring of the sculpture, there can be none as to the ornaments of the mouldings. The traces of colour exist everywhere so strongly, that in taking casts of the mouldings the traces of the pattern are strongly marked on the plaster cast. What the particular colours were, however, is not so certain. Different authorities give them differently: where one will see green, another finds blue,—or imagines gold where another sees brown. We may be quite certain, however, of one point,—all of these ornaments on the mouldings were so high from the ground, and so small in proportion to the distance from which they were seen, that they must have been coloured in a manner to render them distinct and to bring out the pattern. It is with this consideration that we have ventured to supply the colour to 5, 10, 11, 13, 14, which have hitherto been published only as gold or brown ornaments on the white marble.

Plate XV. *(pages 100–01).* In this Plate are given a collection of the different varieties of the Greek fret, from the simple generating form No. 3, to the more complicated meander No. 15. It will be seen, that the variety of arrangement of form that can be produced by the interlacing of lines at right angles in this form is very limited. We have, first, the simple fret, No. 1, running in one direction with a single line; the double fret, No. 14, with the

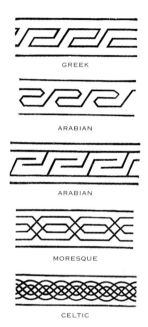

GREEK

ARABIAN

ARABIAN

MORESQUE

CELTIC

second line interlacing with the first; all the others are formed by placing these frets one under the other, running in different directions, as at No. 16; back to back, as at Nos. 17 and 22; or enclosing squares, as at No. 19. All the other kinds are imperfect frets,—that is, not forming a continuous meander. The raking fret, No. 2, is the parent of all the other forms of interlacing ornament in styles which succeeded the Greek. From this was first derived the Arabian fret, which in its turn gave birth to that infinite variety of interlaced ornaments formed by the intersection of equidistant diagonal lines, which the Moors carried to such perfection in the Alhambra.

The knotted work of the Celts differs from the Moresque interlaced patterns only in adding curved terminations to the diagonal intersecting lines. The leading idea once obtained, it gave birth to an immense variety of new forms.

The knotted-rope ornament of the Greeks may also have had some influence in the formation both of these and the Arabian and Moresque interlaced ornaments.

The Chinese frets are less perfect than any of these. They are formed, like the Greek, by the intersection of perpendicular with horizontal lines, but they have not the same regularity, and the meander is more often elongated in the horizontal direction. They are also most frequently used fragmentally,—that is, there is a repetition of one fret after the other, or one below the other, without forming a continuous meander.

The Mexican ornaments and frets, of which we here *(page 99)* give some illustrations from Mexican pottery in the British Museum, have a remarkable affinity with the Greek fret: and in Mr. Catherwood's illustrations of the architecture of Yucatan we have several varieties of the Greek fret: one especially is thoroughly Greek. But they are, in general, fragmentary, like the Chinese: there is also to be found at Yucatan a fret with a diagonal line, which is peculiar.

The ornaments on Plate XVI. *(pages 102–03)* have been selected to show the various forms of conventional leafage to be found on the Greek vases. They are all very far removed from any natural type, and are rather constructed on the general principles which reign in all plants, than attempts to represent any particular one. The ornament No. 2 is the nearest approach to the honeysuckle—that is, the leaves have the peculiar turn upwards of that flower, but it can hardly be called an attempt to represent it. Several of the ornaments on Plate XVII. *(pages 104–05)* are much nearer to Nature: the laurel, the ivy, and vine will be readily distinguished. Plates XVIII., XIX., XX., and XXI. *(pages 106–11)*, present further varieties from borders, necks, and

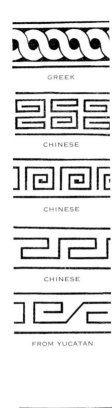

GREEK

CHINESE

CHINESE

CHINESE

FROM YUCATAN

FROM YUCATAN

lips of vases in the British Museum and the Louvre. Being produced by one or two colours, they all depend for their effect on pure form: they have mostly this peculiarity, that the groups of leaves or flowers all spring from a curved stem, with a volute at either end, and all the lines grow out of this parent stem in tangential curves. The individual leaves all radiate from the centre of the group of leaves, each leaf diminishing in exquisite proportion as it approaches the springing of the group.

When we consider that each leaf was done with a single stroke of the brush, and that from the differences which appear we may be sure no mechanical aids were employed, we must be astonished at the high state of the Arts which must have existed for artists to be found in such numbers able to execute with unerring truth what it is almost beyond the skill of modern times even to copy with the same happy result.

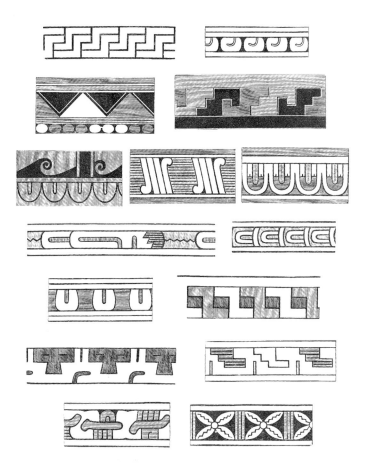

ORNAMENTS FROM MEXICAN POTTERY
IN THE BRITISH MUSEUM

GREEK

Most Victorians felt a nostalgic kinship with ancient Greece, regarding it as the cradle of Western civilization. This was reflected in the neoclassical movement *(see also page 120)*—a major style, celebrating the glories of the ancient, classical world—which had proved a dominant force in European culture since the late eighteenth century. Ironically, the movement gained its greatest momentum from Roman finds, particularly those at Pompeii and Herculaneum. Greece itself remained part of the Ottoman Empire and, as such, was comparatively inaccessible for Western travelers. Curiously, too, the Greek temples in Sicily and at Paestum in Italy attracted little attention from scholars. The fretwork or Greek key patterns shown here lay at the heart of Hellenic design. Their versatility made them extremely popular with neoclassical architects, who often employed them in friezes and string courses.

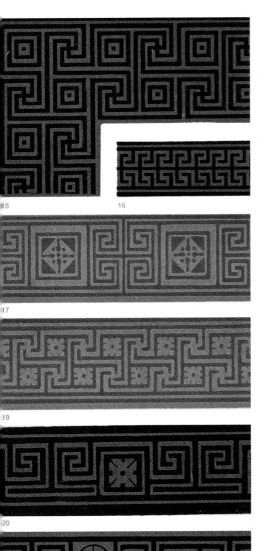

PLATE XV

1–22 A collection of the various forms of the Greek Fret from Vases and Pavements.

15

16

17

18

19

20

21

22

The Greeks were very fond of depicting stylized plants in their artworks. One of their favorite motifs was the anthemion, a flowerlike cluster of foliage resembling a honeysuckle (Nos. 1, 5, 6). This was often used in friezes, alternating with lotus buds or palmettes. Jones employed the motif himself in several of his architectural commissions.

The rediscovery of ancient Greece was a slow and painstaking process. Some of the earliest efforts were made under the auspices of the Dilettanti Society. Founded in 1732, this began as a dining club whose members professed an interest in antique art. It did sponsor serious expeditions, however, among them the Greek tour of James "Athenian" Stuart and Nicholas Revett in 1748. Their survey, *The Antiquities of Athens* (1762), became the recognized source book for the area.

1

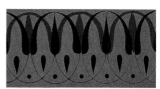

2

3

4

5

6

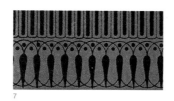

7

8

9

10

11

12

13

14

PLATE XVI

1–24 Ornaments from Greek and Etruscan Vases in the British Museum and the Louvre.

15

16

17

18

19

20

21

22

23

24

GREEK

The Greek War of Independence (1821–30) brought this ancient nation to the forefront of European consciousness. For centuries, the Greeks had been under Turkish control, until the bishop of Patras instigated an uprising in 1821. Their struggle was championed by many Westerners, who regarded the Greeks as their spiritual and cultural ancestors. In particular, it became a *cause célèbre* of the romantic movement, evoking a similar response to the Spanish Civil War in the twentieth century. Artists such as Eugène Delacroix (1798–1863) painted scenes of the conflict, while Lord Byron (1788–1824) went out to join the fighting, but died of a fever before striking a blow.

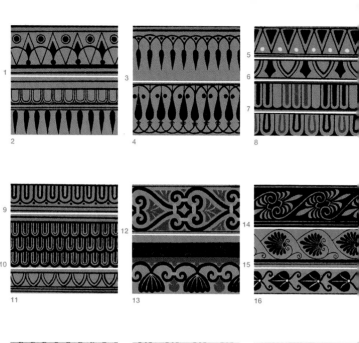

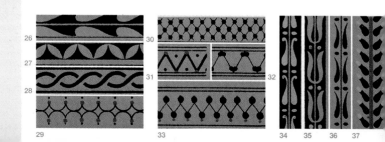

8   39   40   41   42   43   44   45

PLATE XVII

1–65 Ornaments from Greek and Etruscan Vases in the British Museum and the Louvre.

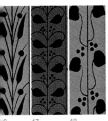

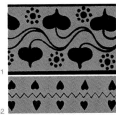

6   47   48   49   50   51   52

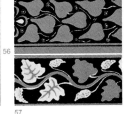

3   54   55   56   57   58

59   60   61   62   63   64   65

Purely in terms of quantity, the most familiar examples of Greek ornament came from antique vases. By Jones's day, thousands of these had been imported into Britain and could be seen in public museums. The greatest collector was Sir William Hamilton (1730–1803), a British envoy in Naples. He began to specialize in vases, after purchasing the Porcinari collection in 1766. By 1772 his stock had grown so large that he sold much of it—some 730 vases— to the British Museum for 8,000 guineas. A second batch was later sold to a private collector, Thomas Hope (1769–1831). In spite of his immense antiquarian knowledge, Sir William is best remembered today as the husband of Lord Nelson's mistress, Emma Hamilton.

2

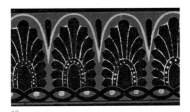

13

15

17

19

21

PLATE XVIII

1–21 Ornaments from Greek and Etruscan Vases in the British Museum and the Louvre.

The Etruscans were an Italian people who came from Etruria (roughly equivalent to present-day Tuscany). Their lavish tombs were first explored in the sixteenth century. These yielded up a huge number of vases, most of which had been imported from Greece, although there was also a local ware known as *bucchero*. For many years, however, there was confusion about the origins of these vases, enabling the Etruscans to gain a very high reputation in this field. As a result, the English potter Josiah Wedgwood (1730–95) dubbed his workshop "Etruria" and, from 1768, produced a line of "Etruscan" wares, which were actually based on Greek models.

29

33

36

PLATE XIX

1–36 Ornaments from Greek and Etruscan Vases in the British Museum and the Louvre.

GREEK

The Elgin Marbles have always been the focus of great controversy, both now and in Victorian times. They were removed from the Parthenon in Athens in 1801, after Thomas Bruce, the seventh earl of Elgin (1766–1841), had received permission from the ruling Turkish authorities. The marbles were then shipped back to London, where they were initially displayed in a "damp, dirty penthouse" in Piccadilly. Opinions differed as to the merits of the sculptures, with some regarding them as sublime, while others deemed them inferior Roman copies. In the end they were only purchased for the nation in 1816, largely to prevent them from being sold abroad.

PLATE XX

1–13 Ornaments from Greek and Etruscan Vases in the British Museum and the Louvre.

PLATE XXI

1–22 Ornaments from Greek and Etruscan Vases in the British Museum and the Louvre.

GREEK

The furor surrounding the Elgin Marbles *(see page 110)* inspired a renewed passion for classical architecture in Britain. Known as the "Greek revival," this trend reached a peak in the 1820s and 1830s, but was still a vital force in Jones's day. As their nicknames suggest, James "Athenian" Stuart (1713–88) and Alexander "Greek" Thomson (1817–75) were leading exponents, although the most celebrated figures were John Nash (1752–1835) and Sir John Soane (1753–1837). The popularity of the style ensured that many new public buildings were built to resemble Grecian temples. Typical examples include the British Museum (1823–47), the Bank of England (1804–26), and the National Gallery (1834–38).

1

2

5

3

4

8

9

6

7

11

10

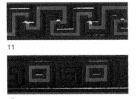
12

13

14

16

17

19

20

22

23

25

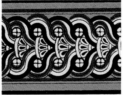
26

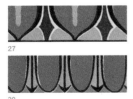
27

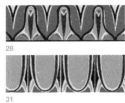
28

30

31

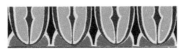
33

PLATE XXII

1–7, 21, 24, 27, 28, 30–33
From the Propylæa,
Athens.—HITTORFF.
1–4, 6, 7 From the Coffers
of the Ceiling of the
Propylæa.—PENROSE.
5 String-course over the
Panathenaic Frieze.
Published by Mr. PENROSE
in gold only, we have
supplied the blue and red.
10 Painted Ornament from
the Cymatium of the raking
Cornice of the Parthenon.—
L. VULLIAMY, the blue and
red supplied.
11–14 Various Frets, the
traces of which exist on all
the Temples at Athens. The
colours supplied.
15, 29 From a Sarcophagus
in Sicily.—HITTORFF.
16, 17, 19, 22, 23, 25
Painted Ornaments.—
HITTORFF.
20, 26 Ornaments in
Terra Cotta.

CHAPTER V

POMPEIAN ORNAMENT

T he ornament of Pompeii has been so ably and so fully illustrated in Zahn's magnificent work, that we have thought it only necessary for this series to borrow from him the materials for two plates, to illustrate the two distinct styles of ornament which prevail in the decorations of the edifices of Pompeii. The first (Plate XXIII., *pages 120–121*) are evidently of Greek origin, composed of conventional ornaments in flat tints, either painted dark on a light ground, or light on a dark ground, but without shade or any attempt at relief; the second (Plate XXIV., *page 122*) are more Roman in character, based upon the acanthus scroll, and interwoven with ornament in direct imitation of Nature.

We refer the reader to Zahn's work* for a full appreciation of the system of ornamentation in use at Pompeii. An examination of this work will show that this system was carried to the very limit of caprice, and that almost

---

* *Les plus Beaux Ornemens et les Tableaux les plus Remarquables de Pompeii, d'Herculanum, et de Stabiœ, & c.*, par Guillaume Zahn. Berlin, 1828.

any theory of colouring and decoration could be supported by authority from Pompeii.

The general arrangement of the decoration on the walls of the interior of a Pompeian house consists of a dado, about one-sixth of the height of the wall, upon which stand broad pilasters half the width of the dado, dividing the wall into three or more panels. The pilasters are united by a frieze of varying width, about one-fourth of the height of the wall from the top. The upper space is frequently white, and it is always subjected to a much less severe treatment than the parts below, generally representing the open air, and upon the ground are painted those fantastic architectural buildings which excited the ire of Vitruvius. In the best examples there is a gradation of colour from the ceiling downwards, ending with black in the dado, but this is very far from being a fixed law. We select opposite from the coloured illustrations in Zahn's work several varieties, which will show how little this was the result of system:—

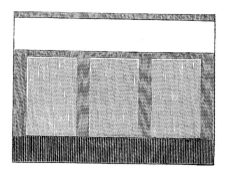

DIAGRAM OF THE SIDE OF A POMPEIAN HOUSE

DADO	PILASTERS	PANELS	FRIEZE
Yellow	Green	Red	Black
Red	Red	Black	Purple
Black	Yellow	Black	Red
Black	Yellow	Green	Green
Blue	Yellow	Green	Green
Blue	Yellow	Blue	Blue
Black	Green	Yellow and Red (alternately)	White
Black	Grey	Yellow and Red (alternately)	Black
Black	Black	Green and Red (alternately)	White

The most effective arrangement appears to be black dado, red pilasters and frieze, with yellow, blue, or white panels, the upper part above the frieze being in white, with coloured decorations upon it. The best arrangement of colours for the ornaments on the ground appears to be, on the black grounds, green and blues in masses, red sparingly, and yellow still more so. On the blue grounds, white in thin lines, and yellow in masses. On the red grounds, green, white and blue in thin lines: the yellow on red is not effective unless heightened with shade.

Almost every variety of shade and tone of colour may be found at Pompeii. Blue, red, and yellow are used, not only in small quantities in the ornaments, but also in large masses as grounds for the panels and pilasters. The yellow of Pompeii, however, nearly approaches orange, and the red is strongly tinged with blue. This neutral character of the colours enables them to be so violently juxtaposed without discord, a result still further assisted by the secondary and tertiary colours by which they are surrounded.

The whole style, however, of the decoration is so capricious that it is beyond the range of true art, and strict criticism cannot be applied to it. It generally pleases, but, if not absolutely vulgar, it oftentimes approaches vulgarity. It owes its greatest charm to the light, sketchy, free-hand manner of its execution, which it is quite impossible to render in any drawing; and which has never been accomplished in any restoration of the style. The reason is obvious; the artists of Pompeii invented as they drew; every touch of their brush had an intention which no copyist can seize.

Mr. Digby Wyatt's restoration of a Pompeian house in the Crystal Palace, Sydenham, admirable and faithful as it is in all other respects, necessarily failed in this; no one could possibly have brought greater knowledge, experience, and zeal to bear upon the realisation of that accuracy in the decorations which was so much desired than did Signor Abbate. The want of his perfect success consisted in the fact, that his paintings were at the same time too well executed and not sufficiently individual.

The ornaments which are given on Plate XXIII. *(pages 120–21)*, and which have evidently a Greek character, are generally borders on the panels, and are executed with stencils. They have a thinness of character compared with Greek models, which show a marked inferiority; we no longer find perfect radiation of lines from the parent stem, nor perfect distribution of masses and proportional areas. Their charm lies in an agreeable contrast of colour, which is still further heightened when surrounded with other colours *in situ*.

The ornaments from pilasters and friezes on Plate XXIV. *(page 122)*, after the Roman type, are shaded to give rotundity, but not sufficiently so to detach them from the ground. In this the Pompeian artists showed a judgment in not exceeding that limit of the treatment of ornament in the round, altogether lost sight of in subsequent times. We have here the acanthus-leaf scroll forming the groundwork, on which are engrafted representations of leaves and flowers interlaced with animals, precisely similar to the remains found in the Roman baths, and which, in the time of Raphael, became the foundation of Italian ornament.

In Plate XXV. *(page 123)* we have gathered together all the forms of mosaic pavement, which was such a feature in every home of the Romans, wherever their dominion extended. In the attempt at relief shown in several of the examples, we have evidence that their taste was no longer so refined as that of their Greek teachers. The borders, formed by a repetition of hexagons at the top and the sides of the page, are the types from which we may directly trace all that immense variety of Byzantine, Arabian and Moresque mosaics.

POMPEIAN

Situated by the Bay of Naples, Pompeii and neighboring Herculaneum were buried under volcanic ash during an eruption of Vesuvius in AD 79. The sites were not forgotten, however, and systematic excavations began in the mid-eighteenth century. These excited great interest throughout Europe, largely because the lava had left the domestic architecture, with its paintings, mosaics, and interior decoration, in a fine state of preservation. This dramatic insight into ancient life was a key factor in the development of neoclassicism, inspiring a number of architects. Robert Adam (1728–92) visited the excavations at Herculaneum in 1755, while Joseph Bonomi (the father of Jones's friend, see page 64) used Pompeian motifs in some of his designs.

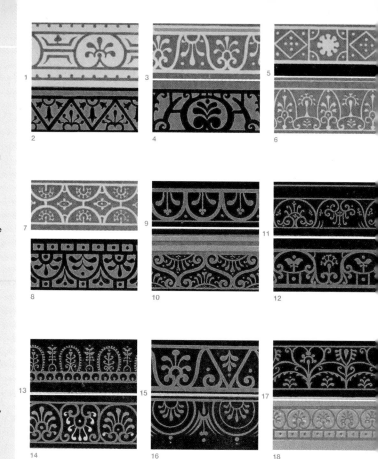

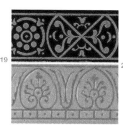

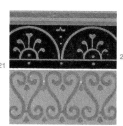

25 26 27 28 29 30

PLATE XXIII

1–48 Collection of Borders from different Houses in Pompeii.—ZAHN'S *Pompeii*.

31 32 33 34 35 36

37 38 39 40 41 42

43 44 45 46 47 48

POMPEIAN

Jones devoted comparatively little space to Pompeian art in his *Grammar of Ornament*, a telling sign of its fluctuating reputation. In the second half of the eighteenth century there was huge public interest in Pompeii, and a visit to the excavated site was an essential element of the Grand Tour. After this first flush of enthusiasm, however, the merits of its decorations were reassessed. As Jones suggests in his introduction, there was a growing view that Pompeii's paintings and mosaics were routine copies of Hellenistic art. To some extent this critical pendulum swung back again in the twentieth century.

1–15 Various Pilasters and Friezes from different Houses in Pompeii.— ZAHN'S *Pompeii*.

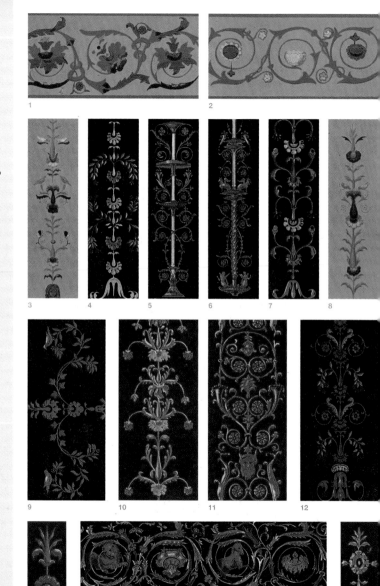

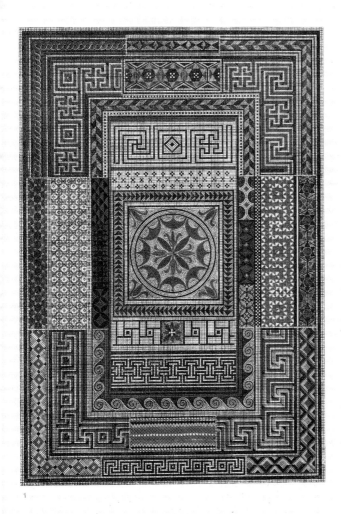

1

PLATE XXV

Collection of Mosaics from Pompeii and the Museum at Naples.—From the Author's Sketches.

CHAPTER VI

ROMAN ORNAMENT

The real greatness of the Romans is rather to be seen in their palaces, baths, theatres, aqueducts, and other works of public utility, than in their temple architecture, which being the expression of a religion borrowed from the Greeks, and in which probably they had little faith, exhibits a corresponding want of earnestness and art-worship.

In the Greek temple it is everywhere apparent that the struggle was to arrive at a perfection worthy of the gods. In the Roman temple the aim was self-glorification. From the base of the column to the apex of the pediment every part is overloaded with ornament, tending rather to dazzle by quantity than to excite admiration by the quality of the work. The Greek temples when painted were as ornamented as those of the Romans, but with a very different result. The ornament was so arranged that it threw a coloured bloom over the whole structure, and in no way disturbed the exquisitely designed surfaces which received it.

FRAGMENT IN WHITE MARBLE
FROM THE MATTEL PALACE, ROME.—L. VULLIAMY*

The Romans ceased to value the general proportions of the structure and the contours of the moulded surfaces, which were entirely destroyed by the elaborate surface-modelling of the ornaments carved on them; and these ornaments do not grow naturally from the surface, but are applied on it. The acanthus leaves under the modillions, and those round the bell of the Corinthian capitals, are placed one before the other most unartistically. They are not even bound together by the necking at the top of the shaft, but rest upon it. Unlike in this the Egyptian capital, where the stems of the flowers round the bell are continued through the necking, and at the same time represent a beauty and express a truth.

* *Examples of Ornamental Sculpture in Architecture*, by Lewis Vulliamy. Architect. London

The fatal facilities which the Roman system of decoration gives for manufacturing ornament, by applying acanthus leaves to any form and in any direction, is the chief cause of the invasion of this ornament into most modern works. It requires so little thought, and is so completely a manufacture, that it has encouraged architects in an indolent neglect of one of their especial provinces, and the interior decorations of buildings have fallen into hands most unfitted to supply their placè.

In the use of the acanthus leaf the Romans showed but little art. They received it from the Greeks beautifully conventionalised; they went much nearer to the general outline, but exaggerated the surface-decoration. The Greeks confined themselves to expressing the principle of the foliation of the leaf, and bestowed all their care in the delicate undulations of its surface.

The ornament engraved opposite is typical of all Roman ornament, which consists universally of a scroll growing out of another scroll, encircling

FRAGMENT OF THE FRIEZE OF THE
TEMPLE OF THE SUN, COLONNA PALACE, ROME.—L. VULLIAMY

FROM THE ABBEY OF ST. DENIS, PARIS

a flower or group of leaves. This example, however, is constructed on Greek principles, but is wanting in Greek refinement. In Greek ornament the scrolls grow out of each other in the same way, but they are much more delicate at the point of junction. The acanthus leaf is also seen, as it were, in side elevation. The purely Roman method of using this is seen in the Corinthian capitals, and in the examples on Plates XXVI. and XXVII *(pages 132–35)*. The leaves are flattened out, and they lay one over the other, as in the cut.

The various capitals which we have engraved from Taylor and Cresy's work have been placed in juxtaposition, to show how little variety the Romans were able to produce in following out this application of the acanthus. The only difference which exists is in the proportion of the general form of the mass; the decline in this proportion from that of Jupiter Stator may be seen readily. How different from the immense variety of Egyptian capitals which arose from the modification of the general plan of the capital, even the introduction of the Ionic volute in the Composite order fails to add a beauty, but rather increases the deformity.

The pilasters from the Villa Medici, Nos. 4 and 5, Plate XXVI. *(pages 132–33)*, and the fragment, No. 6, are as perfect specimens of Roman ornament as could be found. As specimens of modelling and drawing they have strong claims to be admired, but as ornamental accessories to the architectural features of a building they most certainly, from their excessive relief and elaborate surface treatment, are deficient in the first principle, viz. adaptation to the purpose they have to fill.

The amount of design that can be obtained by working out this principle of leaf within leaf and leaf over leaf is very limited; and it was not till this principle of one leaf growing out of another in a continuous line was abandoned for the adoption of a continuous stem throwing off ornaments on either side, that pure conventional ornament received any development. The earliest examples of the change are found in St. Sophia at Constantinople; and we introduce here an example from St. Denis, where, although the swelling at the stem and the turned-back leaf at the junction of stem and stem have entirely disappeared, the continuous stem is not yet fully developed, as it appears in the narrow border top and bottom. This principle became very common in the illuminated MSS. of the eleventh, twelfth, and thirteenth centuries, and is the foundation of Early English foliage.

The fragments on Plate XXVII. *(pages 134–35)*, from the Museo Bresciano, are more elegant than those from the Villa Medici; the leaves more sharply accentuated and more conventionally treated. The frieze from the Arch of the Goldsmiths is, on the contrary, defective from the opposite cause.

We have not thought it necessary to give in this series any of the painted decorations of the Romans, of which remains exist in the Roman baths. We had no reliable material at command; and, further, they are so similar to those at Pompeii, and show rather what to avoid than what to follow, that we have thought it sufficient to introduce the two subjects from the Forum of Trajan, in which figures terminating in scrolls may be said to be the foundation of that prominent feature in their painted decorations.

THE ACANTHUS, FROM A PHOTOGRAPH

ARCH OF SEPTIMIUS
SEVERUS, ROME

INTERIOR OF
PANTHEON, ROME

PANTHEON,
ROME

PANTHEON, ROME,
PORTICO

TEMPLE OF MARS
VICTOR, ROME

ARCH OF
TITUS, ROME

ARCH OF
CONSTANTINE, ROME

ARCH OF
TRAJAN, ANCONA

TEMPLE OF
VESTA, TIVOLI

TEMPLE OF JUPITER
STATOR, ROME

CORINTHIAN AND COMPOSITE CAPITALS
REDUCED FROM TAYLOR AND CRESY'S *ROME* †

† *The Architectural Antiquities of Rome*, by G. L. Taylor and Cresy, Architects. London, 1821.

The Forum of Trajan is one of the most imposing remains of imperial Rome. Its highlight is Trajan's Column, which was regarded by Victorians as the finest example of Roman carving. A copy of this (No. 3) was made for the plaster court at London's Victoria and Albert Museum (which, in Jones's day, was still known as the South Kensington Museum). The Villa Medici is a Renaissance building dating from *ca.* 1540. For a time it was a museum, housing a fine collection of classical statuary, but in 1801 it was purchased by Napoleon for the French Academy.

1

2

3

4

5

6

PLATE XXVI

1, 2 Fragments from the Forum of Trajan, Rome.
3, 6 Fragments from the Villa Medici, Rome.
4 Pilasters from the Villa Medici, Rome.
5 Pilaster from the Villa Medici, Rome.

Nos. 1, 2, 4–6 are from Casts in the Crystal Palace; No. 3 from a Cast at South Kensington Museum.

Jones was largely unimpressed by Roman ornament, treating it as an adjunct of Greek art. In part this may be due to the fact that Roman sculpture was not represented particularly well in Britain's public collections. The chief source of material came from Charles Townley (1737–1805), an enthusiastic amateur who had built up a sizable collection of antique statuary and friezes. These were displayed to the public in his Westminster home. After his death "Townley's marbles" were purchased by the British Museum for the staggering sum of £20,000 ($30,000). They were housed in a specially built gallery (1808) within the museum.

PLATE XXVII

4

5

6

1, 2, 6 Fragments of the Frieze of the Roman Temple at Brescia.
3 From the Frieze of the Arch of the Goldsmiths, Rome.
4, 5 Fragment of the Soffits of the Architraves of the Roman Temple at Brescia.

Nos. 1, 2, 4, 6 from the Museo Bresciano;[§]
No. 5 from TAYLOR and CRESY'S *Rome.*

[§] *Museo Bresciano, illustrato.* Brescia, 1838.

CHAPTER VII

Byzantine Ornament

The vagueness with which writers on Art have treated the Byzantine and Romanesque styles of Architecture, even to within the last few years, has extended itself also to their concomitant decoration. This vagueness has arisen chiefly from the want of examples to which the writer could refer; nor was it until the publication of Herr Salzenberg's great work on Sta. Sofia at Constantinople, that we could obtain any complete and definite idea of what constituted pure Byzantine ornament. San Vitale at Ravenna, though thoroughly Byzantine as to its architecture, still afforded us but a very incomplete notion of Byzantine ornamentation: San Marco at Venice represented but a phase of the Byzantine school; and the Cathedral of Monreale, and other examples of the same style in Sicily, served only to show the influence, but hardly to illustrate the true nature, of pure Byzantine Art: fully to understand that, we required what the ravages of time and the whitewash of the Mahommedan had deprived us of, namely, a Byzantine building on a grand

A

B

scale, executed during the best period of the Byzantine epoch. Such an invaluable source of information has been opened to us through the enlightenment of the present Sultan, and been made public to the world by the liberality of the Prussian Government; and we recommend all those who desire to have a graphic idea of what Byzantine decorative art truly was, to study Herr Salzenberg's beautiful work on the churches and buildings of ancient Byzantium.

In no branch of art, probably, is the observation, *ex nihilo nihil fit*, more applicable than in decorative art. Thus, in the Byzantine style, we perceive that various schools have combined to form its peculiar characteristics, and we shall proceed to point out briefly what were the principal formative causes.

Even before the transfer of the seat of the Roman Empire from Rome to Byzantium, at the commencement of the fourth century, we see all the arts in a state either of decline or transformation. Certain as it is that Rome had given her peculiar style of art to the numerous foreign peoples ranged beneath her sway, it is no less certain that the hybrid art of her provinces had powerfully reacted on the centre of civilisation; and even at the close of the third century had materially affected that lavish style of decoration which characterised the magnificent baths and the other public buildings of Rome. The necessity which Constantine found himself under, when newly settled in Byzantium, of employing Oriental artists and workmen, wrought a still more vital and marked change in the traditional style; and there can be little doubt but that each surrounding nation aided in giving its impress to the newly-formed school, according to the state of its civilisation and its capacity for Art, until at last the motley mass became fused into one systematic whole during the long and (for Art) prosperous reign of the first Justinian.

In this result we cannot fail to be struck with the important influence exercised by the great temples and theatres built in Asia Minor during the rule of the Cæsars; in these we already see the tendency to elliptical curved outlines, acute-pointed leaves, and thin continuous foliage without the springing-ball and flower, which characterise Byzantine ornament. On the frieze of the theatre at Patara (A), and at the Temple of Venus at Aphrodisias (Caria), are to be seen examples of flowing foliage such as we allude to. On the doorway of the temple erected by the native rulers of Galatia at Ancyra (B), in honour of Augustus, is a still more characteristic type, and the pilaster capital of a small temple at Patara (C), inscribed by Texier to the first century of the Christian era, is almost identical with one drawn by Salzenberg at Smyrna (D, *see overleaf*), which he believes to be of the first part of Justinian's reign, or about the year 525 A.D.

In the absence of authentic dates we cannot decide satisfactorily how far Persia influenced the Byzantine style, but it is certain that Persian workmen and artists were much employed at Byzantium; and in the remarkable monuments at Tak-i-Bostan, Bi-Sutoun, and Tak-i-Ghero, and in several ancient capitals at Ispahan— given in Flandin and Coste's great work on Persia— we are struck at once with their thoroughly Byzantine character; but we are inclined to believe that they are posterior, or at most contemporaneous, with the best period of Byzantine art, that is, of the sixth century. However that may be, we find the forms of a still earlier period reproduced so late as the year 363 A.D.; and in Jovian's column at Ancyra (E), erected during or shortly after his retreat with Julian's army from their Persian expedition, we recognise an application of one of the most general ornamental forms of ancient Persepolis. At Persepolis also are to be seen the pointed and channelled leaves so characteristic of Byzantine work, as seen in the accompanying example from Sta. Sofia (F); and at a later period, *i.e.* during the rule of the Cæsars, we remark at the Doric temple of Kangovar (G) contours of moulding precisely similar to those affected in the Byzantine style.

Interesting and instructive as it is to trace the derivation of these forms in the Byzantine style, it is no less so to mark the transmission of them and of others to later epochs. Thus in

No. 1, Plate XXVIII. *(pages 146–47)*, we perceive the peculiar leaf, as given in Texier and in Salzenberg, reappear at Sta. Sofia; at No. 3, Plate XXVIII., is the foliated St. Andrew's cross within a circle, so common as a Romanesque and Gothic ornament. On the same frieze is a design repeated with but slight alteration at No. 20 from Germany. The curved and foliated branch of No. 4 of the sixth century (Sta. Sofia) is seen reproduced, with slight variation, at No. 11 of the eleventh century (St. Mark's). The toothings of the leaves of No. 22 (Germany) are almost identical with those of No. 1 (Sta. Sofia); and between all the examples of 24–29

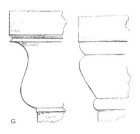

(Plate XXVIII.) is to be remarked a generic resemblance in subjects from Germany, Italy, and Spain, founded on a Byzantine type.

Two of the subjects in this plate illustrate more especially the Romanesque style (Nos. 30 and 36), showing the interlaced ornament so affected by the Northern nation, founded mainly on a native type; whilst at No. 35 (St. Denis) we have one instance out of numbers of the reproduction of Roman models; the type of the present subject,—a common one in the Romanesque style,—being found on the Roman column at Cussy, between Dijon and Chalons-sur-Saone.

Thus we see that Rome, Syria, Persia, and other countries, all took part as *formative* causes in the Byzantine style of art, and its accompanying decoration, which complete as we find it in Justinian's time, reacted in its new and systemised form upon the Western world, undergoing certain changes in its course; and these *modifying* causes, arising from the state of religion, art, and manners in the countries where it was received, frequently gave it a specific character, and produced in some cases co-relative and yet distinct styles of ornament in the Celtic, Anglo-Saxon, Lombardic, and Arabian schools. Placing on one side the question of how far Byzantine workmen or artists were employed in Europe, there can be no possible doubt that the character of the Byzantine school of ornament is very strongly impressed on all the earlier works of central and even Western Europe, which are generically termed Romanesque.

Pure Byzantine ornament is distinguished by broad-toothed and acute-pointed leaves, which in sculpture are bevelled at the edge, are deeply channelled throughout, and are drilled at the several springings of the teeth with deep holes; the running foliage is generally thin and continuous, as at Nos. 1, 14, and 20, Plate XXIX*., Plate XXIX *(pages 148–51)*. The ground, whether in mosaic or painted work, is almost universally gold; thin interlaced patterns are preferred to geometrical designs. The introduction of animal or other figures is very limited in sculpture, and in other colour is confined principally to holy subjects, in a stiff, conventional style, exhibiting little variety or feeling; sculpture is of very secondary importance.

Romanesque ornament, on the other hand, depended mainly on sculpture for effect: it is rich in light and shade, deep cuttings, massive projections, and a great intermixture of figure-subjects of every kind with foliage and conventional ornament. The place of mosaic work is generally supplied by paint; in coloured ornament, animals are as freely introduced as in sculpture, *vide* No. 26, Plate XXIX*. *(pages 150–51)*; the ground is no longer gold alone, but blue, red, or green, as at Nos. 26, 28, 29, Plate XXIX*. In other respects, allowing for local differences, it retains much of the Byzantine character; and in the case of painted glass, for example, handed it down to the middle, and even the close of the thirteenth century.

One style of ornament, that of geometrical mosaic work, belongs particularly to the Romanesque period, especially in Italy; numerous examples of it are given in Plate XXX *(pages 152–53)*. This art flourished principally in the twelfth and thirteenth centuries, and consists in the arrangement of small diamond-shaped pieces of glass into a complicated series of diagonal lines; the direction of which is now stopped, now defined, by means of different colours. The examples from central Italy, such as Nos. 7, 11, 13, 29, 31, are much simpler than those of the southern provinces and Sicily, where Saracenic artists introduced their innate love of intricate designs, some ordinary examples of which are to be seen in Nos. 1, 6, 37, from Monreale, near Palermo. It is to be remarked that there are two distinct styles of design coexistent in Sicily: the one, such as we have noted, consisting of diagonal interlacings, and eminently Moresque in character, as may be seen by reference to Plate XXIX. *(pages 148–49)*; the other, consisting of interlaced curves, as at Nos. 37, 38, 39, also from Monreale, in which we may recognise, if not the hand, at least the influence, of Byzantine artists. Altogether of a different character, though of about the same period, are Nos. 18, 20, 21, 34, 36, which serve as examples of the Veneto-Byzantine style; limited in its range, being almost local, and peculiar in style. Some are more markedly Byzantine, however, as No. 35, with interlaced circles; and the step ornament, so common at Sta. Sofia, as seen at Nos. 3, 10, and 11, Plate XXIX *(pages 148–49).*

The *opus Alexandrinum*, or marble mosaic work, differs from the *opus Grecanicum*, or glass mosaic work, chiefly from the different nature of the material; the principle (that of complicated geometric design) is still the same. The pavements of the Romanesque churches in Italy are rich in examples of this class; the tradition of which was handed down from the Augustan age of Rome; a good idea of the nature of this ornament is given in Nos. 23, 24, 40, 41, and 42.

Local styles, on the system of marble inlay, existed in several parts of Italy during the Romanesque period, which bear little relation either to Roman or Byzantine models. Such is No. 25, from San Vitale, Ravenna; such are the pavements of the Baptistery and San Miniato, Florence, of the eleventh, twelfth, and thirteenth centuries; in these the effect is produced by black and white marble only; with these exceptions, and those produced by Moresque influence in the South of Italy, the principles both of the glass and marble inlay ornament are to be found in ancient Roman inlay, in every province under Roman sway, and especially is it remarkable in the various mosaics found at Pompeii, of which striking examples are given in Plate XXV *(page 123).*

Important as we perceive the influence of Byzantine Art to have been in Europe, from the sixth to the eleventh century, and still later, there is no people whom it affected more than the great and spreading Arab race, who propagated the creed of Mahomet, conquered the finest countries of the

East, and finally obtained a footing even in Europe. In the earlier buildings executed by them at Cairo, Alexandria, Jerusalem, Cordova, and Sicily, the influence of the Byzantine style is very strongly marked. The traditions of the Byzantine school affected more or less all the adjacent countries; in Greece they remained almost unchanged to a very late period, and they have served, in a great degree, as the basis to all decorative art in the East and in Eastern Europe.

J. B. WARING.

September, 1856.

For more information on this subject, see "Handbook" to Byzantine and Romanesque Court at Sydenham.— WYATT and WARING.

BOOKS REFERRED TO FOR ILLUSTRATIONS

SALZENBERG. *Alt Christliche Baudenkmale von Constantinopel.*

FLANDIN ET COSTE. *Voyage en Perse.*

TEXIER. *Description de l'Arménie, Perse, &c.*

HEIDELOFF. *Die Ornamentik des Mittelalters.*

KREUTZ. *La Basilica di San Marco.*

GAILHABAUD. *L'Architecture et les Arts qui en dépendent.*

DU SOMMERARD. *Les Arts du Moyen Age.*

BARRAS ET LUYNES (DUC DE). *Recherches sur les Monuments de Normands en Sicile.*

CHAMPOLLION FIGEAC. *Palœographie Universelle.*

WILLEMIN. *Monuments Français inédits.*

HESSEMER. *Arabische und alt Italiänische Bau-Verzierungen.*

DIGBY WYATT. *Geometrical Mosaics of the Middle Ages.*

WARING AND MACQUOID. *Architectural Arts in Italy and Spain.*

WARING. *Architectural Studies at Burgos and its Neighbourhood.*

BYZANTINE

Jones chose many of his illustrations for this section from sites that lay outside the Byzantine Empire. Indeed, several are from buildings that would normally be classified as Romanesque. Byzantine artists had a formative influence on the development of this style. Many Greek craftsmen migrated to the West, and Byzantine artifacts were often taken there, particularly after 1204, when the Crusaders sacked Constantinople.

PLATE XXVIII

1, 2, 3 Stone Sculptured Ornament, Sta. Sofia, Constantinople. 6th century.—SALZENBERG.
4, 5 From the Bronze Gates, Sta. Sofia.—SALZENBERG.
6, 7 Portions of Ivory Diptychs, Beauvais Cathedral.—WILLEMIN.
8 Portion of Bronze Door, Basilica of the Nativity, Bethlehem. 3rd or 4th century.—GAILHABAUD.
9–11, 16, 31 Stone Sculptures, from St. Mark's, Venice. 11th century.— J.B.W. *Casts at Sydenham.*
12 From St. Denis (Porch), near Paris. 12th century.— J.B.W.
13 From the Cloisters of Sant' Ambrogia, Milan.— J.B.W.

7 18 19 20 21

2 23 24 25 26

  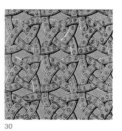

7 28 29 30

32 33

34 35 36

PLATE XXVIII

14 From the Chapel of Heilsbronn, Bavaria.— HEIDELOFF.

15 From St. Denis.— J.B.W.

17, 18, 19 Portion of a Capital, St. Michael's Church, Schwäbisch Hall. 12th Century.—HEIDELOFF.

20 From a Doorway, Murrhard Monastery.— HEIDELOFF.

21 Bosses, from St. Sebald, Nuremberg, and Nosson, Saxony.— HEIDELOFF.

22, 23 Friezes from the Church of St. John, Gmund, Swabia.—HEIDELOFF.

24 Romanesque Wood and Ivory Carving, in the Collection of Herr Leven, Cologne.—HEIDELOFF.

25 From the principal Bronze Door, Monreale, near Palermo.—J.B.W. 11th and 12th centuries.

26 From the Bronze Door of the Duomo, Ravello, near Amalfi.—J.B.W.

27, 28 From the Bronze Door of the Duomo, Trani. 12th century.—BARRAS ET LUYNES.

29 Stone Sculpture, from Huelgas Monastery, Burgos, Spain. 12th century.—J.B.W.

30 From the Porch of Lucca Cathedral. 1204 A.D.— J.B.W.

32 From Bayeux Cathedral. 12th century.— PUGIN, *Antiquities of Normandy*.

33 From St. Denis.—J.B.W.

34 Bayeux Cathedral.— PUGIN.

35 From Lincoln Cathedral Porch. Close of 12th century. J.B.W.

36 From the Kilpeck Porch, Herefordshire.—J.B.W.

Mosaic was the single most important medium in the decoration of Byzantine churches and palaces, assuming a status similar to painting in the West. The artists who worked in this field became adept at creating abstract patterns, largely because the depiction of living creatures was prohibited for a time in the East. These patterns were later mimicked by craftsmen, who added ornamental details to the margins of illuminated manuscripts. The latter were highly sought after in the West; indeed, the demand for manuscripts helped to transmit Byzantine styles of decoration to many parts of Europe.

1

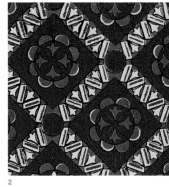

2

3

4

5

6

7

9

10   11

2

13

14

16

17

5

18

The sumptuous appearance of Byzantine decoration, with its heavy emphasis on rich materials and gold trappings, had great appeal for the Victorians. This gave rise to a fashion for neo-Byzantine architecture. Sir Matthew Digby Wyatt (1820–77), whose *Geometrical Mosaics of the Middle Ages* (1848) was one of Jones's chief sources for this section, was among the architects who worked in this vein. The most celebrated example, however, was John Bentley's Westminster Cathedral (1894–1903). The style was also very popular in Germany, where it was known as the *Rundbogenstil* ("round-arched style").

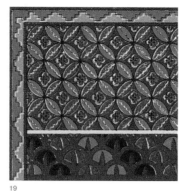

19

20

21

22

23

24

25

26

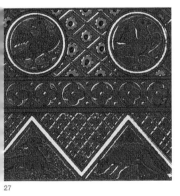

27

28

29

30

PLATE XXIX*

19 From a Greek MS., British Museum.— J.B.W. The border beneath from Monreale.—DIGBY WYATT's *Mosaics*.

20 From the Homilies of Gregory Nazianzen. 12th century.—CHAMPOLLION FIGEAC, *u.a.*

21, 22 From Greek MSS., British Museum.— J.B.W.

23 From the Acts of the Apostles, Greek MS., Vatican Library, Rome.— DIGBY WYATT, *u.a.*

24 St. Mark's, Venice.— DIGBY WYATT, *u.a.*

25 Portion of a Greek Diptych. 10th century. Florence—J.B.W. (The *fleurs-de-lys* are believed to be of later workmanship.)

26 Enamel of the 13th century (French).— WILLEMIN, *Monuments Français inédits.*

27 From an Enamelled Casket (the centre from the Statue of Jean, son of St. Louis).—DU SOMMERARD. *Les Arts du Moyen Age.*

28 From the Enamelled Tomb of Jean, son of St. Louis, A.D. 1247.— WILLEMIN, *u.a.*

29 Limoges Enamel, probably of the close of the 12th century.—WILLEMIN, *u.a.*

30 Portion of Mastic Pavement, 12th century. Preserved at St. Denis, near Paris.—WILLEMIN.

These pages include details from three of the finest Byzantine buildings in the West. The Italian city of Ravenna was briefly the capital of the Roman Empire before coming under Byzantine rule in AD 540. Work began on the spectacular church of San Vitale in 547. The magnificent architecture of St. Mark's in Venice is also Byzantine in all but name. Similarly, Byzantine artists were imported to provide decorations for the Sicilian cathedral of Monreale (*ca.* 1190), most notably its superb cycle of mosaics.

PLATE XXX

1, 2 Mosaics from Monreale Cathedral near Palermo. Close 12th century.—J.B.W.
3 Mosaics from the Church of Ara Cœli, Rome.—J.B.W.
4 Marble Pavement, St. Mark's, Venice.— J.B.W.
5, 6 Monreale.—J.B.W.
7, 8, 11, 12 From San Lorenzo Fuori, Rome. Close of 12th century.— J.B.W.
9 Marble Pavement, St. Mark's, Venice.—J.B.W.
10 Ara Cœli, Rome.—J.B.W.
13 San Lorenzo Fuori, Rome.—J.B.W.
14 San Lorenzo Fuori, Rome.—WARING AND MACQUOID.
15, 16 Palermo.—DIGBY WYATT.

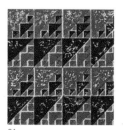
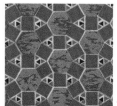

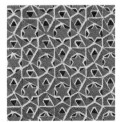

PLATE XXX

17 From the Cathedral, Monreale.—J.B.W.
18 St. Mark's, Venice.— DIGBY WYATT.
19 From Ara Cœli.— J.B.W.
20 From the Baptistery, St. Mark's, Venice.—J.B.W.
21 From St. Mark's, Venice.—WARING AND MACQUOID.
22 From the Duomo, Monreale.—J.B.W.
23 Marble Pavement, S.M. Maggiore, Rome.— HESSEMER.
24 Marble Pavement, S.M. in Cosmedin, Rome.— HESSEMER, *u.a.*
25 Marble Pavement, San Vitale, Ravenna.— HESSEMER, *u.a.*
26 San Giovanni Laterano, Rome.—DIGBY WYATT.
27 San Lorenzo, Rome— WARING AND MACQUOID.
28 The Duomo, Civita Castellana.—DIGBY WYATT.
29 Ara Cœli, Rome.— J.B.W.
30 San Lorenzo, Rome.— WARING AND MACQUOID.
31 San Lorenzo Fuori, Rome.—J.B.W.
32 Ara Cœli, Rome. — WARING AND MACQUOID.
33 San Giovanni Laterano, Rome.—DIGBY WYATT.
34, 35 Mosaic, St. Mark's, Venice.—*Specimens of the Mosaics of the Middle Ages,* DIGBY WYATT.
36 Baptistery of St. Mark, Venice.—WARING AND MACQUOID.
37–39 Monreale Cathedral.—J.B.W.
40–42 Marble Pavement, S.M. Maggiore, Rome.— HESSEMER, *u.a.*

CHAPTER VIII

ARABIAN ORNAMENT

FROM CAIRO

When the religion of Mohammed spread with such astounding rapidity over the East, the growing wants of a new civilisation naturally led to the formation of a new style of Art; and whilst it is certain that the early edifices of the Mohammedans were either old Roman or Byzantine buildings adapted to their own uses, or buildings constructed on the ruins and with the materials of ancient monuments, it is equally certain that the new wants to be supplied, and the new feelings to be expressed, must at a very early period have given a peculiar character to their architecture.

In the buildings which they constructed partly of old materials, they endeavoured, in the new parts of the structure, to imitate the details borrowed from old buildings. The same result followed as had already taken place in the transformation of the Roman style to the Byzantine: the imitations were crude and imperfect. But this very imperfection gave birth to a new order of ideas; they never returned to the original model, but gradually threw off the shackles which the original model imposed. The Mohammedans, very early in their history, formed and perfected a style of art peculiarly their own. The ornaments on Plate XXXI. *(pages 164–65)* are from the Mosque of Tooloon in Cairo, which was erected in 876, only 250 years after the establishment of Mohammedanism, and we in this mosque already find a style of architecture complete in itself,—retaining, it is true, traces of its origin, but being entirely freed from any direct imitation of the previous style. This result is very remarkable when compared with the results of the Christian religion in another direction. It can hardly be said that Christianity produced an architecture peculiarly its own, and entirely freed from traces of paganism, until the twelfth or thirteenth century.

The mosques of Cairo are amongst the most beautiful buildings in the world. They are remarkable at the same time for the grandeur and simplicity of their general forms, and for the refinement and elegance which the decoration of these forms displays.

This elegance of ornamentation appears to have been derived from the Persians, from whom the Arabs are supposed to have derived many of their arts. It is more than probable that this influence reached them by a double process. The art of Byzantium already displays an Asiatic influence. The remains at Bi-Sutoun, published by Flandin and Coste, are either Persian under Byzantine influence, or, if of earlier date, there must be much of Byzantine art which was derived from Persian sources, so similar are they in general character of outline. We have already, in Chapter III., referred to an ornament on a Sassanian capital, No. 16, Plate XIV. *(pages 86–87),*

SPANDRIL OF AN ARCH
FROM STA. SOPHIA—SALZENBERG

which appears to be the type of the Arabian diapers; and on the spandril of
the arch which we here introduce from Salzenberg's work on Sta. Sofia, will
be seen a system of decoration totally at variance with much of the Græco-
Roman features of that building, and which it may not be impossible are the
result of some Asiatic influence. Be that as it may, this spandril is itself the
foundation of the surface decoration of the Arabs and Moors. It will be
observed that, although the leafage which surrounds the centre is still a
reminiscence of the acanthus leaf, it is the first attempt at throwing off the
principle of leafage growing out one from the other: the scroll is continuous

without break. The pattern is distributed all over the spandril, so as to produce one even tint, which was ever the aim of the Arabs and Moors. There is also another feature connected with it,—the mouldings on the edge of the arch are ornamented from the surface, and the soffit of the arch is decorated in the same way as the soffits of Arabian and Moresque arches.

The collection of ornaments from the Mosque of Tooloon, on Plate XXXI. *(pages 164–65)*, are very remarkable, as exhibiting in this early stage of Arabian art the types of all those arrangements of form which reach their culminating point in the Alhambra. The differences which exist result from the less perfection of the distribution of the forms, the leading principles are the same. They represent the first stage of surface decoration. They are of plaster, and the surface of the part to be decorated being first brought to an even face, the patterns were either stamped or traced upon the material, whilst still in a plastic state, with a blunt instrument, which in making the incisions slightly rounded the edges. We at once recognised that the principles of the radiation of the lines from a parent stem and the tangential curvature of those lines had been either retained by Græco-Roman tradition, or was felt by them from observation of nature.

Many of the patterns, such as 2–5, 21, 22, 36, 38, still retain traces of this Greek origin: two flowers, or a flower turned upwards and another downwards, from either end of a stalk; but there was this difference, that with the Greeks the flowers or leaves do not form part of the scroll but grow out of it, whilst with the Arabs the scroll was transformed into an

ARABIAN

ARABIAN

ARABIAN

ARABIAN

GREEK

MORESQUE

intermediate leaf. No. 31 shows the continuous scroll derived from the Romans, with the division at each turn of the scroll, so characteristic of Roman ornament, omitted. The ornament we engrave here from Sta. Sophia would seem to be one of the earliest examples of the change.

The upright patterns on this Plate, chiefly from the soffits of windows, and therefore having all an upright tendency in their lines, may be considered as the germs of all those exquisitely-designed patterns of this class, where the repetition of the same patterns side by side produces another or several others. Many of the patterns on this Plate should be doubled in the lateral direction: our anxiety to exhibit as many varieties as possible preventing the engraving of the repeat.

With the exception of No. 14 on Plate XXXII. *(pages 166–67)*, which is from the same mosque as the ornament on the last plate, the whole of the ornaments on Plates XXXIII. and XXXIV. *(pages 168–71)* are of the thirteenth century, *i.e.* four hundred years later than those of the Mosque of Tooloon. The progress which the style had made in this period may be seen at a glance. As compared, however, with the Alhambra, which is of the same period, they are very inferior. The Arabs never arrived at that state of perfection in the distribution of the masses, or

in the ornamenting of the surfaces of the ornaments, in which the Moors so excelled. The guiding instinct is the same, but the execution is very inferior. In Moresque ornament the relation of the areas of the ornament to the ground is always perfect; there are never any gaps or holes; in the decoration of the surfaces of the ornaments also they exhibited much greater skill,—there was less monotony. To exhibit clearly the difference, we repeat the Arabian ornament, No. 16, from Plate XXXIII. *(pages 168–69)*, compared with two varieties of lozenge diapers from the Alhambra.

The Moors also introduced another feature into their surface ornament, viz. that there were often two and sometimes three planes on which the patterns were drawn, the ornaments on the upper plane being boldly distributed over the mass, whilst those on the second interwove themselves with the first, enriching the surface on a lower level; by which admirable contrivance a piece of ornament retains its breadth of effect when viewed at a distance, and affords most exquisite, and oftentimes most ingenious, decoration for close inspection. Generally there was more variety in their surface treatment; the feathering which forms so prominent a feature on the ornaments on Plates XXXII., XXXIII. *(pages 166–69)*, was intermixed with plain surfaces, such as we see at Nos. 21, 23, Plate XXXII. The ornament No. 18, Plate XXXIII., is in pierced metal, and is a very near approach to the perfection of distribution on the Moorish forms; it finely exhibits the proportionate diminution of the forms towards the centre of the pattern, and that fixed law, never broken by the Moors, that however distant an ornament, or however intricate the pattern, it can always be traced to its branch and root.

Generally, the main differences that exist between the Arabian and Moresque styles may be summed up thus,—the constructive features of the Arabs possess more grandeur, and those of the Moors more refinement and elegance.

ARABIAN   MORESQUE   MORESQUE

The exquisite ornaments on Plate XXXIV. *(pages 170–71),* from a copy of the Koran, will give a perfect idea of Arabian decorative art. Were it not for the introduction of flowers, which rather destroy the unity of the style, and betray a Persian influence, it would be impossible to find a better specimen of Arabian ornament. As it is, however, it is a very perfect lesson both in form and colour.

The immense mass of fragments of marble derived from Roman ruins must have very early led the Arabs to seek to imitate the universal practice of the Romans, of covering the floors of their houses and monuments with mosaic patterns, arranged on a geometrical system; and we have on Plate XXXV. *(pages 172–73)* a great number of the varieties which this fashion produced with the Arabs. No better idea can be obtained of what style in ornament consists than by comparing the mosaics on Plate XXXV. with the Roman mosaics, Plate XXV. *(page 123)*; the Byzantine, Plate XXX. *(pages 152–53)*; the Moresque, Plate XLIII *(pages 220–21)*. There is scarcely a form to be found in any one which does not exist in all the others. Yet how strangely different is the aspect of these plates! It is like an idea expressed in four different languages. The mind receives from each the same modified conception, by the sounds so widely differing.

The twisted cord, the interlacing of lines, the crossing of two squares ⬡, the equilateral triangle arranged within a hexagon, are the starting-points in each; the main differences resulting in the scheme of colouring, with the material employed and the uses to which they were applied, mainly suggested. The Arabian and the Roman are pavements, and of lower tones; the Moresque are dados; whilst those of the brighter hues, on Plate XXX. *(pages 152–53)*, are decorations on the constructive features of the building.

ARABIAN

Jones was eager to show that the architects of Islam had evolved a distinctive language for their holy buildings, long before their Christian counterparts. Part of his argument stemmed from the famous Mosque of Ibn Tulun (876–79). Built by the son of a Turkish slave who rose to become governor of Egypt, this early Islamic masterpiece was modeled on the courtyard mosques of Mesopotamia. It is particularly notable for its use of pointed arches, which predates comparable Western examples by around 300 years, and for its exquisite wooden carvings and stucco decoration.

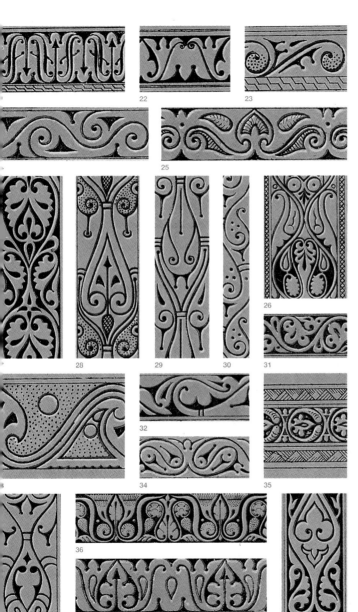

PLATE XXXI

1-39 This Plate consists of the ornamented Architraves and Soffits of the Windows in the interior of the Mosque of Tooloon, Cairo. They are executed in plaster, and nearly all the windows are of a different pattern. The main arches of the building are decorated in the same way; but only a fragment of one of the soffits now remains, sufficiently large to make out the design. This is given in Plate XXXIII., No. 12. Nos. 1–7, 16–25, 30–32, 34, 38, are designs from architraves round the windows. The rest of the patterns are from their soffits and jambs.

The Mosque of Tooloon was founded A.D. 876–7, and these ornaments are certainly of that date. It is the oldest Arabian building in Cairo, and is specially interesting as one of the earliest known examples of the pointed arch.

165

ARABIAN

❦ During the romantic era many artists were attracted by the exotic flavor of Arabic culture and sought to capture it in their paintings. They have been loosely described as "Orientalists." J. F. Lewis (1805–76), for example, was a resident in Cairo during the 1840s where, according to William Makepeace Thackeray (1811–63), he "lived in the most complete Oriental fashion." Lewis's pictures were invariably set in highly detailed Arab interiors, and one of them—*The Harem*—caused a sensation when it was exhibited in London in 1850. Lord Leighton (1830–96) went a stage further. He created an Arab hall in his own house, using it as a setting for many paintings.

PLATE XXXII

1–7 From the Parapet of the Mosque of Sultan Kalaoon.

9, 16 Ornaments round Arches in the Mosque En Nasireeyeh.

10, 11, 16, 18, 21–23 Ornaments on the Mosque of Kalaoon.

12, 20, 25 Ornaments round curved Architraves in the Mosque Sultan Kalaoon.

13 Wooden Stringcourse Pulpit.

14 Soffit of one of the Main Arches in the Mosque of Tooloon.

15, 17, 19 From the Mosque of Kalaoon.

The Mosque of Kalaoon was founded in the year 1284–5. All these ornaments are executed in plaster, and seem to have been cut on the stucco while still wet. There is too great a variety on the patterns, and even disparities on the corresponding parts of the same pattern, to allow of their having been cast or struck from moulds.

16

17

19

18

20

21

22

23

24

25

167

ARABIAN

These details come from buildings produced during the Mamluk era (1252–1517), which was a golden age for the arts in Egypt. Qala-un (ruled 1279–90) built a celebrated hospital and mosque (Nos. 1–10, 17). The latter, in common with many other mosques of the period, was intended primarily as a burial place. The sultan al-Nasir Muhammad (ruled 1294–1340) commissioned several fine buildings in Cairo (Nos. 12,16, 22), while other members of the Nasirid dynasty ruled Granada in Spain. The Mamluk reputation for fine architecture was continued by Sultan Barquq (ruled 1382–99), particularly in the mosque that he built for his son (No. 18).

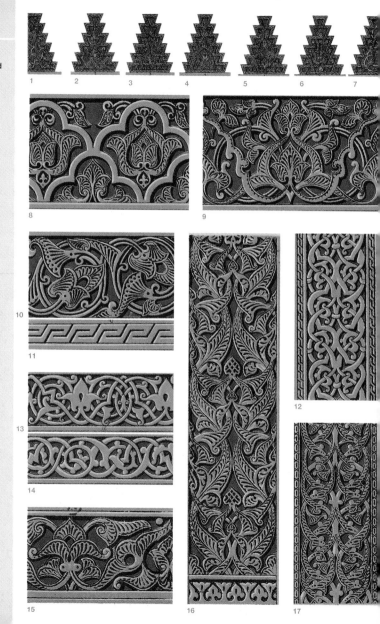

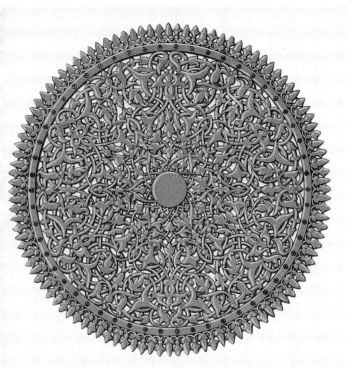

20

22

23

The mysteries of Eastern religion were very much in the news in Jones's day. The holy places of Islam had long been closed to Westerners, but in 1853 the adventurer Sir Richard Burton (1821–90) managed to gain access to Mecca and Medina by disguising himself as an Afghan pilgrim. His account of this expedition was published two years later, delighting Victorian readers. Burton retained close connections with the Islamic world, traveling extensively and working as a diplomat and translator. Today he is best remembered for his exhaustive version of the *Arabian Nights* (16 volumes, 1885–88).

PLATE XXXIV

1–7 These designs were traced from a splendid copy of the Koran in the Mosque El Barkookeyeh, founded A.D. 1384.

4

5

6

7

The architectural ornament in Middle Eastern homes was often extremely decorative, making it a target for Western collectors. Lord Leighton's Arab hall, for example, was composed entirely of genuine Eastern elements. Some of these were purchased directly from Arab manufacturers, but Leighton also made use of his friendship with Sir Richard Burton (see page 170, then the consul in Damascus) to acquire antique examples. The latter confirmed, "I am quite willing to have a house pulled down for you . . . but the difficulty is to find a house with tiles. The bric-à-brac sellers have quite learned their value, and demand extravagant sums for poor articles . . . "

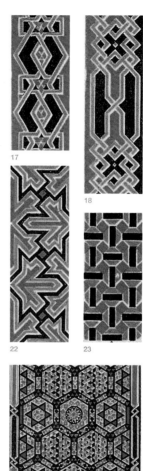

3 14 15 17 18 16 9 20 21 22 23 4 25 26 7 28

PLATE XXXV

1–28 Consists of different Mosaics taken from Pavements and walls in Private Houses and Mosques in Cairo. They are executed in black and white marble, with red tile. Nos. 4–6 are patterns engraved on the white marble slab, and filled in with red and black cement. The ornament on the white marble on the centre of No. 11 is slightly in relief.

The materials for these five Plates have been kindly furnished by Mr. James William Wild, who passed a considerable time in Cairo studying the interior decoration of the Arabian houses, and they may be regarded as very faithful transcripts of Cairean ornament.

CHAPTER IX

TURKISH ORNAMENT

The architecture of the Turks, as seen at Constantinople, is in all its structural features mainly based upon the early Byzantine monuments; their system of ornamentation, however, is a modification of the Arabian, bearing about the same relation to this style as Elizabethan ornament does to Italian Renaissance.

When the art of one people is adopted by another having the same religion, but differing in natural character and instincts, we should expect to find a deficiency in all those qualities in which the borrowing people are inferior to their predecessors. And thus it is with the art of the Turks as compared with the art of the Arabs; there is the same difference in the amount of elegance and refinement in the art of the two people as exists in their national character.

We are, however, inclined to believe that the Turks have rarely themselves practised the arts; but that they have rather commanded the execution than been themselves executants. All their mosques and public

TURKISH

buildings present a mixed style. On the same building, side by side with ornaments derived from Arabian and Persian floral ornaments, we find debased Roman and Renaissance details, leading to the belief that these buildings have mostly been executed by artists differing in religion from themselves. In more recent times, the Turks have been the first of the Mohammedan races to abandon the traditional style of building of their forefathers, and to adopt the prevailing fashions of the day in their architecture; the modern buildings and palaces being not only the work of European artists, but designed in the most approved European style.

The productions of the Turks at the Great Exhibition of 1851 were the least perfect of all the Mohammedan exhibiting nations.

In Mr. M. Digby Wyatt's admirable record of the state of the Industrial Arts of the Nineteenth Century, will be found specimens of Turkish embroidery exhibited in 1851, and which may be compared with the many valuable specimens of Indian embroidery represented in the same work. It will readily be seen, from the simple matter of their embroidery, that the art-instinct of the Turks must be very inferior to that of the Indians. The Indian embroidery is as perfect in distribution of form, and in all the principles of ornamentation, as the most elaborate and important article of decoration.

The only examples we have of perfect ornamentation are to be found in Turkey carpets; but these are chiefly executed in Asia Minor, and most probably not by Turks. The designs are thoroughly Arabian, differing from Persian carpets in being much more conventional in the treatment of foliage.

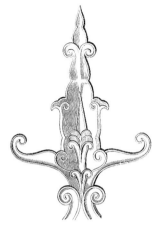

TURKISH

By comparing Plate XXXVII. *(page 182)* with Plates XXXII. and XXXIII. *(pages 166–69)* the differences of style will be readily perceived. The general principles of the distribution of form are the same, but there are a few minor differences that it will be desirable to point out. The surface of an ornament both in the Arabian and Moresque styles is only slightly rounded, and the enrichment of the surface is obtained by sinking lines on this surface; or where the surface was left plain, the additional pattern upon pattern was obtained by painting.

The Turkish ornament, on the contrary, presents a carved surface, and such ornaments as we find painted in the Arabian MSS., Plate XXXIV. *(pages 170–71),* in black lines on the gold flowers, are here carved on the surface, the effect being not nearly so broad as that produced by the sunk feathering of the Arabian and Moresque.

Another peculiarity, and one which at once distinguishes a piece of Turkish ornament from Arabian, is the great abuse which was made of the re-entering curve A A *(page 179)*.

ELIZABETHAN

This is very prominent in the Arabian, but more especially in the Persian styles. See Plate XLVI *(pages 232–33)*.

With the Moors it is no longer a feature, and appears only exceptionally.

This peculiarity was adopted in the Elizabethan ornament, which, through the Renaissance of France and Italy, was derived from the East, in imitation of the damascened work which was at that period so common.

It will be seen on reference to Plate XXXVI. *(pages 180–81)* that this swell always occurs on the inside of the spinal curve of the main stem; with Elizabethan ornament the swell often occurs indifferently on the inside and on the outside.

It is very difficult, nay, almost impossible, thoroughly to explain by words differences in style of ornament having such a strong family resemblance as the Persian, Arabian, and Turkish; yet the eye readily detects them, much in the same way as a Roman statue is distinguished from a Greek. The general principles remaining the same in the Persian, the Arabian, and the

TURKISH

Turkish styles of ornament, there will be found a peculiarity in the proportions of the masses, more or less grace in the flowing of the curves, a fondness for particular directions in the leading lines, and a peculiar mode of interweaving forms, the general form of the conventional leafage ever remaining the same. The relative degree of fancy, delicacy, or coarseness, with which these are drawn, will at once distinguish them as the works of the refined and spiritual Persian, the not less refined but reflective Arabian, or the unimaginative Turk.

Plate XXXVIII. *(page 183)* is a portion of the decoration of the dome of the tomb of Soliman I. at Constantinople; it is the most perfect specimen of Turkish ornament with which we are acquainted, and nearly approaches the Arabian. One great feature of Turkish ornament is the predominance of green and black; and, in fact, in the modern decoration of Cairo the same thing is observed. Green is much more prominent than in ancient examples where blue is chiefly used.

When Constantinople fell to the Turks in 1453, its new ruler Mehmed II (ruled 1451–81) declared himself the rightful heir of both the Byzantine emperors and the Muslim sultans. Accordingly, he employed Greek artists alongside Turkish ones, creating an unusual hybrid of Christian and Islamic styles. This blend has not proved popular with critics, although Jones's lack of enthusiasm may have been colored by Victorian attitudes to Turkey. Known as "the sick man of Europe," its political decline had destabilized central Europe. This in turn had prompted Britain to become involved in the Crimean War (1853–6), in a bid to prevent Russian expansion into the Ottoman territories.

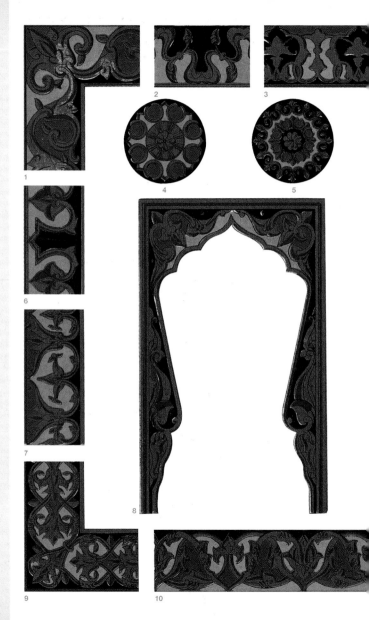

PLATE XXXVI

1, 7, 9, 13, 14 From a Fountain at Pera, Constantinople.
2, 3, 6, 11, 19 From Tombs at Constantinople.
4, 5, 12, 18 From the Tomb of Sultan Soliman I., Constantinople.
8, 15, 16, 17, 21 From the Yeni D'jami, or new mosque, Constantinople.
10 From the Mosque of Sultan Achmet, Constantinople.
20, 22 From a Fountain at Tophana, Constantinople.

The one Turkish building that was universally acknowledged as a masterpiece was the Mosque of Suleyman the Magnificent (ruled 1520–66). Built in 1550–57, it was regarded as the finest work of Sinan (1489–*ca.* 1578), the most famous of the Ottoman architects. Loosely based on the Byzantine church of Santa Sophia, it was notable above all for its glorious array of Iznik tiles. In common with other major mosques, Sinan's creation became the focus for a series of smaller, satellite buildings, such as colleges and mausoleums. The most striking of these was the tomb of Suleyman and his wife (Plate XXXVIII, *far right*), which was added in 1566.

PLATE XXXVII

1, 2, 6, 7, 8 From The Yeni D'jami, Constantinople.
3 Rosace in the Centre of the Dome of the Mosque of Soliman I., Constantinople.
4, 5 Ornaments in Spandrils under the Dome of the Mosque of Soliman I., Constantinople.

PLATE XXXVIII

Portion of the Decoration of
the Dome of the Tomb of
Soliman I., Constantinople.

CHAPTER X

MORESQUE ORNAMENT

FROM THE ALHAMBRA

O ur illustrations of the ornament of the Moors have been taken exclusively from the Alhambra, not only because it is the one of their works with which we are best acquainted, but also because it is the one in which their marvellous system of decoration reached its culminating point. The Alhambra is at the very summit of perfection of Moorish art, as is the Parthenon of Greek art. We can find no work so fitted to illustrate a Grammar of Ornament as that in which every ornament contains a grammar in itself. Every principle which we can derive from the study of the ornamental art of any other people is not only ever present here, but was by the Moors more universally and truly obeyed.

We find in the Alhambra the speaking art of the Egyptians, the natural grace and refinement of the Greeks, the geometrical combinations of the Romans, the Byzantines, and the Arabs. The ornament wanted but one charm, which was the peculiar feature of the Egyptian ornament, symbolism. This the religion of the Moors forbade; but the want was more than supplied by the inscriptions, which, addressing themselves to the eye by their outward beauty, at once excited the intellect by the difficulties of deciphering their curious and complex involutions, and delighted the imagination when read, by the beauty of the sentiments they expressed and the music of their composition.

"THERE IS NO CONQUEROR BUT GOD."
ARABIC INSCRIPTION FROM THE ALHAMBRA

To the artist and those provided with a mind to estimate the value of the beauty to which they gave a life they repeated, *Look and learn*. To the people they proclaimed the might, majesty, and good deeds of the king. To the king himself they never ceased declaring that there was none powerful but God, that He alone was conqueror, and that to Him alone was for ever due praise and glory.

The builders of this wonderful structure were fully aware of the greatness of their work. It is asserted in the inscriptions on the walls, that this building surpassed all other buildings; that at sight of its wonderful domes all other domes vanished and disappeared; in the playful exaggeration of their poetry, that the stars grew pale in their light through envy of so much beauty; and, what is more to our purpose, they declare that he who should study them with attention would reap the benefit of a commentary on decoration.

We have endeavoured to obey the injunctions of the poet, and will attempt here to explain some of the general principles which appear to have guided the Moors in the decoration of the Alhambra—principles which are not theirs alone, but common to all the best periods of art. The principles which are everywhere the same, the forms only differ.

1.* The Moors ever regarded what we hold to be the first principle in architecture to *decorate construction, never to construct decoration*: in Moorish architecture not only does the decoration arise naturally from the construction, but the constructive idea is carried out in every detail of the ornamentation of the surface.

We believe that true beauty in architecture results from that *"repose which the mind feels when the eye, the intellect, and the affections are satisfied, from the absence of any want."* When an object is constructed falsely, appearing to derive or give support without doing either the one or the other, it fails to afford this repose, and therefore never can pretend to true beauty, however harmonious it may be in itself: the Mohammedan races, and Moors especially, have constantly regarded this rule; we never

* This essay on the general principles of the ornamentation of the Alhambra is partially reprinted from the "Guide Book to the Alhambra Court in the Crystal Palace," by the Author.

find a useless or superfluous ornament; every ornament arises quietly and naturally from the surface decorated. They ever regard the useful as a vehicle for the beautiful; and in this they do not stand alone: the same principle was observed in all the best periods of art: it is only when art declines that true principles come to be disregarded; or, in any age of copying, like the present, when the works of the past are reproduced without the spirit which animated the originals.

2. All lines grow out of each other in gradual undulations; there are no excrescences; nothing could be removed and leave the design equally good or better.

In a general sense, if construction be properly attended to, there could be no excrescences; but we use the word here in a more limited sense: the general lines might follow truly the construction, and yet there might be excrescences, such as knobs or bosses, which would not violate the rule of construction, and yet would be fatal to beauty of form, if they did not grow out gradually from the general lines.

There can be no beauty of form, no perfect proportion or arrangement of lines, which does not produce repose.

All transitions of curved lines from curved, or of curved lines from straight, must be gradual. Thus the transition would cease to be agreeable if the break at A were too deep in proportion to the curves, as at B. Where two curves are

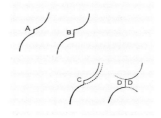

separated by a break (as in this case), they must, and with the Moors always do, run parallel to an imaginary line (C) where the curves would be tangential to each other: for were either to depart from this, as in the case at D, the eye, instead of following gradually down the curve, would run outwards, and repose would be lost.[†]

3. The general forms were first cared for; these were subdivided by general lines; the interstices were then filled in with ornament, which was again subdivided and enriched for closer inspection. They carried out this principle with the greatest refinement, and the harmony and beauty of all their ornamentation derive their chief success from its observance. Their main divisions contrast and balance admirably: the greatest distinctness is obtained; the detail never interferes with the general form. When seen at a distance, the main lines strike the eye; as we approach nearer, the detail comes into the composition; on a closer inspection, we see still further detail on the surface of the ornaments themselves.

4. Harmony of form appears to consist in the proper balancing and contrast of the straight, the inclined, and the curved.

As in colour there can be no perfect composition in which either of the three primary colours is wanting, so in form, whether structural or decorative, there can be no perfect composition in which either of the three primary figures is wanting; and the varieties and harmony in composition

[†] These transitions were managed most perfectly by the Greeks in all their mouldings, which exhibit this refinement in the highest degree; so do also the exquisite contours of their vases.

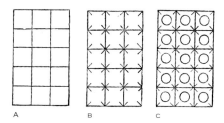

A   B   C

and design depend on the various predominance and subordination of the three.§

In surface decoration, any arrangement of forms, as at A, consisting only of straight lines, is monotonous, and affords but imperfect pleasure; but introduce lines which tend to carry the eye towards the angles, as at B, and you have at once an increased pleasure. Then add lines giving a circular tendency, as at C, and you have now complete harmony. In this case the square is the leading form or tonic; the angular and curved are subordinate.

We may produce the same result in adopting an angular composition, as at D: add the lines as at E, and we at once correct the tendency to follow only the angular direction of the inclined lines; but unite these by circles, as

§ There can be no better example of this harmony than the Greek temple, where the straight, the angular, and the curved are in most perfect relation to each other. Gothic architecture also offers many illustrations of this principle; every tendency of lines to run in one direction is immediately counteracted by the angular or the curved: thus, the capping of the buttress is exactly what is required to counteract the upward tendency of the straight lines: so the gable contrasts admirably with the curved windowhead and its perpendicular mullions.

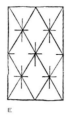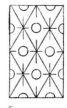

D   E   F

at F, and we have still more perfect harmony, *i.e.* repose, for the eye has now no longer any want that could be supplied.**

5. In the surface decorations of the Moors all lines flow out of a parent stem: every ornament, however distant, can be traced to its branch and root. They have the happy art of so adapting the ornament to the surface decorated, that the ornament as often appears to have suggested the general form as to have been suggested by it. In all cases we find the foliage flowing out of a parent stem, and we are never offended, as in modern practice, by the random introduction of an ornament just dotted down,

** It is to the neglect of this obvious rule that we find so many failures in paper-hangings, carpets, and more especially articles of costume: the lines of papers generally run through the ceiling most disagreeably, because the straight is not corrected by the angular, or the angular by the curved: so of carpets; the lines of carpets are constantly running in one direction only, carrying the eye right through the walls of the apartment. Again, to this we owe all those abominable checks and plaids which constantly disfigure the human form—a custom detrimental to the public taste, and gradually lowering the tone of the eye for form of this generation. If children were born and bred to the sound of hurdy-gurdies grinding out of tune, their ears would no doubt suffer deterioration, and they would lose their sensibility to the harmonious in sound. This, then, is what is certainly taking place with regard to form, and it requires the most strenuous efforts to be made by all who would take an interest in the welfare of the rising generation to put a stop to it.

without a reason for its existence. However irregular the space they have to fill, they always commence by dividing it into equal areas, and round these trunk-lines they fill in their detail, but invariably return to their parent stem.

They appear in this to work by a process analogous to that of nature, as we see in the vine-leaf; the object being to distribute the sap from the parent stem to the extremities, it is evident the main stem would divide the leaf as near as may be into equal areas. So, again, of the minor divisions; each area is again subdivided by intermediate lines, which all follow the same law of equal distribution, even to the most minute filling-in of the sap-feeders.

6. The Moors also follow another principle; that of radiation from the parent stem, as we may see in nature with the human hand, or in a chestnut leaf.

We may see in the example how beautifully all these lines radiate from the parent stem; how each leaf diminishes towards the extremities, and how each area is in proportion to the leaf. The Orientals carry out this principle with marvellous perfection; so also did the Greeks in their honeysuckle ornament. We have already remarked, in Chapter IV., a peculiarity of Greek ornament, which appears to follow the principle of the plants of the cactus tribe, where one leaf grows out of

another. This is generally the case with Greek ornament; the acanthus-leaf scrolls are a series of leaves growing out one from the other in a continuous line, whilst the Arabian and Moresque ornaments always grow out of a continuous stem.

7. All junctions of curved lines with curved, or of curved with straight, should be tangential to each other; this also we consider to be a law found everywhere in nature, and the Oriental practice is always in accordance with it. Many of the Moorish ornaments are on the same principle which is observable in the lines of a feather and in the articulations of every leaf; and to this is due that additional charm found in all perfect ornamentation,  which we call the graceful. It may be called the melody of form, as what we have before described constitutes its harmony.

We shall find these laws of *equal distribution, radiation from a parent stem, continuity of line*, and *tangential curvature*, ever present in natural leaves.

8. We would call attention to the nature of the exquisite curves in use by the Arabs and Moors.

As with proportion, we think that those proportions will be the most beautiful which it will be most difficult for the eye to detect;†† so we think that those compositions of curves will be most agreeable, where the

†† All compositions of squares or of circles will be monotonous, and afford but little pleasure, because the means whereby they are produced are very apparent. So we think that compositions distributed in equal lines or divisions will be less beautiful than those which require a higher mental effort to appreciate them.

mechanical process of describing them shall be least apparent; and we shall find it to be universally the case, that in the best periods of art all mouldings and ornaments were founded on curves of the higher order, such as the conic sections; whilst, when art declined, circles and compass-work were much more dominant.

The researches of Mr. Penrose have shown that the mouldings and curved lines in the Parthenon are all portions of curves of a very high order, and that segments of circles were very rarely used. The exquisite curves of the Greek vases are well known, and here we never find portions of circles. In Roman architecture, on the contrary, this refinement is lost; the Romans were probably as little able to describe as to appreciate curves of a high order, and we find, therefore, their mouldings mostly parts of circles, which could be struck with compasses.

In the early works of the Gothic period, the tracery would appear to have been much less the offspring of compass-work than in the later period, which has most appropriately been termed the *Geometrical*, from the immoderate use of compass-work.

Here is a curve (A) common to Greek Art, to the Gothic period, and so much delighted in by the Mohammedan races. This becomes graceful the

more it departs from the curve which the union of two parts of circles would give.

9. A still further charm is found in the works of the Arabs and Moors from their conventional treatment of ornament, which, forbidden as they were by their creed to represent living forms, they carried to the highest perfection. They ever worked as nature worked, but always avoided a direct transcript; they took her principles, but did not, as we do, attempt to copy her works. In this, again, they do not stand alone: in every period of faith in art, all ornamentation was ennobled by the ideal; never was the sense of propriety violated by a too faithful representation of nature.

Thus, in Egypt, a lotus carved in stone was never such an one as you might have plucked, but a conventional representation perfectly in keeping with the architectural members of which it formed a part; it was a symbol of the power of the king over countries where the lotus grew, and added poetry to what would otherwise have been a rude support.

The colossal statues of the Egyptians were not little men carved on a large scale, but architectural representations of Majesty, in which were symbolised the power of the monarch, and his abiding love of his people.

In Greek art, the ornaments, no longer symbols, as in Egypt, were still further conventionalised; and in their sculpture applied to architecture, they adopted a conventional treatment both of *pose* and relief very different to that of their isolated works.

In the best periods of Gothic art the floral ornaments are treated conventionally, and a direct imitation of nature is never attempted; but as art declined, they became less idealised, and more direct in imitation.

The same decline may be traced in stained glass, where both figures and ornaments were treated at first conventionally; but as the art declined, figures and draperies, through which light was to be transmitted, had their own shades and shadows.

In the early illuminated MSS. the ornaments were conventional, and the illuminations were in flat tints, with little shade and no shadow; whilst in those of a later period highly-finished representations of natural flowers were used as ornament, casting their shadows on the page.

ON THE COLOURING OF MORESQUE ORNAMENT

When we examine the system of colouring adopted by the Moors, we shall find, that as with form, so with colour, they followed certain fixed principles, founded on observations of nature's laws, and which they held in common with all those nations who have practised the arts with success. In all archaic styles of art, practised during periods of faith, the same true principles prevail; and although we find in all somewhat of a local or temporary character, we yet discern in all much that is eternal and immutable; the same grand ideas embodied in different forms, and expressed, so to speak, in a different language.

10. The ancients always *used colour to assist in the development of form*, always employed it as a further means of bringing out the constructive features of a building.

Thus, in the Egyptian column, the base of which represented the root—the shaft, the stalk—the capital, the buds and flowers of the lotus or papyrus, the several colours were so applied that the appearance of strength in the column was increased, and the contours of the various lines more fully developed.

In Gothic architecture, also, colour was always employed to assist in developing the forms of the panel-work and tracery; and this is effected to an extent of which it is difficult to form an idea, in the present colourless condition of the buildings. In the slender shafts of their lofty edifices, the idea of elevation was further increased by upward-running spiral lines of colour, which, while adding to the apparent height, also helped to define its form.

In Oriental art, again, we always find the constructive lines of the building well defined by colour; an apparent additional height, length, breadth, or bulk, always results from its judicious application; and with the ornaments in relief it develops constantly new forms which would have been altogether lost without it.

The artists have in this but followed the guiding inspiration of Nature, in whose works every transition of form is accompanied by a modification of colour, so disposed as to assist in producing distinctness of expression. For example, flowers are separated by colour from their leaves and stalks, and these again from the earth in which they grow. So also in the human figure every change of form is marked by a change of colour; thus the colour of the hair, the eyes, the eyelids and lashes, the sanguine complexion of the lips, the rosy bloom of the cheek, all assist in producing distinctness, and in more visibly bringing out the form. We all know how much the absence or impairment of these colours, as in sickness, contributes to deprive the features of their proper meaning and expression.

Had nature applied but one colour to all objects, they would have been indistinct in form as well as monotonous in aspect. It is the boundless variety of her tints that perfects the modelling and defines the outline of each; detaching equally the modest lily from the grass from which it springs, and the glorious sun, parent of all colour, from the firmament in which it shines.

11. The colours employed by the Moors on their stucco-work were, in all cases, *the primaries, blue, red, and yellow (gold). The secondary colours, purple, green, and orange, occur only in the Mosaic dados*, which, being near the eye, formed a point of repose from the more brilliant colouring above. It is true that, at the present day, the grounds of many of the ornaments are found to be green; it will always be found, however, on a minute examination, that the colour originally employed was blue, which being a metallic pigment, has become green from the effects of time. This is proved by the presence of the particles of blue colour, which occur everywhere in the crevices: in the restorations, also, which were made by the Catholic kings, the grounds of the ornaments were repainted both green and purple. It may be remarked that, among the Egyptians and the Greeks, the Arabs and the Moors, the primary colours were almost entirely, if not exclusively, employed during the early periods of art; whilst during the decadence, the secondary colours became of more importance. Thus, in Egypt, in Pharaonic temples, we find the primary colours predominating; in the Ptolemaic temples, the secondary; so also on the early Greek temples are found the primary colours, whilst at Pompeii every variety of shade and tone was employed.

In modern Cairo, and in the East generally, we have green constantly appearing side by side with red, where blue would have been used in earlier times.

This is equally true of the works of the Middle Ages. In the early manuscripts and in stained glass, though other colours were not excluded, the primaries were chiefly used; whilst in later times we have every variety of shade and tint, but rarely used with equal success.

12. *With the Moors, as a general rule, the primary colours were used on the upper portions of objects, the secondary and tertiary on the lower.* This also appears to be in accordance with a natural law; we have the primary blue in the sky, the secondary green in the trees and fields, ending with the tertiaries on the earth; as also in flowers, where we generally find the primaries on the buds and flowers, and the secondaries on the leaves and stalks.

The ancients always observed this rule in the best periods of art. In Egypt, however, we do see occasionally the secondary green used in the upper portions of the temples, but this arises from the fact, that ornaments in Egypt were symbolical; and if a lotus leaf were used on the upper part of a building, it would necessarily be coloured green; but the law is true in the main; the general aspect of an Egyptian temple of the Pharaonic period gives the primaries above and the secondaries below; but in the buildings of the Ptolemaic and Roman periods more especially, this order was inverted, and the palm and lotus-leaf capitals give a superabundance of green in the upper portions of the temples.

In Pompeii we find sometimes in the interior of the houses a gradual gradation of colour downwards from the roof, from light to dark, ending with black; but this is by no means so universal as to convince us that they felt it as a law. We have already shown in Chapter V. that there are many examples of black immediately under the ceiling.

13. Although the ornaments which are found in the Alhambra, and in the *Court of the Lions* especially, are at the present day covered with several thin coats of the whitewash which has at various periods been applied to them, we may be said to have authority for the whole of the colouring of our reproduction; for not only may the colours be seen in the interstices of the ornaments in many places by scaling off the whitewash, but the colouring of the Alhambra was carried out on so perfect a system, that any one who will make this a study can, with almost absolute certainty, on being shown for the first time a piece of Moorish ornament in white, define at once the manner in which it was coloured. So completely were all the architectural forms designed with reference to their subsequent colouring, that the surface alone will indicate the colours they were destined to receive. Thus, in using the colours blue, red, and gold, they took care to place them in such positions that they should be best seen in themselves, and add most to the general effect. *On moulded surfaces they placed red, the strongest colour of the three, in the depths*, where it might be softened by shadow, never on the surface; *blue in the shade*, and *gold on all surfaces exposed to light*: for it is evident that by this arrangement alone could their true value be obtained. The several colours are either separated by white bands, or by

the shadow caused by the relief of the ornament itself—and this appears to be an absolute principle required in colouring—*colours should never be allowed to impinge upon each other.*

14. In colouring the grounds of the various diapers the blue always occupies the largest area; and this is in accordance with the theory of optics, and the experiments which have been made with the prismatic spectrum. The rays of light are said to neutralise each other in the proportions of 3 yellow, 5 red, and 8 blue; thus, it requires a quantity of blue equal to the red and yellow put together to produce a harmonious effect, and prevent the predominance of any one colour over the others. As in the "Alhambra," yellow is replaced by gold, which tends towards a reddish-yellow, the blue is still further increased, to counteract the tendency of the red to overpower the other colours.

INTERLACED PATTERNS

We have already suggested, in Chapter IV., the probability that the immense variety of Moorish ornaments, which are formed by the intersection of equidistant lines, could be traced through the Arabian to the Greek fret. The ornaments on Plate XXXIX. *(pages 206–07)* are constructed on two general principles; Nos. 1–13, 17, 18, are constructed on one principle (Diagram No. 1, *see overleaf*), No. 15 on the other (Diagram No. 2). In the first series the lines are equidistant, diagonally crossed by horizontal and perpendicular lines on each square. But by the system on which No. 15 is constructed, the perpendicular and horizontal lines are equidistant, and the diagonal lines

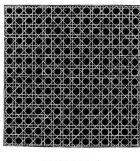
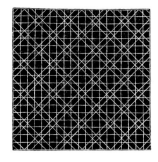

DIAGRAM NO. 1   DIAGRAM NO. 2

cross only each alternate square. The number of patterns that can be produced by these two systems would appear to be infinite; and it will be seen, on reference to Plate XXXIX. *(pages 206–07)*, that the variety may be still further increased by the mode of colouring the ground or the surface lines. Any one of these patterns which we have engraved might be made to change its aspect, by bringing into prominence different chains or other general masses.

LOZENGE DIAPERS

The general effect of Plate XLI. and XLI*. *(pages 210–13)* will, we think, at once justify the superiority we have claimed for the ornament of the Moors. Composed of but three colours, they are more harmonious and effective than any others in our collection, and possess a peculiar charm which all the others fail to approach. The various principles for which we have contended, the constructive idea whereby each leading line rests upon another, the gradual transitions from curve to curve, the tangential curvatures of the lines, the flowing off of the ornaments from a parent stem, the tracing of each flower to its branch and root, the division and subdivision of general lines, will readily be perceived in every ornament on the page.

SQUARE DIAPERS

The ornament No. 1, on Plate XLII. *(pages 214–15)*, is a good example of the principle we contend for, that to produce repose the lines of a composition should contain in equilibrium the *straight*, the *inclined*, and the *curved*. We have lines running horizontally, perpendicularly, and diagonally, again contrasted by circles in opposite directions. So that the most perfect repose is obtained, the tendency of the eye to run in any direction is immediately corrected by lines giving an opposite tendency, and wherever the eye strikes upon the patterns it is inclined to dwell. The blue ground of the inscriptions and ornamental panels and centres, being carried over the red ground by the blue feathers, produces a most cheerful and brilliant effect.

The leading lines of the ornaments Nos. 2–4, Plates XLII. and XLII* *(pages 214–17)*, are produced in the same way as the interlaced ornaments on Plate XXXIX *(pages 206–07)*. In Nos. 2 and 4 it will be seen how the repose of the pattern is obtained by the arrangement of the coloured grounds; and how, also, by this means an additional pattern besides that produced by form results from the arrangement of the colours.

Pattern No. 6, Plate XLII[†]. *(pages 218–19)*, is a portion of a ceiling, of which there are immense varieties in the Alhambra, produced by divisions of the circle crossed by intersecting squares. It is the same principle which exists in the copy from the illuminated Koran, Plate XXXIV. *(pages 170–71)*, and is also very common on the ceilings of Arabian houses.

The ornament No. 5, Plate XLII[†] *(pages 218–19)*, is of extreme delicacy, and is remarkable for the ingenious system on which it is constructed. All the pieces being similar, it illustrates one of the most important principles in Moorish design,—one which, more perhaps than any other, contributed to the general happy results, viz. that by the repetition of a few simple elements the most beautiful and complicated effects were produced.

However much disguised, the whole of the ornamentation of the Moors is constructed geometrically. Their fondness for geometrical forms is evidenced by the great use they made of mosaics, in which their imagination had full play. However complicated the patterns on Plate XLIII. *(pages 220–21)* may appear, they are all very simple when the principle of setting them out is once understood. They all arise from the intersection of equidistant lines round fixed centres. No. 5 is constructed on the principle of Diagram No. 2, cited on the other side, and is the principle which produces the greatest variety; in fact, geometrical combinations on this system may be said to be infinite.

MORESQUE

Jones's section on Moorish motifs is the most lavish, but also perhaps the most inconsistent, part of *The Grammar of Ornament*. In it, he devotes more space to a single building (the Alhambra in Granada) than to some entire cultures. The author was well aware of this discrepancy. In part, it stemmed from his enormous respect for Moorish decoration, which in his view was superior even to that of the Greeks and Egyptians. In his Crystal Palace catalog, for example, he wrote, "The grace and refinement of Greek ornament is here surpassed. Possessing, equally with the Greeks, an appreciation of pure form, the Moors excelled them in variety and imagination."

1

2

3

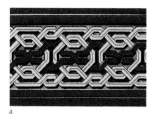

4

5

7

6

8

9

10

206

14

16

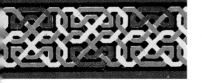

12

15

18

PLATE XXXIX

INTERLACED ORNAMENTS
1–3, 9, 10, 12, 18, are
Borders on Mosaic Dados.
4–8, 11, 13, 15 Plaster
Ornaments, used as
upright and horizontal
Bands enclosing Panels on
the walls.
14, 16 Square Stops in the
Bands of the Inscriptions.
17 Painted Ornament from
the Great Arch in the Hall of
the Boat.

Jones had considerable firsthand experience of the glories of the Alhambra at Granada. In 1834, he spent considerable time there, collaborating with a French architect, Jules Goury, on a massive study of the place. Goury died prematurely during an outbreak of cholera, and Jones was obliged to complete his research alone. The results were published in a massive two-volume work entitled *Plans, Elevations, Sections, and Details of the Alhambra* (1836–45). The illustrations were printed in "litho-chrysography," a form of chromolithography, which enabled Jones to discuss his controversial views about color. These revolved around his unfounded belief that the palace columns had originally been gilded.

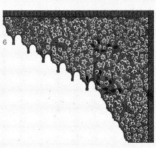

PLATE XL

SPANDRILS OF ARCHES
1 From the centre Arch of
the Court of the Lions.
2, 3 From the Arches of the
Hall of Justice.
4 From the Entrance to the
Court of the Lions from the
Court of the Fish-ponds.
5 From the Entrance to
the Divan Hall of the Two
Sisters.
6 From the Entrance to the
Court of the Fish-pond from
the Hall of the Boat.

Not surprisingly, Jones was eager to introduce Moorish elements into his own architectural work. In particular he submitted an ambitious design "in the Alhambra style" for the new premises of the Army and Navy club in London. In the event, this commission did not materialize, but Jones was able to incorporate many of the ideas into the spectacular "Alhambra Court" that he created at the Crystal Palace exhibition at Sydenham. This consisted of a partial reconstruction of the Spanish masterpiece, together with a cast room. The latter contained many of the plaster impressions of ornamental detail that Jones and his pupils had taken in the 1830s.

1

2

3

4

5

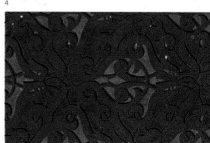

6

7

8

PLATE XLI

LOZENGE DIAPERS
1 Ornament in Panels, Hall of the Abencerrages.
2 Ornament over Arches, entrance to the Court of Lions.
3 Ornament in Panels from the Hall of the Ambassadors.
4 Ornament in Panels from the Hall of the Boat.
5 Ornament in Spandril of Arch, entrance to Court of Lions.
6 Ornament in Doorway of the Divan, Hall of the Two Sisters.
7 Ornament in Panels of the Hall of the Ambassadors.
8 Ornament in Panels of the Courts of the Mosque.

Many writers have celebrated the glories of the Alhambra, but for English-speaking readers the most influential figure was Washington Irving (1783–1859). Today he is best remembered as the creator of *Rip Van Winkle* (1820), but he also wrote several books on Granada during the 1820s and 1830s. These did not focus solely on the architectural finery, but also included thumbnail sketches of the palace's eccentric inhabitants, most of them "poor as rats," though they gave themselves grand, aristocratic titles. More vivid still were his accounts of the Alhambra's legends, complete with pining infantas, ghostly horses, and hoards of Moorish gold. Irving attempted to explain the origin of the Hall of the Two Sisters by concocting a tale about a pair of princesses, who fell in love with Christian captives. One eloped with her lover, while the other remained a spinster, languishing alone at the Alhambra.

9

10

11

13

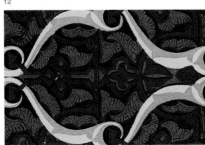

12

14

15

16

The Court of Lions takes its name from its spectacular centerpiece —a stone fountain adorned with 12 heraldic lions. Legend has it that the object was transferred here from the palace of an eleventh-century Jewish vizier. Today, this section of the Alhambra is immaculate, but in Jones's time the entire complex was in a very different state; it was a sorry, dilapidated place. During the Napoleonic Wars it had been used as a jail for French prisoners of war. Worse was to follow, as a motley assortment of tinkers and vagrants took up residence. Don Ignacio Montilla kept sheep and donkeys in the palace, while another family set up looms in the private apartments. Early tourists chipped off ornaments as souvenirs, while the daughters of a local governor sold off some of the tiles to finance a bullfight. The decay was reversed only at the end of the nineteenth century, when a full restoration program was launched.

1

2

PLATE XLII

SQUARE DIAPERS
1 Frieze over Columns,
Court of the Lions.
2 Panelling in Windows,
Hall of the Ambassadors.

Spain was rediscovered by the romantics, following a long period of isolation. Artists and writers celebrated it in their work, enchanted by the combination of a country that was European and yet retained an exotic, African appeal. The Moors had finally been driven out in 1609, but their culture still dominated Andalusia and the south. Nowhere was this more apparent than at Granada, where the magnificence of the Alhambra remained unsurpassed. Built by successive generations of the Nasirid dynasty —most notably Muhammad III (ruled 1302–08)—it was finally ceded to Christian forces in 1492. The Hall of the Ambassadors is arguably the most impressive of all the rooms. It was created during the reign of Yusuf I (1333–54), who used it as his audience chamber and throne room.

3

PLATE XLII*

3 Panelling of the centre Recess of the Hall of the Ambassadors.
4 Panelling on the Walls, Tower of the Captive.

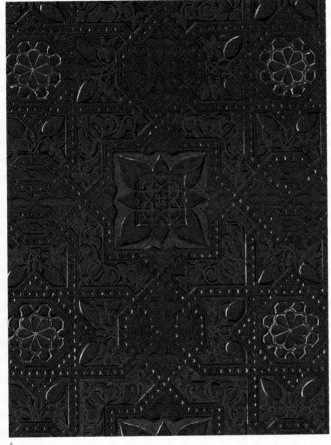

4

🎔 Jones may not have secured any official architectural commissions for work in this style, but at least one significant "Moorish" building dated from this time, for in 1858 the Alhambra Palace opened in London's Leicester Square. Designed by T. Hayter Lewis, its twin minarets soon became synonymous with light entertainment. In its day it was a circus, music-hall, and theater, its star performers including Blondin, the tightrope walker, and Leotard, the trapeze artist. The true revival of the Moorish style did not occur until the Art Deco period (1920s/1930s), when it was mainly applied to motion picture theaters. The best surviving example is London's Northfields Odeon (1932), which was nicknamed "Spanish City."

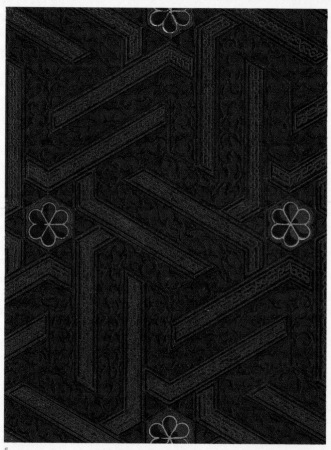

5

6

Jones's detailed, personal study of the Alhambra inspired other people to create their own Moorish fantasies. At Sammezzano in Tuscany the Marquese Ferdinando d'Aragona transformed his castle into a Moorish wonderland, complete with horseshoe arches, stalactite corbeling, and elaborate marble and mosaic pavements, using Jones's books as his source. Closer to home, the Pre-Raphaelite painter William Holman Hunt (1827–1910) used the Alhambra Court at Sydenham when he was sketching in the architectural background for his painting *The Finding of the Savior in the Temple* (1854–55).

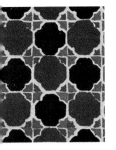

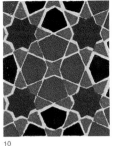

10

11

12

13

14

15

16

PLATE XLIII

MOSAICS
1 Pilaster, Hall of the
Ambassadors.
2 Dado, ditto.
3, 8 Dados, Hall of the
Two Sisters.
4 Pilaster, Hall of Justice.
5 Dado, Hall of the Two
Sisters.
6 Dado, Hall of the Two
Sisters.
7 Pilaster, Hall of the
Ambassadors.
9 Dado in the Baths.
10 From a Column, Hall
of Justice.
11, 12 Dados, Hall of the
Ambassadors.
13 Dado in centre Window,
Hall of the Ambassadors.
14 Dado in Divan, Court of
the Fish-pond.
15 Pilaster, Hall of the
Ambassadors.
16 Dado, Hall of Justice.

CHAPTER XI

PERSIAN ORNAMENT

The Mohammedan architecture of Persia, if we may judge from the representations published in Flandin and Coste's "Voyages en Perse," does not appear to have ever reached the perfection of the Arabian buildings of Cairo. Although presenting considerable grandeur in the main features, the general outlines are much less pure, and there would appear to be a great want of elegance in all the constructive features as compared with those of Cairo. Their system of ornamentation also appears to us much less pure than the Arabian and Moresque. The Persians, unlike the Arabs and the Moors, were free to introduce animal life, and this mixing up of subjects drawn from real life in their decoration led to a much less pure style of ornament. With the Arabs and Moors, ornaments with their inscriptions had to supply every want, and therefore it became of more importance in their structures, and reached a higher point of elaboration. Persian ornament is a mixed style; combining the conventional, which is similar to the Arabian, and probably derived from a common origin, with an attempt at the natural, which sometimes has influenced both the Arabian and Turkish styles, and is even felt in portions of the Alhambra. The great attention paid to the illuminating of manuscripts in Persia, which, doubtless, were widely disseminated in Mohammedan countries, would readily spread the influence of this mixed style. The decorations of the houses of Cairo and Damascus, the mosques and fountains of Constantinople more especially, exhibit this mixed style; groups of natural flowers are constantly found growing from a vase and enclosed in panels of conventional Arabian ornament. The ornament of modern India also feels this ever-present influence of the Persian mixed style. In a book-cover from the India House (Plates LIII. and LIV., *pages 256, 258*) is an example of this; the outside is treated in the pure Arabian manner, whilst the inside (Plate LIV.) is quite Persian in character.

The ornaments on Plate XLIV. *(pages 228–29)*, from illuminated MSS. in the British Museum, present also the mixed character we have referred to. The geometrical patterns are purely conventional ornament, and have great affinity with the Arabian, but are less perfect in distribution. Nos. 2–8, 10, 12, 13, on the contrary, are from backgrounds of pictures, representing tapestry on the walls; they possess great elegance, and the masses are well contrasted with the grounds.

The patterns on Plate XLV. *(pages 230–31)* are chiefly representations of pavements and dados, and probably were intended for glazed tiles, so abundantly used by the Persians. Compared with the Arabian and

Moresque mosaics, they exhibit a marked inferiority, both in the distribution of form and in the arrangement of colour. It will be observed that, throughout our Persian subjects, the secondary and tertiary colours are much more dominant than in the Arabian (Plate XXXIV., *pages 170–71*), or in the Moresque, where blue, red, and gold, are the prevailing harmonies, and, as may be seen at a glance, with much increased effect.

The ornaments on Plate XLVI. *(pages 232–33)* have a much greater affinity with the Arabian; Nos. 11, 13, 15, 22–25, are very common ornaments for the heads of chapters in Persian MSS.: indeed there is but little variety to be found in these, numerous as they are. Compared with the Arabian MSS. (Plate XXXIV.), a great similarity will be found in all the leading lines of the construction of the ornaments, and also in the surface decoration of the ornaments themselves; but the masses are much less evenly distributed. However, the same general principles prevail.

Plates XLVII. and XLVII*. *(pages 234–37)* are arranged from a very curious Persian book at South Kensington Museum, which appears to be a manufacturer's pattern-book. The designs exhibit much elegance, and there is great simplicity and ingenuity displayed in the conventional rendering of natural flowers. Both these Plates and Plate XLVIII. *(pages 238–39)* are very valuable, as showing the extreme limit of this conventional rendering, reached, but not exceeded. When natural flowers are used as decoration, and subjected to a geometrical arrangement, they can have neither shade nor shadow, as was the case with the later MSS. of the Mediæval School—see Plate LXXIII. *(pages 340–41)*—

without falling under that reproach so justly due to the floral papers and floral carpets of modern times. The ornament No. 3 of Plate XLVIII. *(pages 238–39)*, as well as the borders throughout, present that mixed character of pure ornament, arranged in conjunction with the ornamental rendering of natural forms, which we have considered as characteristic of the Persian style, and which, we think, renders it so much inferior to the Arabian and the Moresque.

PERSIAN

The culture of Persia may have seemed very exotic to the Victorian public, but the same could not be said of its political status. With the empire at its height, British influence even extended to these far-flung regions. In Jones's day there was increasing concern about the disintegration of Ottoman authority, coupled with the growing threat from Russia. From the British point of view, Persia was of great strategic importance because it lay on the overland route to India. So, even though it was an independent kingdom, ruled by the Qajar shahs, European influence remained strong. Indeed, in 1843 Britain and Russia reached an agreement to share power in the region.

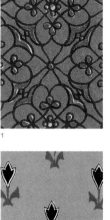

1

5

2

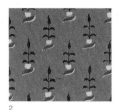

3

8

6

4

7

9

10

11

12

13

PLATE XLIV

1–19 Ornaments from Persian MSS. in the British Museum.

14

15

16

17

18

19

PERSIAN

✥ Jones believed (despite the caption given opposite) that many of these designs were intended for glazed tiles *(see page 224)*, which, in spite of his reservations, were among the chief glories of Persian art. In particular, Persian potters excelled at producing lusterware ceramics, utilizing a firing technique that gave their work a brilliant, metallic sheen. This effect was reproduced in England by William De Morgan (1839–1917). He had close links with the Pre-Raphaelite circle and was a key figure in the Arts and Crafts Movement, designing tiles for William Morris's firm. He also created a stunning range of iridescent blue tiles for Lord Leighton's Arab hall.

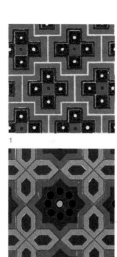

1

4

5

7

8

9

10

2

3

6

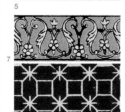

11

PLATE XLV

1–23 Ornaments from Persian MSS. in the British Museum.

PERSIAN

One of the great literary successes of the Victorian era came from a Persian source. This was the *Rubáiyát of Omar Khayyám*, which was translated into English by the Suffolk poet Edward Fitzgerald (1809–83). The original manuscript was a book of verse epigrams (a *rubái* is a four-line poem) by a twelfth-century scholar, mathematician, and astronomer. Some nineteenth-century critics described him as "the Voltaire of the East." Fitzgerald's very loose translation was published in 1859 and, initially, sold rather poorly. However, its hedonistic spirit struck a chord with the Pre-Raphaelite circle and, with their support, its ultimate success was assured.

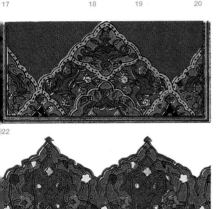

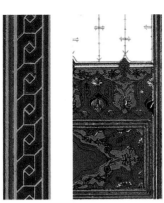

PLATE XLVI

1–25 Ornaments from Persian MSS. in the British Museum.

17

18

19

20

21

22

23

24

25

Today, the *Rubáiyát (see page 232)* is undoubtedly regarded as the most significant example of Anglo-Persian literature from the Victorian world, but in Jones's day there was an even more famous piece, for in 1853 Matthew Arnold (1822–88) published his epic poem *Sohrab and Rustum*. This told the tale of a father and son who faced each other on the battlefield, during a war between the Persians and the Tartars. Arnold took his subject matter from the *Shahnama* ("Book of Kings," 1010), a monumental verse anthology of ancient Persian tales by Firdawsi. This was hugely popular in its native country and, over the centuries, was illustrated in scores of different manuscripts.

1

2

3

4

5

6

7

8

9

10

11

12

13

14

15

16

17

18

19

20

PLATE XLVII

1–27 From a Persian Manufacturer's Pattern-Book, South Kensington Museum.

21

22

23

24

25

26

27

235

PERSIAN

Fabrics with Persian designs were often used to adorn one of the most popular items of Victorian furniture, the ottoman. As the name suggests, this originated in the Ottoman Empire. Usually, it took the form of a backless, upholstered bench, although smaller examples were also employed as storage boxes or footstools. Either way, the chief area of decoration was the padded top. Occasionally ottomans were given a European flavor—some were made to resemble medieval, Gothic chests —but more often they were covered in an ornate, oriental fabric. In more lavish households ottomans were a typical feature of the smoking room, which was invariably decorated in an Eastern style.

28

29

30

31

34

32

33

35

36

37

38

39

PLATE XLVII*

28–61 From a Persian
Manufacturer's
Pattern-Book, South
Kensington Museum.

237

PERSIAN

Persian textiles were highly sought after in the West during the Victorian era. In particular there was a strong demand for rugs and carpets. These had a very long history in Persia, although the most elaborate examples probably dated from the Safavid period (1499–1722). Many of the carpets incorporated floral or bird motifs. These were traditionally interpreted as scenes of Paradise, although some included depictions of hunting parties. The supply was fitful until the later years of the nineteenth century, when Liberty's opened its Oriental Bazaar (1875) and Zieglers of Manchester set up their own workshop in the Persian center of Arak (1883).

1

2

3

4

5

PLATE XLVIII

1–10 From a Persian MS.
South Kensington Museum.

CHAPTER XII

INDIAN ORNAMENT

FROM THE EXHIBITIONS OF 1851 AND 1855

The Exhibition of the Works of Industry of all Nations in 1851 was barely opened to the public ere attention was directed to the gorgeous contributions of India. Amid the general disorder everywhere apparent in the application of Art to manufactures, the presence of so much unity of design, so much skill and judgment in its application, with so much of elegance and refinement in the execution as was observable in all the works, not only of India, but of all the other Mohammedan contributing countries,—Tunis, Egypt, and Turkey,—excited a degree of attention from artists, manufacturers, and the public, which has not been without its fruits.

Whilst in the works contributed by the various nations of Europe there was everywhere to be observed an entire absence of any common principle in the application of Art to manufactures,—whilst from one end to the other of the vast structure there could be found but a fruitless struggle after novelty, irrespective of fitness, that all design was based upon a system of copying and misapplying the received forms of beauty of every bygone style of Art, without one single attempt to produce an Art in harmony with our present wants and means of production—the carver in stone, the worker in metal, the weaver and the painter, borrowing from each other, and alternately misapplying the forms peculiarly appropriate to each—there were to be found in isolated collections at the four corners of the transepts all the principles, all the unity, all the truth, for which we had looked elsewhere in vain, and this because we were amongst a people practising an art which had grown up with their civilisation, and strengthened with their growth. United by a common faith, their art had necessarily a common expression, this expression varying in each according to the influence to which each nation was subject. The Tunisian still retaining the art of the Moors who created the Alhambra; the Turk exhibiting the same art, but modified by the character of the mixed population over which they rule; the Indian uniting the severe forms of Arabian art with the graces of Persian refinement.

All the laws of the distribution of form which we have already observed in the Arabian and Moresque Ornament are equally to be found in the productions of India. From the highest work of embroidery, or most elaborate work of the loom, to the constructing and decorating of a child's toy or earthen vessel, we find everywhere at work the same guiding principles,—there is always the same care for the general form, the same absence of all excrescences or superfluous ornament; we find nothing that has been added without purpose, nor that could be removed without disadvantage. The same division and subdivision of their general lines, which forms the charms of Moresque ornament, is equally to be found here; the difference which creates the style is not one of principle, but of individual expression. In the Indian style ornaments are somewhat more flowing and less conventionalised, and have, doubtless, been more subjected to direct Persian influence.

The ornaments on Plate XLIX. *(pages 248–49)* are chiefly taken from Hookhas, of which there was an immense variety exhibited in 1851, and all remarkable for great elegance of outline, and for such a judicious treatment of the surface decoration that every ornament tended to further develope the general form.

It will be seen that there are two kinds of ornament,—the one strictly architectural and conventional: such as Nos. 1, 4, 5, 6, 8, which are treated as diagrams; and the other, such as Nos. 13, 14, 15, in which a more direct imitation of nature is attempted: these latter are to us very valuable lessons, showing how unnecessary it is for any work of decoration to more than indicate the general idea of a flower. The ingenious way in which the full-blown flower is shown in No. 15, in three positions in Nos. 14 and 15, the folding back of the leaf in No. 20, are very suggestive. The intention of the artist is fully expressed by means as simple as elegant. The unity of the surface of the object decorated is not destroyed, as it would be by the European method of making the flower as near like a natural flower as possible, with its own light and shade and shadow, tempting you to pluck it from the surface. On the Persian,

Plate XLVII. *(pages 234–35)*, will be seen a similar treatment of natural flowers; the comparison shows how much of Persian influence there is in this floral style of India.

In the application of the various ornaments to the different portions of the objects the greatest judgment is always shown. The ornament is invariably in perfect scale with the position it occupies; on the narrow necks of the Hookhas are the small pendent flowers, the swelling forms of the base are occupied by the larger patterns; at the lower edge, again, appear ornaments having an upward tendency, and, at the same time, forming a continuous line round the form to prevent the eye running out of it. Whenever narrow flowing borders are used, they are contrasted by others, with lines flowing in an opposite direction; the general repose of the decoration is never for a moment lost sight of.

In the equal distribution of the surface ornament over the grounds, the Indians exhibit an instinct and perfection of drawing perfectly marvellous. The ornament No. 3, on Plate L. *(pages 250–51)*, from an embroidered saddle-cloth, excited universal admiration in 1851. The exact balance obtained by the gold embroidery on the green and red grounds was so perfect, that it was beyond the power of a European hand to copy it with the same complete balance of form and colour. The way in which the colours are fused in all their woven fabrics, so as to obtain what they always appear to seek, viz. that coloured objects when viewed at a distance should present a neutralised bloom, is very remarkable. A due regard to economy in the production of our Plates has necessarily limited the number of printings, and we have not always, therefore, been able to obtain the proper balance of colour. The Indian collection at South Kensington Museum should be visited and studied by all in any way connected with the production of woven fabrics. In this collection will be found the most brilliant colours perfectly harmonised—it is impossible to find there a discord. All the examples show the nicest adjustment of the massing of the ornament to the colour of the ground; every colour or tint, from the palest and most delicate to the deepest and richest shades, receiving just the amount of ornament that it is adapted to bear.

The following general rules, which are applicable to all woven fabrics, may be observed:—

1. When gold ornaments are used on a coloured ground, where gold is used in large masses, there the ground is darkest. Where the gold is used more thinly, there the ground is lighter and more delicate.

2. When a gold ornament alone is used on a coloured ground, the colour of the ground is carried into it by ornaments or hatchings worked in the ground-colours on the gold itself.

3. When ornaments in one colour are on a ground of contrasting colour, the ornament is separated from the ground by an edging of a lighter colour, to prevent all harshness of contrast.

4. When, on the contrary, ornaments in a colour are on a gold ground, the ornaments are separated from the gold ground by an edging of a darker colour, to prevent the gold overpowering the ornament.— See No. 8, Plate L.

5. In other cases, where varieties of colour are used on a coloured ground, a general outline of gold, of silver, or of white or yellow silk, separates the ornament from the ground, giving a general tone throughout.

In carpets and low-toned combinations of colour, a black general outline is used for this purpose.

The object always appears to be, in the woven fabrics especially, that each ornament should be softly, not harshly, defined; that coloured objects viewed at a distance should present a neutralised bloom; that each step nearer should exhibit fresh beauties; and a close inspection, the means whereby these effects are produced.

In this they do but carry out the same principles of surface decoration which we find in the architecture of the Arabs and Moors. The spandril of a Moorish arch, and an Indian shawl, are constructed precisely on the same principles.

The ornament on Plate LIII. *(page 256),* from a book-cover at the India House, is a very brilliant example of painted decoration. The general proportions of the leading lines of the pattern, the skilful distribution of the flowers over the surface, and, notwithstanding the intricacy, the perfect continuity of the lines of the stalks, place it far before any European effort of this class. On the inside of the same cover, Plate LIV. *(page 258),* the ornaments are less conventional in their treatment; but how charmingly is observed the limit of the treatment of flowers on a flat surface! This book-cover offers in itself a specimen of two marked styles: the outside, Plate LIII., being after the Arabian manner, and the inside after the Persian.

These details were taken from works displayed at the Great Exhibition of 1851. As Jones indicated in his introduction *(see page 241)*, the Indian section drew particular praise from visitors to the show. Its centerpiece was a magnificent howdah, perched on top of a stuffed elephant. The exhibition committee experienced considerable difficulty in procuring the latter, finding a suitable example in Saffron Walden museum only at the very last minute. The ornamental patterns are mostly from hookahs—long, water-cooled pipes. These never became popular with smokers in the West, although Lewis Carroll's inclusion of a hookah-smoking caterpillar in the *Alice* adventures underlines their exotic appeal.

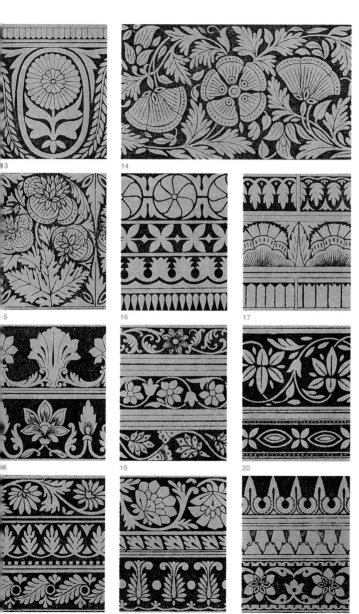

PLATE XLIX

1–23 Ornaments from
Works in Metal, exhibited
in the Indian Collection
in 1851.

⅍ The Indian displays at the Great Exhibition *(see page 248)* evoked considerable pride, due to Britain's influence in the subcontinent. The country was not yet, however, part of the empire. British interests were administered through the East India Company, which used native soldiers (sepoys) to maintain its authority. It was these sepoys who took part in the Indian Mutiny of 1857–58. After order was restored, power was transferred from the East India Company to the Crown. A viceroy was appointed and most westernizing policies were discontinued. In 1876 Queen Victoria assumed the title of empress of India.

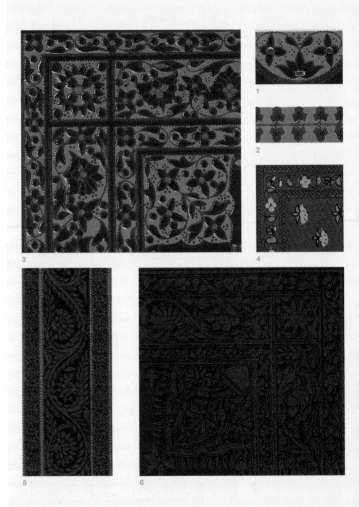

PLATE L

1–11 Ornaments from Embroidered and Woven Fabrics, and paintings on Vases, exhibited in the Indian Collection in 1851, and now at South Kensington Museum.

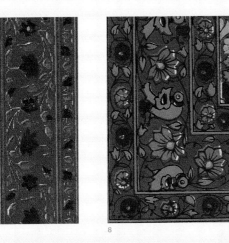

7

8

9

10

11

🐾 Above all else, most British people associated India with lavish fabrics. In particular there was a widespread fashion for cashmere shawls. As the name suggests, these luxury items originated in Kashmir, where they were worn by men. They became popular in Europe in the early nineteenth century, when their warmth made them the ideal accessories for skimpy Empire fashions. Prices were prohibitive, however, so attempts were made to copy the shawls in France and Britain. The versions produced at the Scottish center of Paisley proved especially successful, lending their name to the "paisley" pattern.

1

2

3

4

5

6

7

8

9

10

11

12

PLATE LI

1–24 Ornaments from Embroidered and Woven Fabrics, and paintings on Vases, exhibited in the Indian Collection in 1851, and now at South Kensington Museum.

13

14

15

16

17

18

19

20

21

22

23

24

The taste for cashmere shawls *(see page 252)* was a passing trend, but there was a long-term demand for Indian chintzes. Deriving from a Hindi word *(chint)*, these colored cotton fabrics had been popular since the seventeenth century. Initially they were used as barter goods by the British and Dutch East India companies, but, by the end of the seventeenth century, production was being geared toward Europe. Patterns and color schemes were sent out from the West so that local manufacturers could copy them. The favorite design was the "flowering tree," which came from Indo-Persian sources, but was adapted to European taste. The chintz trade flourished until the late nineteenth century, when improved printing techniques favored Western manufacturers.

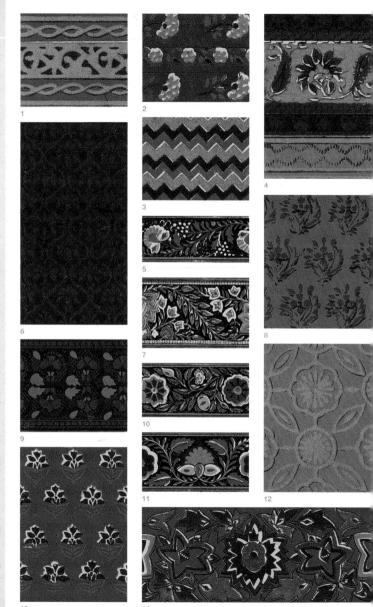

1

2

3

4

5

6

7

8

9

10

11

12

13

14

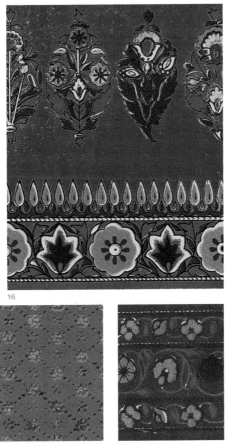

15

16

PLATE LII

1–22 Ornaments from Embroidered and Woven Fabrics, and paintings on Vases, exhibited in the Indian Collection in 1851, and now at South Kensington Museum.

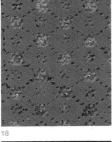

17

18

19

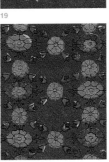

20

21

22

🎨 Early examples of wooden artworks from India are comparatively rare, perhaps because of the damaging effects of the climate. The finest pieces are writing cabinets or caskets, inlaid with mother-of-pearl or ivory. These have elaborate floral designs, similar to those shown here. Painted lacquerware seems to have been a relatively late development. The technique was imported from Persia and older examples have a pronounced Iranian flavor. Later it became a specialty of artists of the Deccan region and its school of painting, such as Rahim Deccani. The most popular format appeared on small jewel boxes. These consisted of painted and lacquered papier-mâché, finished off with ivory trimmings.

1

1–8 Specimens of
Painted Lacquer-work,
from the Collection at the
India House.

🪷 Although there was a long history of British involvement in India, it was only in the late eighteenth and early nineteenth centuries that the English public gained a clear visual impression of the place. This was due to the work of artist-travelers, such as William Hodges (1744–97) and the Daniells. Hodges gained acclaim for his *Selected Views of India* (1785–88), which chronicled his tour of the subcontinent in 1780–83. The fine aquatint engravings of Thomas Daniell (1749–1840) and his nephew William (1769–1837) proved even more popular, when they were published in their *Oriental Scenery* (1808) and *Picturesque Voyage to India* (1810). The tear-shaped motif illustrated here (No. 3) is the *buta* or "Kashmir cone." This stemmed from Persian and Mogul art, but became a popular feature of Indian design. From there, it was exported to Britain, where it came to form the basis of the "paisley" pattern *(see page 252).*

1

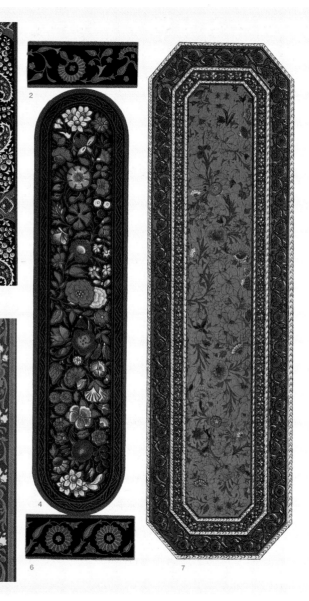

PLATE LIV, LIV*

1–7 Specimens of
Painted Lacquer-work,
from the Collection at the
India House.

INDIAN

The Daniells' aquatints of India *(see page 258)* created a huge impression in Britain, inspiring many artworks in other fields. In the 1820s, for example, the Staffordshire pottery marketed a wide range of blue-and-white porcelain with Indian designs, based on the Daniells' prints. There was also a growing taste for "Hindoo" architecture—a very general term, which could embrace almost any oriental style. The best-known building in this vein is Nash's Royal Pavilion in Brighton (1815–21), which marries an Indian exterior with a Chinese interior. The finest example, however, is probably Sezincote (*ca.* 1805) in Gloucestershire, a country house that was designed by Samuel Pepys Cockerell (1753–1827).

1

2

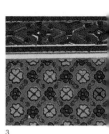

3

1

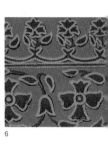

4

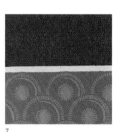

7

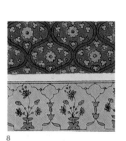

10

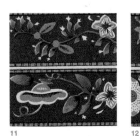

11

12

3

14

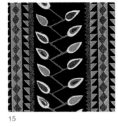

15

PLATE LV

1–26 Ornaments from Woven and Embroidered Fabrics and Painted Boxes, exhibited in the Indian Collection at Paris in 1855.

6

17

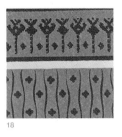

18

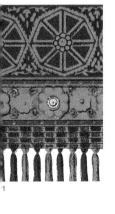

1

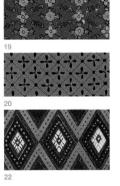

19

20

22

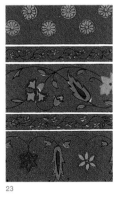

23

4

25

26

CHAPTER XIII

HINDOO ORNAMENT

We have not been able, with the materials at command in this country, to procure sufficient illustrations for a fair appreciation of the nature of Hindoo ornament. In the works hitherto published on the ancient architecture of India, sufficient attention has not been directed to the ornamental portions of the buildings to enable us to recognise the true character of Hindoo ornament.

In early publications on the art of Egypt all the works of sculpture and ornament were so falsely rendered, that it has taken considerable time for the European public to become persuaded that there existed so much grace and refinement in the works of the Egyptians.

The Egyptian remains, however, which have been transported to this country, the casts of others existing in Egypt, and the more trustworthy representations which have of late been published, have placed this beyond doubt, and Egyptian art is taking its true place in the estimation of the public.

When the same thing shall have been done for the ancient architecture of India, we shall be in a better position than we are at present to form an opinion how far it is entitled to take rank as a really fine art, or whether the Hindoos are only heapers of stone, one over the other, adorned with grotesque and barbaric sculpture.

Had we possessed only picturesque views of the Parthenon and the Temples of Balbeck and Palmyra, we should unhesitatingly have said that the Romans were far greater architects than the Greeks. But the contour of a single moulding from the Parthenon would at once reverse the judgment, and proclaim loudly that we were viewing the works of a people who had reached the highest point in civilisation and refinement.

Although ornament is most properly an accessory to architecture, and never should be allowed to usurp the place of proper structural features, or to overload or disguise them, it is in all cases the very soul of an architectural monument; and by the ornament alone can we judge truly of the amount of care and mind which has been devoted to the work. All else in any building may be the result of rule and compass, but by the ornament of a building we can best discover how far the architect was at the same time an artist.

No one can peruse the Essay on Hindoo Architecture by Ram Raz[*] without feeling that a higher state of architectural perfection has been reached than the works published up to the present time would lead us to

[*] "History of the Architecture of the Hindoos." By Ram Raz. London, 1834.

believe. In this work not only are precise rules laid down for the general arrangement of structures, but also minute directions are given for the divisions and subdivisions of each ornament.

One of the precepts quoted by Ram Raz deserves to be cited, as showing how much the general perfection was cared for: "Woe to them who dwell in a house not built according to the proportions of symmetry! In building an edifice, therefore, let all its parts, from the basement to the roof, be duly considered."

Among the directions for the various proportions of columns, bases, and capitals, is a rule for finding the proper diminution of the upper diameter of a column in proportion to the lower.

Ram Raz says, that the general rule adopted by the Hindoo architects was to divide the diameter of the column at the base by as many parts as there were diameters in the whole height of the column, and that one of these parts was invariably deducted to form the upper diameter. From which it is apparent that the higher the column the less it will diminish; and that this was done because the apparent diminution of the diameter in columns of the same proportion is always greater according to the height.

The best specimens of Hindoo ornament we have been able to procure are represented in Plate LVI. *(pages 268–69)*, from a statue of Surga, or the Sun, in basalt, at the house of the Asiatic Society, and supposed to belong to a period between the fifth and ninth century A.D. The ornaments are very beautifully executed, and evidently betray Greek influence. The ornament

No. 9 represents the lotus, seen as it were in plan, with the buds in side-elevation: it is held in the hand of the god.

In the sacred books quoted by Ram Raz are several directions to ornament the various architectural members with lotuses and jewels; which seem to be the chief types of the decoration on the mouldings.

The architectural features of Hindoo buildings consist chiefly of mouldings heaped up one over the other. Definite instructions are quoted by Ram Raz for the varying proportions of each, and it is evident that the whole value of the style will consist in the more or less perfection with which these transitions are effected; but, as we said before, we have no opportunity of judging how far this is the case.

On Plate LVII. *(pages 270–71)* we have gathered together all the examples of decorative ornament that we could find on the copies of the paintings from the Caves of Ajunta, exhibited by the East India Company at the Crystal Palace. As these copies, notwithstanding that they are said to be faithful, are yet by a European hand, it is difficult to say how far they may be relied upon. In the subordinate portions, such as the ornaments, at all events, there is so little marked character, that they might belong to any style. It is very singular, that in these paintings there should be so little ornament; a peculiarity that we have observed in several ancient paintings in the possession of the Asiatic Society. There is a remarkable absence of ornament even on the dresses of the figures.

HINDOO

These ornamental details come from a statue of Surya, an Indian Sun god. He is one of the five solar deities listed in the *Rig-Veda* (an ancient Hindu text), each of whom traversed the sky in their sun chariot. In many images he was portrayed with a lotus in each hand. As in Egypt, this flower was a traditional symbol of the Sun, since it opened at dawn and closed at sunset. This is emphasized in No. 9, where both states are shown. In more elaborate depictions Surya was shown with two female spirits wielding bows, who drove away the powers of darkness.

1

2

3

4

5

6

7

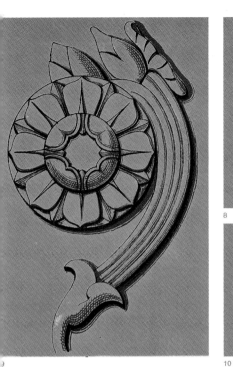

8

10

1

PLATE LVI

1–11 Ornaments from a Statue in Basalt at the House of the Royal Asiatic Society.

HINDOO

In the nineteenth century "Hindoo" was used as a very general term for any oriental style of architecture, including Indian, Chinese, and Moorish forms. It did not refer specifically to Hindu buildings, and indeed, many of the images in this section are actually Buddhist. This is certainly true of the celebrated cave paintings at Ajanta, which adorn a series of Buddhist rock sanctuaries. Dating from the second century BC to the seventh century AD, the complex includes no fewer than 29 caves, which were intended as *viharas* (monasteries). As Jones suggests, most of the decoration is figurative, showing scenes from the life of Buddha, although the ceilings feature some remarkable ornamental panels.

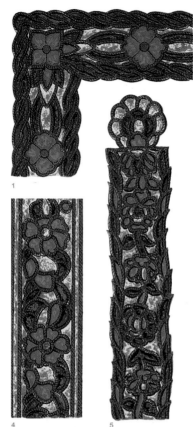

1

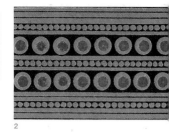

5

4

6

7

2

3

8

9

12

15   16

17

PLATE LVII

1 Burmese, of Glass.—
CRYSTAL PALACE.
2, 3, 6–11, 13, 14
Ornaments from the Copies
of the Paintings on the walls
of the Caves at Ajunta.—C.P.
4 Burmese Shrine.—C.P.
5 Burmese Standard.—C.P.
12, 15, 16 From Burmese
Shrine.—C.P.
17 Burmese, from a
Monastery near Prome.—C.P.

Many of the details in this chapter come from Burma, where the art was predominantly Buddhist. Hindu settlers arrived from India in the early Middle Ages, but their religion never became firmly established in the country. In Jones's day there was a strong European presence in the area as France and Britain competed for control. In 1852, the governor general of India ordered the occupation of Rangoon, following an attack on some English merchants. After this, the British exercised authority over the Burmese coastline. The entire country was subsequently annexed in 1886, becoming a province of British India.

1

2

3

4

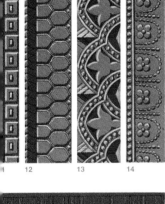

CHAPTER XIV

CHINESE ORNAMENT

Notwithstanding the higher antiquity of the civilisation of the Chinese, and the perfection which all their manufacturing processes reached ages before our time, they do not appear to have made much advance in the Fine Arts. Mr. Fergusson, in his admirable "Handbook of Architecture," observes that "China possesses scarcely anything worthy of the name of Architecture," and that all their great engineering works, with which the land is covered, "are wholly devoid of either architectural design or ornament."

In their ornamentation, with which the world is so familiar through the numerous manufactured articles of every kind which have been imported into this country, they do not appear to have gone beyond that point which is reached by every people in an early stage of civilisation: their art, such as it is, is fixed, and is subject neither to progression nor retrogression. In the conception of pure form they are even behind the New Zealander; but they possess, in common with all Eastern nations, the happy instinct of harmonising colours. As this is more a faculty than an acquirement, it is just what we should expect; the arriving at an appreciation of pure form is a more subtle process, and is the result of either more highly endowed natural instincts, or of the development of primitive ideas by successive generations of artists improving on each other's efforts.

The general forms of many of the Chinese porcelain vases are remarkable for the beauty of their outline, but not more so than the rude water-bottles of porous clay which the untutored Arabian potter fashions daily on the banks of the Nile, assisted only by the instincts of his gentle race; and the pure form of the Chinese vases is often destroyed by the addition of grotesque or other unmeaning ornaments, built up upon the surface, not growing from it: from which we argue, that they can possess an appreciation of form, but in a minor degree.

In their decoration, both painted and woven, the Chinese exhibit only just so much art as would belong to a primitive people. Their most successful efforts are those in which geometrical combinations form the basis; but even in these, whenever they depart from patterns formed by the intersection of equal lines they appear to have a very imperfect idea of the distribution of spaces. Their instinct of colour enables them, in some measure, to balance form, but when deprived of this aid they do not appear to be equally successful. The diapers on Plate LIX. *(pages 280–81)* will furnish us with examples. Patterns 1, 8, 13, 21, 35, being generated by figures which ensure an equal distribution, are more perfect than Nos. 2, 4–7, 41, where the arrangement depends more upon caprice; on the other hand, Nos. 23, 29, 30, and the other patterns of this class on the Plate, are examples in which the instinct of the amount of balancing colour required would determine the mass. The Chinese share with the Indian this happy power in their woven fabrics; and the tone of the ground of any fabric is always in harmony with the quantity of ornament which it has to support. The Chinese are certainly colourists, and are able to balance with equal success both the fullest tones of colour and the most delicate shades.

They are not only successful in the use of the primaries, but also of the secondaries and tertiaries; most successful, perhaps, of all in the management of the lighter tones of pure colours,—pale blue, pale pink, pale green, prevailing.

Of purely ornamental or conventional forms, other than geometric patterns, the Chinese possess but very few. On Plate LX. *(pages 282–83)* are some examples in 1–3, 5, 7, 8. They have no flowing conventional ornament—such as we find in all other styles; the place of this is always supplied by a representation of natural flowers interwoven with lineal ornament: such as Nos. 17, 18, Plate LXI. *(pages 284–85)*; or of fruit, see Plate LXII *(pages 286–87)*. In all cases, however, their instinct restrains them within the true limit; and although the arrangement is generally unnatural and unartistic, they never, by shades and shadows, as with us, violate consistency. In their printed paper-hangings, the whole treatment, both of figures, landscape and ornament, is so far conventional, that however we may feel it to be unartistic, we are not shocked by an overstepping of the legitimate bounds of decoration. In their floral patterns, moreover, they always observe the natural laws of radiation from the parent stem, and tangential curvature: it could not well be otherwise, as the peculiarity of the Chinese is their fidelity in copying; and we hence infer that they must be close observers of nature. It is the taste to idealise upon this close observation which is wanting.

We have already referred in the Greek chapter to the peculiarities of the Chinese fretwork. No. 1, Plate LXI. *(pages 284–85),* is a continuous meander like the Greek; Nos. 4–10, 13, 18, specimens of irregular frets; No. 4, Plate LX. *(pages 282–83)*, a curious instance of a fret with a curved termination.

On the whole, Chinese ornament is a very faithful expression of the nature of this peculiar people; its characteristic feature is oddness,—we cannot call it capricious, for caprice is the playful wandering of a lively imagination; but the Chinese are totally unimaginative, and all their works are accordingly wanting in the highest grace of art,—the ideal.

———◦———

CHINESE

Jones's unflattering comments *(see page 276)* about Chinese culture may well have been colored by the country's political weakness. China had long pursued a policy of isolation, allowing foreigners to trade only through the port of Canton. This changed after their defeat in the Opium Wars (1839–42 and 1856–60). Hong Kong was ceded to Britain by the Treaty of Nanking (1842), which also obliged the Chinese authorities to open up five ports to UK traders. In addition, the ruling Manchu dynasty came under threat from a series of internal uprisings and only clung on to power with the aid of Western support.

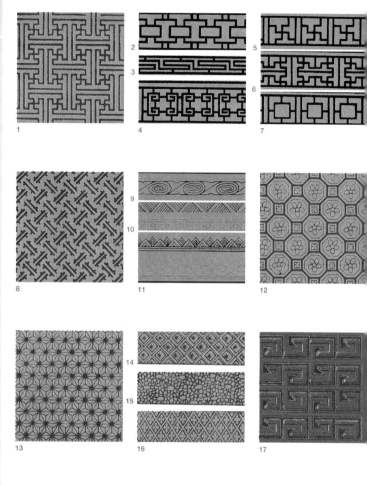

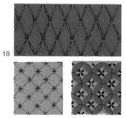

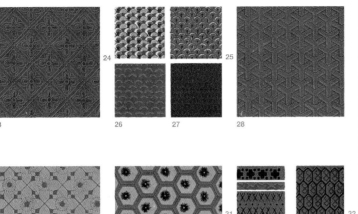

24

25

26

27

28

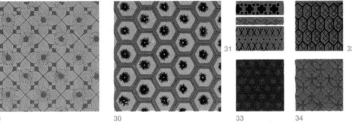

29

30

31

32

33

34

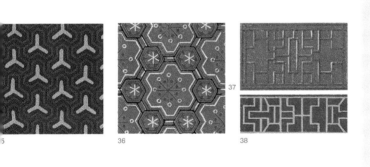

35

36

37

38

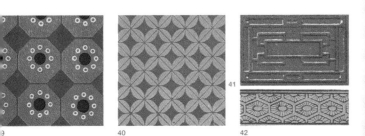

39

40

41

42

PLATE LIX

The Ornaments, Nos. **1,
8–17, 23–30, 40, 42,** are
Painted on Porcelain.
Nos. **2–7, 18–22, 31–39,
41,** are from Paintings.

CHINESE

Although trading links with the Orient were limited prior to the nineteenth century, the Chinese had maintained a long tradition of producing goods for export to the West. In particular they knew that there was a great demand for their porcelain. The shape of these export pieces was generally European, and they were normally designed for display rather than use, but the decoration was entirely oriental. In turn, Westerners produced their own imitations of Chinese goods, which they termed *chinoiserie*. This style was particularly popular in the eighteenth century, when it exerted a strong influence on both architecture and furniture. By Jones's day, however, it had fallen out of fashion.

1

2

3

4

5

6

7

8

9

10

11

12

PLATE LX

The Ornaments, Nos. **1–12, 16, 19–24,** are Painted on Porcelain.
Nos. **17, 18,** from Pictures.
Nos. **13, 22, 23,** from Woven Fabrics.
Nos. **14, 15,** Painted on Wooden Boxes.

13

14

15

16

17

18

19

20

21

22

23

24

The increasing availability of Chinese wares after the 1840s had a significant impact on British art. Following the lead of Dante Gabriel Rossetti (1828–82), several members of the Pre-Raphaelite circle began to collect Chinese blue-and-white porcelain. Soon it became an essential interest for any self-respecting devotee of the aesthetic movement. This trend is clearly reflected in the work of the American artist James Whistler (1834–1903). After settling in London, he became a neighbor of Rossetti and swiftly acquired a passion for Chinese artworks. Items from his collection are displayed in such paintings as *The Princess from the Land of Porcelain* (1864).

10

11

12

13

PLATE LXI

The Ornaments, Nos. **1, 4, 5,** are Painted on Wood.
Nos. **2, 3, 6, 7, 9, 12–15, 17, 18,** are Painted on Porcelain.
Nos. **8, 10, 11,** Woven Fabrics.
No. **16,** from a Picture.

14

15

16

7

8

From a British perspective, fine porcelain and lavish silks were the most important Chinese artworks. Both were highly prized by the aesthetes, a group of nineteenth-century artists and writers who advocated a policy of "art for art's sake." Their mecca was the London store of Liberty's, which specialized in delicate, oriental fabrics. The affected sensibilities of some aesthetes, epitomized by the dandified attitudes of Oscar Wilde (1854–1900) and James Whistler *(see page 284),* were mercilessly lampooned in the press. *Punch* ran a series of cartoons on the Cimabue Browns from Passionate Brompton, who were obsessed with their collection of blue-and-white china, while Gilbert and Sullivan satirized them in *Patience* (1881).

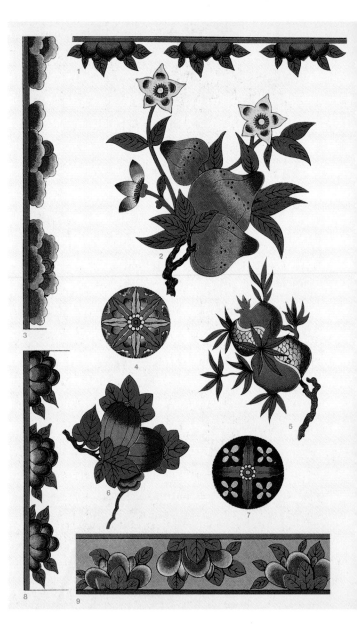

PLATE LXII

1–20 Conventional Renderings of Flowers and Fruit, Painted on Porcelain.

CHAPTER XV

CELTIC ORNAMENT

The genius of the inhabitants of the British Islands has, in all ages, been indicated by productions of a class or style singularly at variance with those of the rest of the world. Peculiar as are our characteristics at the present time, those of our forefathers, from the remotest ages, have been equally so. In the Fine Arts, our immense Druidical temples are still the wonder of the beholder; and in succeeding ages gigantic stone crosses, sometimes thirty feet high, most elaborately carved and ornamented with devices of a style unlike those of other nations, exhibited the old genius for lapidary erections under a modified form inspired by a new faith.

The earliest monuments are relics of ornamental art which we possess (and they are far more numerous than the generality of persons would conceive) are so intimately connected with the early introduction of Christianity into these islands* *(see overleaf for footnote)*, that we are compelled to refer to the latter in our endeavours to unravel the history and peculiarities of Celtic Art; a task which has hitherto been scarcely attempted to be performed, although possessing, from its extreme nationality, a degree of interest equal, one would have thought, to that connected with the history of ornamental art in other countries.

1. HISTORICAL EVIDENCE. — Without attempting to reconcile the various statements which have been made by historians as to the precise manner of the introduction of religion into Britain, we have the most ample evidence, not only that it had been long established previous to the arrival of St. Augustine in A.D. 596, but that in several important points of doctrine the old British religionists differed from the missionary sent by St. Gregory the Great. This statement is most completely borne out by still existing artistic evidences. St. Gregory sent into England various copies of the Holy Scriptures, and two of these are still preserved; one in the Bodleian Library at Oxford, and the other in the Library of Corpus Christi College, Cambridge. They are copies of the Holy Gospels, written in Italy, in the large uncial or rounded characters common in that country, and destitute of ornament; the initial letter of each Gospel scarcely differing from the ordinary writing of the text, the first line or two being merely written in red ink, each Gospel preceded by a portrait of the Evangelist (one only still remains, namely, that of St. Luke), seated under a round-headed arch, supported upon marble columns, and ornamented with foliage arranged in

* The Pagan Celtic remains at Gavr' Innis, in Brittany, New Grange, in Ireland, and, I believe, one Druidical monument near Harlech, in Wales, exhibit a very rude attempt at ornamentation, chiefly consisting of incised spiral or circular and angulated lines.

a classical manner. All the most ancient Italian manuscripts are entirely destitute of ornamental elaboration.

The case is totally different with the most ancient manuscripts known to have been written in these islands; and as these are the chief supports of our theory of the independent origin of Celtic ornament, and as, moreover, we are constantly opposed by doubts as to the great age which has been assigned to these precious documents, we must enter into a little palæographical detail in proof of their venerable antiquity. It is true, indeed, that none of them are dated; but in some the scribe has inserted his name, which the early annals have enabled us to identify, and thus to fix the period of the execution of the volume. In this manner the autograph Gospels of St. Columba; the Leabhar Dhimma, or Gospels of St. Dimma Mac Nathi; the Bodleian Gospels, written by Mac Regol; and the Book of Armagh, have been satisfactorily assigned to periods not later than the ninth century. Another equally satisfactory evidence exists, in proof of the early date of the volumes, in the unrivalled collection of contemporary Anglo-Saxon Charters existing in the British Museum and other libraries, from the latter half of the seventh century up to the Norman Conquest; and although, as Astle observes, "these Charters are generally written in a more free and expeditious manner than the books written in the same ages, yet a similarity of character is observable between Charters and books written in the same century, and they authenticate each other." Now it is quite impossible to compare, for example, the Cottonian MS. Vespasian, A 1, generally known under the name of the Psalter of St.

Augustine, with the Charters of Sebbi King of the East Saxons, A.D. 670 (Casley's *Catal. of MSS.* p. xxiv.); of Lotharius King of Kent, dated at Reculver, A.D. 679; or, again, the Charter of Æthelbald, dated A.D. 769, with the Gospels of Mac Regol or St. Chad; without being perfectly convinced that the MSS. are coeval with the Charters.

A third species of evidence of the great antiquity of our very ancient national manuscripts is afforded by the fact of many of them being still preserved in various places abroad, whither they were carried by the Irish and Anglo-Saxon missionaries. The great number of monastic establishments founded by our countrymen in different parts of Europe is matter of historical record; and we need only cite the case of St. Gall, an Irishman, whose name has not only been given to the monastic establishment which he founded, but even to the Canton of Switzerland in which it is situated. The monastic books of this establishment, now transferred to the public library, comprise many of the oldest manuscripts in Europe, and include a number of fragments of elaborately-ornamented volumes executed in these islands, and long venerated as relics of the founder. In like manner, the Book of the Gospels of St. Boniface is still preserved at Fulda with religious care; and that of St. Kilian (an Irishman), the Apostle of Franconia, was discovered in his tomb, stained with his blood, and is still preserved at Wurtzburgh, where it is annually exhibited on the altar of the cathedral on the anniversary of his martyrdom.

Now, all these manuscripts, thus proved to have been written in these islands at a period prior to the end of the ninth century, exhibit peculiarities of ornamentation totally at variance with those of all other countries, save only in places where the Irish or Anglo-Saxon missionaries may have introduced their own, or have modified the already existing styles. And here we may observe that, although our arguments are chiefly derived from the early manuscripts, the results are equally applicable to the contemporary ornamental metal or stone-work; the designs of which are in many cases so entirely the counterparts of those of the manuscripts, as to lead to the conclusion that the designers of the one class of ornaments supplied also the designs for the other. So completely, indeed, is this the case in some of the great stone crosses, that we might almost fancy we were examining one of the pages of an illuminated volume with a magnifying glass.

2. PECULIARITIES OF CELTIC ORNAMENT. — The chief peculiarities of the Celtic ornamentation consist, first, in the entire absence of foliage or other phyllomorphic or vegetable ornament,—the classical acanthus being entirely ignored; and secondly, in the extreme intricacy, and excessive minuteness and elaboration, of the various patterns, mostly geometrical, consisting of interlaced ribbon-work, diagonal or spiral lines, and strange, monstrous animals and birds, with long top-knots, tongues, and tails, intertwining in almost endless knots.

The most sumptuous of the manuscripts, such for instance as the Book of Kells, the Gospels of Lindisfarne and St. Chad, and some of the manuscripts at St. Gall, have entire pages covered with the most elaborate patterns in compartments, the whole forming beautiful cruciform designs, one of these facing the commencement of each of the four Gospels. The labour employed in such a mass of work[†] must have been very great; the care infinite, since the most scrutinizing examination with a magnifying glass will not detect an error in the truth of the lines, or the regularity of the interlacing; and yet, with all this minuteness, the most harmonious effect of colouring has been produced.

Contrary to the older plan of commencing a manuscript with a letter in noways or scarcely differing from the remainder of the text, the commencement of each Gospel opposite to these grand tessellated pages was ornamented in an equally elaborate manner. The initial letter was often of gigantic size, occupying the greater part of the page, which was completed by a few of the following letters or words, each letter generally averaging about an inch in height. In these initial pages, as in those of the cruciform designs, we find all the various styles of ornament employed in more or less detail.

The most universal and singularly diversified ornament employed by artificers in metal, stone, or manuscripts, consists of one or more narrow ribbons interlaced and knotted, often excessively intricate in their convolutions, and often symmetrical and geometrical. Plates LXIII. and LXIV. *(pages 306–09)* exhibit numerous examples of this ornament in varied styles. By colouring the ribbons with different tints, either upon a coloured or black ground, many charming effects are produced. Of the curious intricacy of some of these designs, an idea may easily be obtained by

[†] In one of these pages in the Gospels of St. Chad, which we have taken the trouble to copy, there are not fewer than one hundred and twenty of the most fantastic animals.

following the ribbon in some of these patterns; as, for instance, in the upper compartment of Fig. 4 of Plate LXIII. Sometimes two ribbons run parallel to each other, but are interlaced alternately, as in Fig. 3 of Plate LXIV. When allowable the ribbon is dilated and angulated to fill up particular spaces in the design, as in Plate LXIV., Fig. 6. The simplest modification of this pattern of course is the double oval, seen in the angles of Fig. 8, Plate LXIV. This occurs in Greek and Syriac MSS., in Roman tessellated pavements, but rarely in our early MSS. Another simple form is that known as the triquetra, which is extremely common in MSS. and metal-work; an instance in which four of these triquetræ are introduced occurs in Plate LXIV., Fig. 11. Figures 10 and 32 in the same Plate are modifications of this pattern.

Another very distinguishing ornament profusely introduced into early work of all kind consists of monstrous animals, birds, lizards, and snakes of various kinds, generally extravagantly elongated, with tails, top-knots, and tongues, extended into long interlacing ribbons, intertwining together in the most fantastic manner; often symmetrical, but often irregular, being drawn so as to fill up a required space. Occasionally, but of rare occurrence, the human figure is also thus introduced; as on one of the panels of the Monasterboice Cross in the Crystal Palace, where are four figures thus singularly intertwined, and on one of the bosses of the Duke of Devonshire's Lismore crozier are several such fantastic groups. In Plate LXIII. are groups of animals thus intertwined. The most intricate examples are the groups of eight dogs (Plate LXV., *pages 310–11,* Fig. 3) and eight birds (Plate LXV., Fig. 9) from one of the St. Gall MSS., and the most elegant is the marginal ornament (Plate LXV., *pages 310–11*, Fig. 19) from the Gospels of Mac Durnan, at Lambeth Palace. In the later Irish and Welsh MSS. the edges of the interlaced ribbons touch each other, and the designs are far less geometrical and much more confused. The strange design (Plate LXV., Fig. 6) is no other than the initial Q of the Psalm 'Quid Gloriaris,' from the Psalter of Ricemarchus, Bishop of St. David's A.D. 1088. It will be seen that it is intended for a monstrous animal, with one top-knot extended in front over its nose, and a second forming an extraordinary whorl above the head, the neck with a row of pearls, the body long and angulated, terminated by two contorted legs and grim claws, and a knotted tail, which it would be difficult, indeed, for the animal to unravel. Very often, also, the heads alone of birds or beasts form the terminal ornament of a pattern, of which various examples occur in Plate LXIV *(pages 308–09)*., the gaping mouth and long tongue forming a not ungraceful finish.

The most characteristic, however, of all the Celtic patterns, is that produced by two or three spiral lines starting from a fixed point, their opposite extremities going off to the centres of coils formed by other spiral lines. Plate LXV., Figs. 7, 14, 18, are instances of this ornament, all more or less magnified; and Fig. 11. Plate LXIII. *(pages 306–07)*, Fig. 2, shows how ingeniously this pattern may be converted into the diagonal pattern. In the MSS., and all the finer and more ancient metal and stone-work, these spiral lines always take the direction of a C, and never that of an S. It is, therefore, evident, not only from the circumstance, but also from the irregularity of the design itself, that the main ornament in Plate LXIII., Fig.

1, was not drawn by an artist skilled in the genuine Celtic patterns, but indicates a certain amount either of carelessness or of extraneous influence. This pattern has also been called the trumpet pattern, from the spaces between any two of the lines forming a long, curved design, like an ancient Irish trumpet, the mouth of which is represented by the small pointed oval placed transversely at the broad end. Instances in metal-work of this pattern occur in several circular objects of bronze of unknown use, about a foot in diameter, occasionally found in Ireland; also in small, circular, enamelled plates of early Anglo-Saxon work, found in different parts of England. It is more rarely found in stone-work, the only instance of its occurrence in England, as far as we are aware, being on the font of Deerhurst Church. Bearing in mind that this ornament does not appear in MSS. executed in England after the ninth century, we may conclude that this is the oldest ornamental font in this country.

Another equally characteristic pattern is composed of diagonal lines, never interlacing, but generally arranged at equal intervals apart, forming a series of Chinese-like patterns,[§] and which, as the letter Z, or Z reversed, seems to be the primary element, may be termed the Z pattern. It is capable of great modification, as may be seen in Plate LXV. *(pages 310–11)*, Figs. 8, 12, 13, 15, 20, and 21. In the more elaborate MSS. it is purely geometrical and regular, but in rude work it degenerates into an irregular design, as in Plate LXIII., Figs. 1 and 2.

[§] Several of the patterns given in the upper part of the Chinese Plate LIX. occur with scarcely any modification in our stone and metal-work, as well as in our MSS.

Another very simple ornament occasionally used in our MSS. consists of a series of angulated lines, placed at equal distances apart, forming a series of steps. See Plate LXIV. *(pages 308–09)*, Figs. 9 and 11; and Plate LXV. *(pages 310–11)*, Fig. 2. This is, however, by no means characteristic of Celtic ornament occurring elsewhere from the earliest period.

The last ornament we shall notice is, indeed, the simplest of all, consisting merely of red dots or points. These were in great use as marginal ornaments of the great initial letters, as well as of the more ornamental details, and are, indeed, one of the chief characteristics distinguishing Anglo-Saxon and Irish MSS. Sometimes, also, they were even formed into patterns, as in Plate LXIV., Figs. 40 and 44.

3. ORIGIN OF CELTIC ORNAMENT. — The various styles of ornament described above were practised throughout Great Britain and Ireland from the fourth or fifth to the tenth or eleventh centuries; and as they appear in their purest and most elaborate forms in those parts where the old Celtic races longest prevailed, we have not hesitated to give the Celtic as their generic name.

We purposely, indeed, avoid entering into the question, whether the Irish in the first instance received their letters and styles or ornament from the early British Christians, or whether it was in Ireland that the latter were originated, and thence dispersed over England. A careful examination of the local origin of the early Anglo-Saxon MSS., and of the Roman, Romano-British, and early Christian inscribed and sculptured stones of the western parts of England and Wales, would, we think, materially assist in determining this question. It is sufficient for our argument that Venerable Bede informs us, that the British and Irish Churches were identical in their peculiarities, and the like identity occurs in their monuments. It is true, indeed, that the Anglo-Saxons, as well as the Irish, employed all these styles of ornamentation. The famous Gospels of Lindisfarne, or Book of St. Cuthbert, preserved in the Cottonian Library in the British Museum, is an unquestionable proof of such employment; and it is satisfactorily known that this volume was executed by Anglo-Saxon artists at Lindisfarne at the end of the seventh century. But it is equally true that Lindisfarne was an establishment founded by the monks of Iona, who were the disciples of the Irish St. Columba, so that it is not at all surprising that their Anglo-Saxon scholars should have adopted the styles of ornamentation used by their Irish predecessors. The Saxons, pagans as they were when they arrived in England, had certainly no peculiarities of ornamental design of their own; and no such remains exist in the north of Germany as would give the least support to the idea that the ornamentation of Anglo-Saxon MSS., &c., was of a Teutonic origin.

Various have been the conjectures whence all these peculiarities of ornament were derived by the early Christians of these islands. One class of writers, anxious to overthrow the independence of the ancient British and Irish Churches, has referred them to a Roman origin, and has even gone so far as to suppose that some of the grand stand crosses of Ireland were executed in Italy. As, however, not a single Italian MS. older than the ninth century, nor a single piece of Italian stone sculpture having the slightest resemblance to those of this country, can be produced, we at once deny the assertion. An examination of the magnificent work upon the Catacombs of Rome, lately published by the French Government, in which all the inscriptions and mural drawings executed by the early Christians are elaborately represented, will fully prove that the early Christian art and ornamentation of Rome had no share in developing that of these islands. It is true that the grand tessellated pages of the MSS. above described bear a certain general resemblance to the tessellated pavement of the Romans, and had they been found only in Anglo-Saxon MSS. we might have conjectured that such pavements existing in various parts of England, and which in the seventh and eighth centuries must still have remained uncovered, were the originals from which the illuminator of the MSS. had taken his idea; but it is in the Irish MSS., and in the MSS. which are clearly traceable to Irish influence, that we find these pages most elaborately ornamented, and we need hardly say that there are no Roman tessellated pavements in Ireland, the Romans never having visited that island.

It may, again, be said that the interlaced ribbon patterns, so common in the MSS., &c., were derived from the Roman tessellated and mosaic work; but in the latter the interlacing was of the simplest and most inartificial character, bearing no resemblance to such elaborate, interlaced knotwork as is to be seen, for instance, in Plate LXIII. *(pages 306–07)*. In fact, in the Roman remains the ribbons are simply alternately laid over each other, whilst in the Celtic designs they are *knotted*.

Another class of writers insist upon the Scandinavian origin of these ornaments, which we are still perpetually accustomed to hear called Runic knots, and connected with Scandinavian superstitions. It is certainly true that in the Isle of Man, as well as at Lancaster and Bewcastle, we find Runic inscriptions upon crosses, ornamented with many of the peculiar ornaments above described. As, however, the Scandinavian nations were Christianised by missionaries from these islands, and as *our* crosses are quite unlike those still existing in Denmark and Norway; as, moreover, they are several centuries more recent than the oldest and finest of our MSS., there can be no grounds for asserting that the ornaments of the MSS. are Scandinavian. A comparison of our plates with those contained in the very excellent series of illustrations of the ancient Scandinavian relics in the Copenhagen Museum, lately published,** is sufficient to disprove such an assertion. Only one figure (No. 398) in the whole of the 460 representations given in that work exhibits the patterns of our MSS., and we have no hesitation in asserting it to be a reliquary of Irish work. That the Scandinavian artists adopted Celtic ornamentation, especially such as was practised about the end of the tenth or eleventh centuries, is evident from the similarity between their carved wooden churches (illustrated in detail by M. Dahl) and Irish metal-work of the same period, such as the Cross of Cong in the Museum of the Royal Irish Academy in Dublin.

** In the division of this Danish work devoted to the Bronze age we find various examples of spiral ornaments on metal-work, but always arranged in the ∞ manner, and with but very few inartificial combinations. In the second division of the Iron period we also find various examples of fantastical intertwined animals, also represented on metal-work. Nowhere, however, do the interlaced ribbon patterns, or the diagonal Z-like patterns, or the trumpet-like spiral patterns, occur.

Not only the Scandinavian, but also the earlier and more polished artists of the school of Charlemagne and his successors, together with those of Lombardy, adopted many of the peculiar Celtic ornaments in their magnificently illuminated MSS. They, however, interspersed with them classical ornaments, introducing the acanthus and foliage, giving a gracefulness to their pages which we look for in vain in the elaborate, but often absolutely painfully intricate, work of our artists. Our Fig. 16, in Plate LXIV. *(pages 308–09)*, is copied from the Golden Gospels in the British Museum, a magnificent production of Frankish art of the ninth century, in which we perceive such a combination of ornament. The Anglo-Saxon and Irish patterns were, however, so closely copied (always, however, of a much larger size) in some of the grand Frankish MSS. that the term Franco-Saxon has been applied to them. Such is the case with the Bible of St. Denis in the Bibliothèque Nationale, Paris, of which forty pages are preserved in the Library of the British Museum. Plate LXIV., Fig. 13, is copied from this MS. of the real size.

It remains to inquire, whether Byzantium and the East may not have afforded the ideas which the early Celtic Christian artists developed in the retirement of their monasteries into the elaborate patterns which we have been examining. The fact that this style of ornament was fully developed before the end of the seventh century, taken into connexion with that of Byzantium having been the seat of Art from the middle of the fourth century, will suggest the possibility that the British or Irish missionaries (who were constantly travelling to the Holy Land and Egypt) might have there obtained the ideas or principles of some of these ornaments. To prove this assertion will, indeed, be difficult, because so little is known of real Byzantine Art previous to the seventh or eighth century. Certain, however, it is that the ornamentation of St. Sophia, so elaborately illustrated by H. Salzenberg, exhibits no analogy with our Celtic patterns; a much greater resemblance exists, however, between the latter and the early monuments of Mount Athos, representations of some of which are given by M. Didron, in his *Iconographie de Dieu*. In our Egyptian Plate X. *(pages 70–71)*, Figs. 10, 13–16, 18–23, and Plate XI. *(pages 72–73)*, Figs. 1, 4, 6, and 7, will be perceived patterns formed of spiral lines or ropes, which may have suggested the spiral pattern of our Celtic ornaments; but it will be perceived that in the majority of these Egyptian examples the spiral line is arranged like an S. In Plate X., Fig. 11, however, it is arranged C-wise, and thus to a greater degree agrees with our patterns, although wide enough in detail for them. The elaborate interlacements, so common in Moresque ornamentation, agree to a certain extent with the ornaments of Sclavonic, Ethiopic, and Syriac MSS., numerous examples of which are given by Silvestre, and in our *Palœographia Sacra Pictoria*; and as all of these, probably, had their origin in Byzantium or Mount Athos, we might be led to infer a similar origin in the idea,—worked out, however, in a different manner by the Irish and Anglo-Saxon artists.

We have thus endeavoured to prove that, even supposing the early artists of these islands might have obtained the germ of their peculiar styles of ornament from some other source than their own national genius, they had, between the period of the introduction of Christianity and the beginning of the eighth century, formed several very distinct systems of ornamentation, perfectly unlike in their developed state to those of any other country; and this, too, at a period when the whole of Europe, owing to the breaking up of the great Roman empire, was involved in almost complete darkness as regards artistic productions.

4. LATER ANGLO-SAXON ORNAMENT. — About the middle of the tenth century another and equally striking style of ornament was employed by some of the Anglo-Saxon artists, for the decoration of their finest MSS., and equally unlike that of any other country. It consisted of a frame-like design, composed of gold bars entirely surrounding the page, the miniatures or titles being introduced into the open space in the centre. These frames were ornamented with foliage and buds; but, true to the interlaced ideas, the leaves and stems were interwoven together, as well as with the gold bars—the angles being, moreover, decorated with elegant circles, squares, lozenges, or quatrefoils. It would appear that it was in the South of England that this style of ornament was most fully elaborated, the grandest examples having been executed at Winchester, in the Monastery of St. Æthelwold, in the latter half of the tenth century. Of these the Benedictional belonging to the Duke of Devonshire, fully illustrated in the *Archœologia*, is the most magnificent; two others, however, now in the public library of Rouen, are close rivals of it; as is also a copy of the Gospels in the library of Trinity College, Cambridge. The Gospels of King Canute in the British Museum is another example, which has afforded us the Figure 10 in Plate LXV. *(pages 310–11).*

There can be little doubt that the grand MSS. of the Frankish schools of Charlemagne, in which foliage was introduced, were the originals whence our later Anglo-Saxon artists adopted the idea of the introduction of foliage among their ornaments.

J. O. WESTWOOD.

BIBLIOGRAPHICAL REFERENCES

LEDWICK. *Antiquities of Ireland.* 4to.

O'CONOR. *Biblioth. Stowensis.* 2 vols. 4to. 1818. Also, *Rerum Hibernicarum Scriptores veteres.* 4 vols. 4to.

PETRIE. *Essay on the Round Towers of Ireland.* Large 8vo.

BETHAM. *Irish Antiquarian Researches.* 2 vols. 8vo.

O'NEILL. *Illustrations of the Crosses of Ireland.* Folio, in Parts.

KELLER, DR. FERDINAND. *Bilder und Schriftzüge in den Irischen Manuscripten;* in the *Mittheilungen der Antiq. Gesellsch. in Zürich.* Bd. 7, 1851.

WESTWOOD, J.O. *Palœographia Sacra Pictoria.* 4to. 1843–1845.

—— In *Journal of the Archœological Institute,* vols. vii. and x. Also numerous articles in the *Archœologia Cambrensis.*

CUMMING. *Illustrations of the Crosses of the Isle of Man.* 4to.

CHALMERS. *Stone Monuments of Angusshire.* Imp. fol.

SPALDING CLUB. *Sculptured Stones of Scotland.* Fol. 1856.

GAGE, J. *Dissertation on St. Æthelwold's Benedictional, in Archœologia,* vol. xxiv.

ELLIS, SIR H. *Account of Cœdmon's Paraphrase of Scripture History,* in *Archœologia,* vol. xxiv.

GOODWIN, JAMES, B.D. *Evangelia Augustini Gregoriana,* in *Trans. Cambridge Antiq. Soc.* No. 13, 4to. 1847, with eleven plates.

BASTARD, LE COMTE DE. *Ornements et Miniatures des Manuscrits Français.* Imp. fol. Paris.

WORSAAE, J. J. A. *Afbildninger fra det Kong. Museum i Kjöbenhavn.* 8vo. 1854.

And the general works of WILLEMIN, STRUTT, DU SOMMERARD, LANGLOIS, SHAW, SILVESTRE and CHAMPOLLION, ASTLE *(on Writing),* HUMPHREYS, LA CROIX, and LYSONS *(Magna Britannia).*

🦌 These are Pictish
carvings from eastern
Scotland. The Picts
were a Celtic people
who settled in Scotland
during the Iron Age.
Their decorated crosses
date mainly from the
eighth century, although
the purpose of these
was not solely religious.
The Aberlemno Cross
(No. 1), for example,
may have been erected
to celebrate the battle
of Nechtansmere
(685), where the Picts
defeated the Angles
(there is a battle scene
on the reverse of the
stone). The strange
patterns, mentioned by
Jones in his Note *(far
right),* have continued to
puzzle historians. The
popular view, however,
is that these symbol
stones were meant as
territorial markers or
family monuments.

PLATE LXIII

LAPIDARY
ORNAMENTATION
1 The Aberlemno Cross,
formed of a single Slab, 7 ft.
high.— CHALMERS, *Stone
Monuments of Angus.*
2 Central portion of Stone
Cross in the Cemetery in the
Island of Inchbrayoe,
Scotland.

1

PLATE LXIII

3 Ornament on the Cross in the Churchyard of Meigle, Angusshire.—CHALMERS.
4 Ornament of Base of Cross near the old Church of Eassie, Angusshire.—CHALMERS.
5 Circular Ornament on the base of Stone Cross in the Churchyard of St. Vigean's, Angusshire.—CHALMERS.

NOTE.—In addition to the various ornaments observed on the stones here figured, a peculiar ornament occurs only in many of the Scotch crosses, which has been called the Spectacle Pattern, consisting of two circles, connected by two curved lines, which latter are crossed by the oblique stroke of a decorated Z. Its origin and meaning have long puzzled antiquaries: the only other instance which we have ever met with of the occurrence of this ornament is upon a Gnostic Gem engraved in WALSH's *Essay on Christian Coins.*

On some of the Manx and Cumberland crosses—as well as on that at Penmon, Anglesea—a pattern occurs analogous to classical ones. It was probably borrowed from the Roman tessellated pavements, on which it is occasionally found: it never occurs in MSS. or Metal-work.

The study of Celtic art was in its infancy in Jones's day. The two key sites were still in the process of being explored. These were the prehistoric cemetery at Hallstatt in Austria, excavated by Johann Ramsauer between 1846 and 1863, and an important ritual site at La Tène in Switzerland, where the earliest finds were made in 1857.

PLATE LXIV

INTERLACED STYLE
1–7, 12, 14, 19–21, 23, 26, 27, 29, 33, 35, 38, 42, 45, are Borders of Interlaced Ribbon Patterns, copied from Anglo-Saxon and Irish MSS. in the British Museum, the Bodleian Library, Oxford, and the Libraries of St. Gall and Trinity College, Dublin.

8 Angulated Ornament from the Bible of St. Denis. 9th century.

9 Pattern of Angulated Lines, from the Gospels of Lindisfarne. End 7th century.

10 Interlaced Triquetral Pattern, from the Coronation Gospels of the Anglo-Saxon Kings.

11 Circular Ornament of four conjoined Triquetræ, from the Sacramentarium of Rheims.

13 Part of Gigantic Initial Letter, from the Franco-Saxon Bible of St. Denis. 9th century.—SILVESTRE.

PLATE LXIV

15, 34 Initial Letters from the Gospels of Lindisfarne. End of 7th century.
16 Terminal Ornament from the Golden Gospels.—HUMPHRIES.
17 Interlaced Panel, from the Psalter of St. Augustine in the British Museum. 6th or 7th century.
18 Terminal Ornament of Initial Letter, from copy of the Gospels in the Paris Library, No. 693.—SILVESTRE.
22 Interlaced Ornament, from Irish MS. at St. Gall.—KEILER.
24, 25 Interlaced Ribbon Patterns, from the Golden Gospels in the Harleian Library in the British Museum.—HUMPHRIES.
30 Terminal Ornament from the Sacramentarium of Rheims.—SILVESTRE.
31 Quatrefoil Interlaced Ornament, from the Rheims Sacramentarium.—SILVESTRE.
32 Ornament from the Sacramentarium of Rheims. 9th or 10th century.—SILVESTRE.
36 Terminal Interlaced Ornament, from the Tironian Psalter in the Paris Library.—SILVESTRE.
37 Angularly Interlaced Ornament, from the Golden Gospels.
39 Terminal Ornament of Initial Letter, from the Coronation Gospel.
40, 44 Interlaced Ornaments from the Gospels of Lindisfarne.
41, 43 Quadrangular Interlaced Ornaments, Missal of Leofric, Bodleian.

🐾 Several images in this chapter would no longer be classified as Celtic (for instance, Nos. 10 and 22), but these pages do contain details from two leading examples of the style, the Book of Kells and the Lindisfarne Gospels. The Book of Kells—the most famous of all Celtic manuscripts—was produced in *ca.* 800, although in Jones's day it was believed to be much older. There was a tradition that the text had been copied out by St. Columba (*ca.* 521–97). The low regard for Celtic material can be gauged by the fact that, in 1814, the Kells manuscript was temporarily mislaid by the library that owned it.

PLATE LXV

SPIRAL, DIAGONAL, ZOOMORPHIC, AND LATER ANGLO-SAXON ORNAMENTS
1 Interlaced Animals, from the Book of Kells, in the Library of Trinity College, Dublin.
2 Ornament of angulated Lines, from the Gregorian Gospels. British Museum.
3, 9 Panels of Interlaced Beasts and Birds, from Irish Gospels at St. Gall. 8th or 9th century.

PLATE LXV

4 One Quarter of Frame, or Border, of an Illuminated Page of the Benedictional of Æthelgar at Rouen. 10th century.—SILVESTRE.

5 Interlaced Ornament, from Irish MSS. at St. Gall.

6 Initial Q, formed of an elongated Angulated Animal, from Psalter of Ricemarchus, Trinity College, Dublin. End of 11th century.

7, 14 Spiral Patterns, from the Gospels of Lindisfarne.

8 Diagonal Pattern. Gospels of Mac Durnan, in the Library of Lambeth Palace. 9th century.

10 One Quarter of Frame, or Border, from the Gospels of Canute, in British Museum. End of 10th century.

11 Terminal Ornament of Spiral Pattern, with Birds. Part of large Initial Letter in the Gospels of Lindisfarne.—HUMPHRIES.

12 Diagonal Patterns, Irish MSS. at St. Gall. 9th century.

13, 15, 21 Diagonal Patterns. Gospels of Mac Durnan.

16 Terminal Border of Interlaced Animals, from Gospels of Lindisfarne.

17 One Quarter of Frame, or Border, from the Arundel Psalter, No. 155, British Museum.—HUMPHRIES.

18 Initial Letter, from the Gospels of Lindisfarne. End of 7th century. British Museum.

19 Interlaced Animals. Gospels of Mac Durnan.

20 Diagonal Patterns, from Gospels of Lindisfarne.

22 One Quarter of Frame, or Border, from the Benedictional of Æthelgar.

CHAPTER XVI

MEDIÆVAL ORNAMENT

The transition from the round arch, characteristic of the Romanesque style to the Pointed style of the thirteenth century, is readily traced in the buildings in which the two styles are intermingled; but the passage from Romanesque Ornament to that which prevailed so universally in the thirteenth century is not so clear. All traces of the acanthus leaf have disappeared, and we find a purely conventional style of ornament universally prevalent in all the buildings of the time. The nearest approach to this style is found in the illuminated MSS. of the twelfth century, which appear to have been derived in some of their features from the Greek MSS. The ornaments are formed of a continuous stem, throwing off leaves on the outer side, and terminating in a flower. The general disposition and arrangement of the lines in any given space is exactly similar to the arrangement of Early English sculptured ornament.

Early English Ornament is the most perfect, both in principle and in execution, of the Gothic period. There is as much elegance and refinement

EARLY ENGLISH. WELLS.—COLLINS

in modulations of form as there is in the ornament of the Greeks. It is always in perfect harmony with the structural features, and always grows naturally from them. It fulfils every one of the conditions which we desire to find in a perfect style of Art. But it remained perfect only so long as the style remained conventional. As this style became less idealised and more direct in imitation, its peculiar beauties disappeared, and it ceased to be an ornamentation of structural features, but became ornament applied.

In the capitals of the columns in the Early English architecture the ornament arises directly from the shaft, which above the necking splits up into a series of stems, each stem terminating in a flower. This is analogous to the mode of decorating the Egyptian capital. In the Decorated style, on the contrary, where a much nearer approach to Nature was attempted, it was no longer possible to treat a natural leaf as part of the shaft; and, therefore, the shaft is terminated by a bell-shape, round which the leaves are twined. The more and more natural these were made, the less artistic became the arrangement.

The same thing occurs in the bosses which cover the intersections of the ribs. On the vaulting in the Early English bosses the stems of the flowers forming the bosses are continuations of the mouldings of the ribs, whilst in subsequent periods the intersections of the ribs were concealed by the

WARMINGTON CHURCH,
NORTHAMPTONSHIRE.—W. TWOPENY

WARMINGTON CHURCH,
NORTHAMPTONSHIRE.—W. TWOPENY

DECORATED. WELLS.—COLLINS

overlaying of the boss, which was here as much an application as was the acanthus leaf to the bell of the Corinthian capital.

In the spandrils of the arches, so long as the conventional style was retained, one vigorous main stem was distributed over the spandril, from which sprang the leaves and flowers; but when the natural was attempted, the stem ceased to be the guiding form of the ornament, and lost all grace in the endeavour to represent in stone the softness of nature. The main stem as a leading feature gradually disappears, and the spandrils are often filled with three immense leaves springing from a twisted stem in the centre.

From the few remains which still exist of the decorations of the interior of buildings, we are unable to form a very complete idea of this class of ornament of the thirteenth century. The ornaments from illuminated MSS. are not a safe guide, as, after the twelfth century, the style is rarely very architectural, and there were so many schools of illumination, and they borrowed so much one from the other, that there is often great mixture in the same illumination. It is unlikely, that while the sculptured ornament was so universally conventional, that the decorated portion of the same building could have departed from the style.

On Plates LXVII. and LXVII*. *(pages 327–29)* we give a selection of borders found on illuminated MSS., ranging from the ninth to the fourteenth century; and on Plate LXVIII. *(pages 330–31)* diapers from walls, chiefly taken from the back-grounds of illuminations, from the twelfth to the sixteenth. There are very few of either class that could be worthy accompaniments to the pure conventional ornament of the Early English style.

STONE CHURCH, KENT.—
PUBLISHED BY THE TOPOGRAPHICAL SOCIETY

In the thirteenth century, beyond all others, architecture was in its zenith. The mosques of Cairo, the Alhambra, Salisbury, Lincoln, Westminster, all possess the same secret of producing the broadest general effects combined with the most elaborate decoration. In all these buildings there is a family likeness; although the forms widely differ, the principles on which they are based are the same. They exhibit the same care for the leading masses of the composition, the same appreciation of the undulations of form, the same correct observation of natural principles in the ornamentation, the same elegance and refinement in all the decoration.

The attempt to reproduce in our time a building of the thirteenth century must be vain indeed. Whitewashed walls, with stained glass and encaustic tiles, cannot alone sustain the effect which was arrived at when every moulding had its colour best adapted to develope its form, and when, from the floor to the roof, not an inch of space but had its appropriate ornament;

an effect which must have been glorious beyond conception. So glorious a point, indeed, had the style reached that it was exhausted by the effort,— the light burnt out; not only architecture, but all the decorative arts which accompanied it, immediately began to decline,—a decline which never stops till the style dies out.

In the examples of encaustic tiles on Plate LXX. *(page 336)* it will be seen that the broadest in effect, and the best adapted to their purpose, are the earliest, such as Nos. 17, 23. Although there was never so much decline as to attempt an appearance of relief, yet a near approach to a representation of the natural forms of leaves may be seen in No. 16; and a very marked decline is observed in patterns such as No. 28, where tracery and the structural features of buildings were represented.

On Plate LXVI. *(page 326)* are arranged a great variety of conventional leaves and flowers from illuminated MSS. Although many of them are in the originals highly illuminated, we have printed them here in two colours only, to show how possible it is to represent in diagram the general character of leaves. By adapting these leaves or flowers to a volute stem, almost as many styles in appearance could be produced as there are separate ornaments on the page. By a combination of different varieties they might be still further increased, and by adding to the stock by conventionalising the form of any natural leaf or flower on the same principle, there need be no limit to an artist's invention.

In Plates LXXI., LXXII., LXXIII. *(pages 337–41)*, we have endeavoured to gather together types of the various styles of ornamental illumination from the twelfth to the end of the fifteenth century. There is here, also, evidence of decline from the very earliest point. On Plate LXXI. *(page 337)* the letter N is not surpassed by any example in the subsequent styles we have reproduced. Here the true purpose of illumination is fulfilled; in every way, it is pure decorative writing. The letter itself forms the chief ornament; from this springs a main stem, sweeping boldly from the base, swelling out into a grand volute exactly at the point best adapted to contrast with the angular line of the letter: this is beautifully sustained again by the green volute, which embraces the upper part of the N, and prevents it falling over, and is so nicely proportioned that it is able to sustain the red volute which flows from it. The colours also are most beautifully balanced and contrasted; and the way in which the rotundity of the stems is expressed, without attempting positive relief, is a fruitful lesson. There are an immense number of MSS. in this style, and we consider it the finest kind of illumination. The general character of the style is certainly Eastern, and was probably a development of the illumination of the Byzantines. We believe that, from its universal prevalence, it led to the adoption of the same principle so universally in the ornamentation of the Early English, which follows exactly the same laws in the general distribution of form.

This style, from constant repetition, gradually lost the peculiar beauty and fitness which it had derived from first inspiration, and died out by the scroll-work becoming too minute and elaborate, as we see in No. 13 of the same plate. We have no longer the same balance of form, but the four series of scrolls repeating each other most monotonously.

From this period we no longer find the initial letters forming the chief ornament on the page, but the general text becomes enclosed either in borders round the page, as at No. 1, Plate LXXII. *(pages 338–39)*, or with tails on one side of the page, such as 3–6. The border gradually comes to

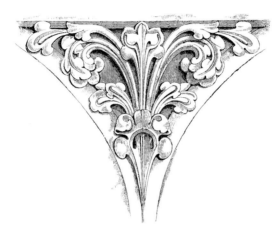

WELLS CATHEDRAL.—COLLINS

be of more importance, and from the vignette form, which was at first general, we gradually arrive through the manner of No. 15 to that of Nos. 7 and 2, where the border is bounded on the outer edge by a red line, and the border is filled up by intermediate stems and flowers, so as to produce an even tint. No. 14 is a specimen of a style very prevalent in the fourteenth century, and which is very architectural in character. It is generally to be found on small missals, and surrounding very beautiful miniatures.

The gradual progress from the flat conventional ornament, Nos. 11 and 12, to the attempt at rendering the relief of natural forms in Nos. 15, 7, 2, will readily be traced through Nos. 3, 4, 5. There is also to be remarked a gradual decline in the idea of continuity of the main stems, and although each flower or group of leaves in Nos. 15, 7, 2, may still be traced to their roots, the arrangement is fragmentary.

Up to this period the ornaments are still within the province of the scribe, and are all first outlined with a black line and then coloured, but on Plate LXXIII. *(pages 340–41)* we shall find that the painter began to usurp the office of the scribe; and the farther we proceed the more does the legitimate object of illumination seem to be departed from.

We have the first stage in No. 2, where a geometrical arrangement is obtained with conventional ornament enclosing gold panels, on which are painted groups of flowers slightly conventionalised. In 1, 3–5, 7, 12, we find conventional ornament intermingled with natural flowers arranged in a fragmentary way. All continuity of design being abandoned, we arrive through this to No. 10, when a natural flower and a conventional ornament appear on the same stem, to Nos. 11, 14, where the painter has full sway, and represents flowers and insects casting their shadow on the page. When the art of illumination has arrived at this stage it could go no farther,— all ideality had fled—and it ends in the desire to copy an insect so faithfully that it should appear to be alighting on the page.

Nos. 9, 13, are specimens of a peculiar style of Italian MSS., which was a revival in the fifteenth century of the system of ornament so prevalent in the twelfth. It led to the style No. 8, where the interlaced pattern became highly coloured on the gold ground. This style also died out in the same way, the interlacings, from being purely geometrical forms, became imitations of natural branches, and, of course, when it arrived thus far there could be no further progress.

The character of the ornament on stained glass appears to follow much more closely that of the illuminated MSS. than it does the sculptured ornament of the monuments of the same period, and, like the ornament of the illuminated MSS., it appears to us to be always in advance of structural ornament. For instance,—the stained glass of the twelfth century possesses the same breadth of effect, and is constructed in the same way, as the sculptured ornament of the thirteenth, whilst the stained glass of the thirteenth century is, according to our view, already in a state of decline. The same change has taken place which we have already observed on comparing No. 13 with No. 12, Plate LXXI. *(page 337).*

The constant repetition of the same forms has gradually led to an over-elaboration of detail, from which the general effect considerably suffers. The ornaments are out of scale with the general masses. Now as it is one of the most beautiful features of the Early English style, that the ornament is in such perfect relation in point of scale and effect to the members which it decorates, this seems a very curious fact, if fact it is. On Plates LXIX. and LXIX*. *(pages 332–35)* Nos. 4, 11, 14–22, 24–29 are of the twelfth century. Nos. 1 and 3 are of the thirteenth. Nos. 2, 5–10, 12, 13, are of the fourteenth, and we think a mere glance at the general effect of the plates will establish what we have here advanced.

In the stained glass of the twelfth century we shall always find all the principles which we have shown to belong to a true style of art. We need only call attention here to the very ingenious way in which the straight, the inclined, and the curved, are balanced and contrasted in all the diapers.

In Nos. 2 and 9 we have an example of a very common principle, which is thoroughly Eastern in character, viz. a continuous ground pattern forms a tint interlacing with a more general surface pattern.

In Nos. 5, 10, 12, 13, of the fourteenth century we see the commencement of the direct natural style, which ended in the total neglect of the true principles of stained glass, when both ornaments and figures through which life was to be transmitted, in the attempt to render them over-true, had their own shades and shadows.

🎋 *The Grammar of Ornament* remained an inspiration to architects long after Jones's death. The American architect Frank Lloyd Wright (1869–1959) was particularly proud of the copies that he made of it as a youth, when he spent many fruitful hours tracing the designs onto onionskin paper. In 1887, when he applied for the post of draftsman in the office of Louis Sullivan (1856–1924), he took some of his copies with him: "I took the onionskin tracing of ornamental details I had made from Owen Jones, mostly Gothic, and made them over into 'Sullivanesque.'" He also mulled over the theories outlined in Jones's "General Principles," using them to develop his own architectural language. "I read the propositions," he declared, "and felt the first five were dead right."

PLATE LXVI

CONVENTIONAL LEAVES AND FLOWERS, from MSS. of different periods.

1

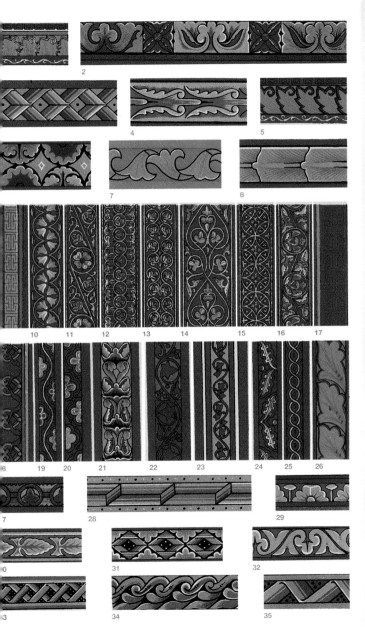

PLATE LXVII

1–35 COLLECTION OF
BORDERS, from Illuminated
MSS., from the 9th to the
14th century.

327

In architecture the rediscovery of the Middle Ages was epitomized by the Gothic revival. Here, the dominant figure was A. W. N. Pugin (1812–52), who drew his inspiration from medieval patterns. In his brief life he managed to revitalize the style, introducing Gothic motifs into virtually every area of design, from architecture and wallpaper to textiles and jewelry. The mainspring of his approach came from his conversion to Catholicism in 1835. This led Pugin to denounce all forms of classicism as essentially pagan, while arguing for the supremacy of the Gothic forms that had inspired the great cathedral builders of the Middle Ages. Not surprisingly, Pugin was heavily involved in church architecture, although he is most famous for his work on the Palace of Westminster.

36
37
38
39
40
41
42
43
44
45
46
47
48
49

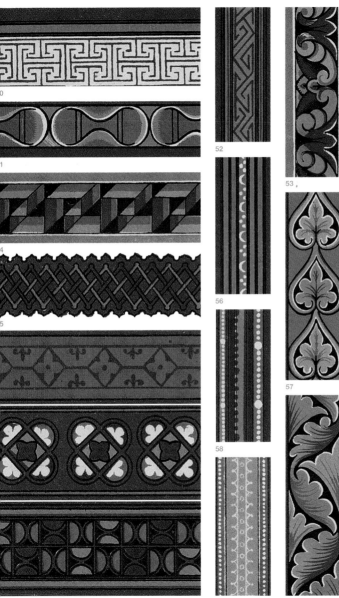

PLATE LXVII*

36–63 COLLECTION OF
BORDERS, from Illuminated
MSS., from the 9th to the
14th century.

52

53 .

56

57

58

62

63

329

In ornamental terms a diaper is a simple pattern, made up of repeated geometrical shapes (usually diamonds). It can appear on textiles, wallpapers, and paving designs, but during the nineteenth century it was most widely used as an ornamental detail in architectural designs. Its chief exponent was William Butterfield (1814–1900), a leading light of the Gothic revival. He created diaper patterns on the walls of many of his buildings by employing bricks with contrasting colors. His favorite combination was dark red and white. Typical examples include All Saints' in London's Margaret Street (1849–59) and Keble College, Oxford (1867–83).

PLATE LXVIII

1–50 DIAPERS ON WALLS, from Miniatures in Illuminated MSS., from the 12th to the 16th century.

MEDIÆVAL

There was a huge upsurge in church building during the Victorian era, which in turn sparked off a renewed interest in all aspects of church furnishings. The momentum came from the Oxford Movement, founded in the 1830s, which heralded a revival of High-Church Anglicanism. The latter proved extremely controversial in religious circles, particularly after 1845, when one of the key members of the movement, John (later Cardinal) Newman (1801–90), converted to Catholicism. During this period the building of new churches was rigorously scrutinized by the Camden Society (founded in 1839) and *The Ecclesiologist* (a Christian journal, 1841–68), both of which advocated the neo-Gothic style.

1

2

3

4

5

6

PLATE LXIX

STAINED GLASS OF
DIFFERENT PERIODS
AND STYLES
1 Southwell Church,
Nottinghamshire.
2, 9 Chapter-house, York
Cathedral.
3 North Transept, York
Cathedral.
4 Cathedral at Troyes.
5, 10, 12, 13 Church at
Attenberg, near Cologne.
6, 8 Cathedral of Soissons.
7 St. Thomas at Strasburg.
11 Canterbury Cathedral.

9

0

11

2

13

333

The increase in church building *(see page 332)* was accompanied by the emergence of a new group of stained-glass firms, which sought to recapture the magnificence of medieval windows. Initially, the most successful outfit was the partnership of J. R. Clayton and Alfred Bell. They began their careers working for the architect Sir George Gilbert Scott (1811–78), before setting up their own studio in London's Regent Street. Eventually, their reputation was overtaken by that of William Morris (1834–96) and his Pre-Raphaelite colleagues, who won many commissions for stained-glass windows in the medieval style. The finest of these designs were produced by Sir Edward Burne-Jones (1833–98).

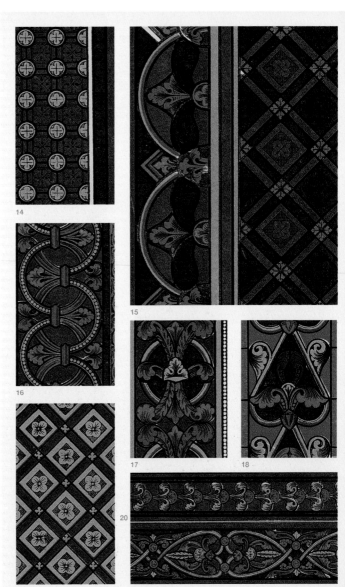

14

15

16

17

18

19

20

21

22

23

24

25

26

27

28

29

PLATE LXIX*

STAINED GLASS OF
DIFFERENT PERIODS
AND STYLES
**14, 15, 19, 20, 23–25,
27–29** Cathedral of
Bourges.
16, 26 St. Cunibert,
Cologne.
17 Canterbury Cathedral.
18, 21 Abbey of St. Denis
22 Cathedral of Angers.

MEDIÆVAL

Deriving from a Greek word for "burnt in," encaustic tiles were notable for their inlaid, colored patterns, which were fixed during the firing process. The technique was revived by A. W. N. Pugin, working in association with the potter Herbert Minton. They met in 1840 and, two years later, the Minton firm produced its influential catalogue of *Early English Tile Patterns*. Initially these medieval-style tiles were used for restoration projects, but they gained a fresh lease on life after Pugin and Minton won the commission to provide a new range of tiles for the Palace of Westminster. Minton & Company were subsequently hired to carry out similar work for the Australian Senate House in Melbourne and the Capitol in Washington, DC.

PLATE LXX

1–36 ENCAUSTIC TILES
13th and 14th centuries.

2

3

PLATE LXXI

ILLUMINATED MSS., No. 1
1–12 are of the 12th
century;
13 is of the 13th century.
12, 13 are from the
*Illuminated Books of the
Middle Ages.*—HUMPHREYS.
The remainder of the
Ornaments on this Plate
from the British Museum.

5

6

7

8

9

10

12

13

❧ In the 1840s advances in the field of chromolithography had a significant impact on the publishing world. For the first time printing in color became a sound, commercial proposition. Jones himself set up in business as a color printer, swiftly gaining a name for lavishly illustrated gift books. Some of these—the *Home Illuminated Diary and Calendar* (1845), for example—made use of images from medieval manuscripts. More ambitiously, he also worked with Henry Noel Humphreys on *The Illuminated Books of the Middle Ages.* This sumptuous study of medieval ornament was initially issued in separate parts (1844–49), before appearing as a complete book in 1849.

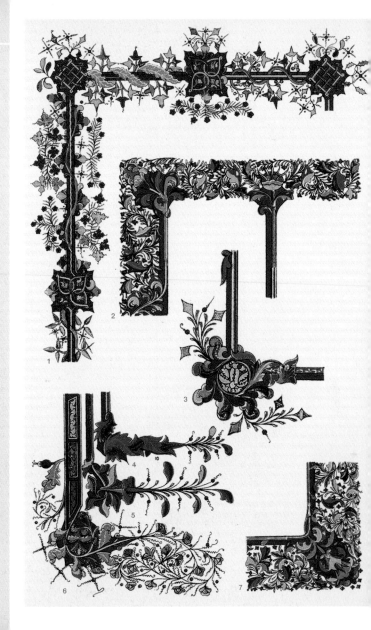

PLATE LXXII

ILLUMINATED MSS., No. 2
11, 12, of the 13th century.
1, 3, 4, 5, 8–10, 13, 14, of
the 14th century.
2, 6, 7, 15, of the 15th
century.
1, 2, 7, 9, 14, 15, are from
the *Illuminated Books of the
Middle Ages.*
15, from a MS. in the
possession of the Author.
The remainder from the
British Museum.

By a happy accident, the advent of chromolithography *(see page 338)* coincided with a heightened awareness of the importance of early manuscripts. Scholars had started to examine their illustrations more carefully, placing them in a proper, art historical context. These studies were greatly assisted by the superb colored reproductions that were now made available in print for the first time. The earliest examples were issued in France, notably Champollion's monumental *Paléographie Universelle* (1841), while in England the pioneering works were J. O. Westwood's *Palaeographia Sacra Pictoria* (1843–45) and *The Illuminated Books of the Middle Ages* (1849), which Humphreys produced in conjunction with Jones.

1

2

3

4

5

6

7

PLATE LXXIII

ILLUMINATED MSS., No. 3
MSS. from the Beginning to
the End of the 15th century.
6, 7, 10, 11, 14, from the
*Illuminated Books of the
Middle Ages.*
The remainder from the
British Museum.

8

9

10

11

12

13

14

15

CHAPTER XVII

RENAISSANCE ORNAMENT

f two intelligent students of Italian Art and Literature diligently set themselves to trace, the one the latest date at which the direct, though lingering, light of Roman greatness waned to its feeblest glimmer in the land over which it had once shed its dazzling rays, and the other the earliest effort made to excite a veneration for what most historians declare to have almost utterly died out in the lapse of ages—classical beauty—there is little doubt that they would not only meet, but cross one another, in the progress of their researches. The truth is, that the material monuments of the ancient Romans, scattered thickly over the soil of Italy, were so substantial and majestic, that it was impossible to live under their shadow and to forget them. Fragments of exquisite beauty, in stone, bronze, and marble, were to be had for the trouble of turning up the soil that scarcely covered them; and thus they were, from time to time, pressed into service for tombs, and as accessories in buildings, in the construction of which the principles of Art to which those fragments owed their beauty had been entirely lost sight of. Hence, the Gothic style was at once slow to take root in Italy, and destined to bloom brilliantly, but for a short season. Almost concurrently with the introduction of the pointed arch into Northern Italy by an Englishman, in the construction of St. Andrea, at Vercelli, early in the thirteenth century, and with the German works of Magister Jacobus, at Assisi, a protest was commenced in favour of the ancients and their arts by that great reviver of antique sculpture, Nicola Pisano. The close of the thirteenth century was further marked by a complete revolution in the world of letters. Dante, in his time, was scarcely less known as a Christian poet than as an emulator of the great Mantuan, and a profound student in classical learning. In the fourteenth century, Petrarch and Boccaccio, intimate friends, spent long and laborious lives, not in writing Italian poetry or prose, as is often fancied, but in labouring incessantly in the preservation and restoration to the world of the long-lost texts of the Roman and Grecian authors. Cino da Pistoia and other learned commentators and jurists brought into fashion the study of the great "Corpus" of ancient law, and maintained academies in which it was adopted as a text. Boccaccio it was who first gave to Italy a lucid account of Heathen Mythology, and who first instituted a chair for the study of the Grecian language at Florence, bringing over Leontius Pilatus, a learned Greek, from Constantinople, to be the first professor. These efforts at a revival of classical learning were seconded by a numerous band of notables, among whom the names of John of Ravenna (Petrarch's pupil), Lionardo Aretino, Poggio Bracciolini, Æneas Sylvius (ultimately Pope Pius II., 1458–1464), and Cosmo, the father of the Medici, are most popularly and familiarly known. It was at a moment when the labours of such men as these had accumulated in public and private libraries all that could be recovered of classical learning, that about the middle of the fifteenth century the art of printing was introduced into Italy. Under the auspices of the Benedictines of Subiaco, the Germans Sweynheim and Pannartz set up their press in the celebrated Monastery of Santa Scholastica, from which issued, in the year 1465, their edition of Lactantius. Removing to Rome in 1467, the first-fruits of their labour was "Cicero de Oratore." Thus, while in Germany and France biblical and ecclesiastical literature, and in England popular, first gave employment to the printer; in Italy, classical, for a time, almost exclusively engaged his attention. Nicholas Jenson, the Frenchman, who was sent by Louis XI. to the *ateliers* of Fust and Scheffer, to learn "le nouvel art par lequel on faisait des livres," carried his acquired knowledge from Mayence to Venice, where he invented the Italic character, subsequently adopted by the learned Aldus Manutius. This remarkable man, who was a no less learned editor than he was a zealous printer, from about the year 1490 gave to the world in rapid succession editions of the Greek and Latin Classics. Among his earliest works is one ever memorable in the history of Art, the "Hypnerotomachia," or dream of Poliphilus, written by the learned ecclesiastic Fra Colonna. It is profusely illustrated with engravings on wood, the design of which has been frequently ascribed to no less great an artist than Andrea Mantegna. Through those illustrations, which display a profound study of ancient ornament, types of form diametrically opposed to those of the middle ages were disseminated over the Continent of Europe. The publication of Vitruvius at Rome, about 1486, at Florence in 1496, and at Venice, with illustrations, in 1511, as well as of Alberti's great work, "De Re Ædificatoriâ," at Florence, in 1485, set the seal upon the classical tendency of the age in matters of Art, and afforded the means of speedily transmitting to other countries the details of ancient design, so warmly taken up throughout Italy. The successors of the first Aldus at Venice, the Gioliti in the same city, and the Giunti at Florence, rapidly multiplied the standard classics; and thus the art of printing speedily caused a movement of revival to become cosmopolitan, which, had that noble art remained undiscovered, would very probably have been limited, to a great extent, to the soil of Italy.

Long, however, as we have already asserted, before the aspirations of the first labourers in the mine of antiquity had been thus brought to fruition, indications had been given in the world of Art of an almost inherent antagonism on the part of the Italians to Gothic forms. In the ornaments which surround the ceilings of the Church of Assisi, ascribed to Cimabue, the father of painting, the acanthus had been drawn with considerable accuracy; while Nicola Pisano and other masters of the trecento, or thirteenth century, had derived many important elements of design from a study of antique remains. It was scarcely, however, until the beginning of the fifteenth century that the movement can be said to have borne really valuable fruit. In its earliest stage the Renaissance of Art in Italy was unquestionably *a revival of principles*, and it was scarcely until the middle of the fifteenth century that it came to be in anywise *a literal revival*.

Conscious as we may be, that in some productions of this earlier stage, when Nature was recurred to for suggestion, and the actual details of classic forms were comparatively unknown and unimitated, there may exist occasional deficiencies, supplied at a later period, and under a more regular system of education; we are yet free to confess a preference for the freshness and *naïveté* with which the pioneers worked, over the more complete but more easily obtained graces of an almost direct reproduction of the antique.

The first great step in advance was taken by the celebrated Jacopo della Quercia, who having been driven from his birth-place, Sienna, to Lucca, executed about the year 1413, in the Cathedral of that city, a monument to Ilaria di Caretto, wife of Giunigi di Caretto, Lord of the City. In this interesting work (of which a good cast may be seen in the Crystal Palace) Jacopo exhibited a careful recourse to nature, both in the surrounding festoons of the upper part of the pedestal and the "puttini," or chubby boys supporting them; the simplicity of his imitation being revealed by the little bandy legs of one of the "puttini." His great work, however, was the fountain in the Piazza del Mercato Siena, which was completed at an expense of two thousand two hundred gold ducats, and even in its present sad state of decay offers unmistakable evidence of his rare ability. After his execution of this *capo d'opera* he was known as Jacopo *della Fonte*. This work brought him much distinction, and he was made Warden of the Cathedral in that city, where, after a life of much labour and many vicissitudes, he died in the year 1424, aged sixty-four. Although one of the unsuccessful candidates for the second bronze door of the Florence Baptistery, as we shall presently see, he was much esteemed during his life, and exercised a great and salutary influence on sculpture after his death. Great, however, as were his merits, he was far surpassed in the correct imitation of nature, and in grace, dexterity, and facility in ornamental combination, by Lorenzo Ghiberti, who was one of his immediate contemporaries.

In the year 1401, Florence, under an essentially democratic form of government, had risen to be one of the most flourishing cities of Europe. In this civic democracy the trades were distinguished as guilds, called "Arti," represented by deputies *(consoli)*. The Consuls resolved in the above-mentioned year to raise another gate of bronze to the Baptistery, as a pendant to that of Andrea Pisano, which had been previously executed in a very noble, but still Gothic style.

The *Signoria*, or executive government, made known this resolve to the best artists of Italy, and a public competition was opened. Lorenzo Ghiberti, a native of Florence, at that time very young (twenty-two), ventured on the trial, and with two others, Brunelleschi and Donatello, was pronounced worthy. These two last-named artists appear to have voluntarily retired in his favour; and in twenty-three years from that date the gate was finished, and put up. The beauty of its design and workmanship induced the *Signoria* to order another of him, which was ultimately finished about the year 1444. It would be impossible to overrate the importance of this work, either as regards its historical influence on art or its intrinsic merit,—standing, as it does, unrivalled by any similar specimen in any age for excellence of design and workmanship. The ornament (for a portion of which see Plate LXXV., *pages 388–89,* Fig. 1), which encloses and surrounds the panels, is worthy of the most careful study. Lorenzo Ghiberti belonged to no school, neither can it be said he founded one; he received his education from his father-in-law, a goldsmith; and his influence on Art is to be seen rather in the homage and study his works received from men such as Buonarotti and Raffaelle than from his formation of any school of pupils. He died in his native city at a good old age, in the year 1455. One of his immediate followers, Donatello, imparted a life and masculine vigour to the art, which, in spite of all their beauty, were often wanting in the compositions of Ghiberti; and the qualities of both these artists were happily united in the person of Luca della Robbia, who, during his long life (which extended from 1400 to 1480), executed an infinity of works, the ornamental details of which were carried out in a style of the freest and most graceful analogy with the antique. In the person of Filippo Brunelleschi the talents of the sculptor and the architect were combined. The former are sufficiently evinced by the excellence of the trial-piece in which he competed with Ghiberti for the execution of the celebrated gates of San Giovanni Battista; and the latter, by his magnificent Cathedral of Sta. Maria della Fiore at Florence. This combination of architectural and sculpturesque ability was, indeed, a distinguishing feature of the period. Figures, foliage, and conventional ornaments, were so happily blended with mouldings and other structural forms, as to convey the idea that the whole sprang to life in one perfect form in the mind of the artist by whom the work was executed.

A development of taste coincident with that noticeable in Tuscany took place at Naples, Rome, Milan, and Venice. At Naples, the torch that was lit by Massuccio was handed on by Andrea Ciccione, Bamboccio, Monaco, and Amillo Fiore.

At Rome, the opulence of the princes, and the great works undertaken by the successive pontiffs, attracted to the Imperial city the highest procurable ability; and hence it is, that in the various palaces and churches fragments of exquisite decorative sculpture are still to be met with. Bramante, Baldassare Peruzzi, and Baccio Pintelli (of whom arabesques on the interior of the Church of Sant' Agostino, one of the earliest

FAR LEFT: ARABESQUES DESIGNED BY BACCIO PINTELLI, FOR THE CHURCH OF SANT' AGOSTINO, ROME

LEFT: PANELS FROM THE PISCINA OF THE HIGH ALTAR OF THE CERTOSA, PAVIA

RIGHT: ARABESQUES DESIGNED BY BACCIO PINTELLI, FOR THE CHURCH OF SANT' AGOSTINO, ROME

BELOW: PANEL FROM THE PISCINA OF THE HIGH ALTAR OF THE CERTOSA, PAVIA

buildings of the pure revival executed in the Imperial, our woodcuts give some elegant examples), and even the great Raffaelle himself did not disdain to design ornaments for carvers, of the purest taste and most exquisite fancy. Of the perfection attained in this department of art by the last-named artist, the celebrated wooden stalls of the choir of San Pietro dei Casinensi, at Perugia, will long remain unquestionable evidence. The carrying out of these carvings by Stefano da Bergamo does full justice to the admirable compositions of Raffaelle.

At Milan, the important works of the Duomo, and the Certosa at Pavia, created a truly remarkable school of art; among the most celebrated masters of which may be noticed, Fusina, Solari, Agrati, Amadeo, and Sacchi. The sculptor's talent had long been traditional in that locality, and there can be no doubt that these artists embodied in the highest forms the lingering traditions of the *Maestri Comaschi*, or Freemasons, of Como; from whose genius many of the most celebrated buildings of the middle ages derived their highest graces of adornment. Of all the Lombard Cinque-centists, however, the highest admiration must be reserved for Agostino Busti, better known as Bambaja, and his pupil Brambilla, whose exquisite works in arabesque at the Certosa must ever remain marvels of execution. Our woodcuts, selected from the Piscina of the High Altar, furnish some idea of the general style of the Pavian arabesques.

At Venice, the first great names which call for notice are those of the Lombardi (Pietro, Tullio, Giulio, Sante, and Antonio), through whose talents that city was adorned with its most famous monuments. They were followed by Riccio, Bernardo, and Domenico di Mantua, and many other sculptors; but their lesser glories are altogether eclipsed by those of the great Jacopo Sansovino. At Lucca, Matteo Civitale (born 1435, died 1501) fully maintained the reputation of the period. Returning to Tuscany, we find, towards the close of the fifteenth century, the greatest perfection of ornamental sculpture, the leading characteristic of which, however, we now no longer find to be the sedulous and simple imitation of nature, but rather a conventional rendering of the antique. The names of Mino de Fiesole—the greatest of the celebrated school of the Fiesolani—

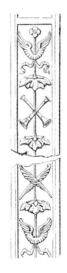

Benedetto da Majano, and Bernardo Rossellini, bring to our recollection many exquisite monuments which abound in the churches of Florence, and the other principal towns of the Grand Duchy. These artists excelled alike in wood, in stone, and in marble, and their works have been surpassed in this style of art only by those of their predecessors we have already named, and by some few others, their contemporaries. Of these, Andrea Contucci, better known as the elder Sansovino, was pre-eminent in his art; and it would appear impossible to carry ornamental modelling to greater perfection than he has exhibited in the wonderful monuments which form the pride of the Church of Sta. Maria del Popolo, at Rome. His pupil, Jacopo Tatti, who subsequently took his master's name, may be regarded as his only rival. Of him, however, more hereafter.

ORNAMENTS FROM
THE PISCINA OF THE
HIGH ALTAR OF THE
CERTOSA, PAVIA

Having thus succinctly traced the historical succession of the great sculptors of Italy, all of whom, it must constantly be borne in mind, were ornamentists also, we proceed to point out some few of those lessons which may, as we conceive, be derived from a study of their works by the artist and art-workman. One of the most peculiar and most fascinating qualities of the best Cinque-cento ornament in relief is the skill with which those by

PORTIONS OF PILASTERS FROM THE CHURCH OF STA. MARIA DEI MIRACOLI, VENICE

whom it was wrought availed themselves of the play of light and shade produced by infinite variations of plane, not only in surfaces parallel to the grounds from which the ornament was raised, but brought to a tangent with it at ever-varying angles of impact.

The difference in effect between a scroll of the volute form, in which the relief gradually diminishes from the starting of the volute to its eye, and one in which the relief is uniform throughout, is very great; and it is to their undeviating preference for the former over the latter, that the Cinque-cento artists are indebted for the infallibly pleasing results they attained alike in their simplest and most complicated combinations of spiral forms.

This refined appreciation of delicate shades of relief in sculpture was carried to its greatest perfection by Donatello, whose authority in matters of taste was held in the highest possible esteem by the contemporary Florentines, and whose example was followed with respect and devotion by all classes of artists. Not only was he the first to practise the *bassissimo relievo*, in which the effect of projection and of rounded modelling is obtained within apparently impracticable limits of relief, but he was the first to combine that style of work with *mezzo* and *alto relievo*; thus maintaining an almost pictorial division of his subject into several planes. Too good a master of his craft to ever overstep the special conventions of sculpture, Donatello enriched the Florentine practice of the Cinque-centisti with many elements derived from the sister art of Painting. These inventions—for they are almost worthy of the name, though arrived at only through a sedulous study of the antique—were adopted and imitated with the greatest avidity by the ornamentists of the period; and hence we may trace some of the most peculiar and striking technical excellence of the best Renaissance carving and modelling.

Ultimately, and at its acme of perfection, this system of regular arrangement of ornament in planes was so ingeniously managed in relation to light and shade, that, viewed from a distance, the relievo presented only certain points symmetrically disposed with reference to some dominant geometrical figures. An approach of a few paces served to bring to the sense of vision the lines and figures connecting the points of greatest salience. A yet nearer approach revealed the leafage and delicate tendrils necessary to convey a tangible idea of the type of nature selected for convention, while no inspection could be too close to test the artist's perfect appreciation of the refinements of surface texture. The "cisellatura," or "chasing," of the best Italian Cinque-cento ornament, such as may be seen in the Church of the Miracoli, Venice (Figs. 1, 5, 7, Plate LXXIV., *pages 386–87*), by the Lombardi; in the Church of Sta. Maria del Popolo (Fig. 9, Plate LXXVI., *pages 390–91*), Rome, by Sansovino; in the gates of the Baptistery, Florence (Fig. 1, Plate LXXV., *pages 388–89*), by Ghiberti; in the carvings of San Michele di Murano (Figs. 3, 4, Plate LXXIV.); the Scuola di San Marco (Fig. 2, Plate LXXIV.); the Scala dei Giganti (Figs. 8, 9, Plate LXXIV.); and other buildings at Venice, is beyond all praise. The fibres of a leaf or tendril are never misdirected, nor is Nature's tendency to grace in growth perverted or misapprehended. Smoothness and detail are never added excepting where they have some specific function to perform; and while labour is so prodigally bestowed as to show that every additional touch was a labour of love, it is never thrown way, as is too often the case in the present day, in converting those portions of a design

SMALL PILASTERS OF MARBLE STAIRCASE IN THE CHURCH OF STA. MARIA DEI MIRACOLI, VENICE, TULLIO LOMBARDO, A.D. 1485, ABOUT

LEFT: SMALL PILASTER
OF MARBLE STAIRCASE IN THE
CHURCH OF STA. MARIA DEI
MIRACOLI, VENICE

RIGHT: SMALL PILASTER OF
THE GIANT'S STAIRCASE, DUCAL
PALACE, VENICE, BY BENEDETTO
AND DOMENICO DA MANTUA

which should be secondaries or tertiaries in point of interest into primaries.

In the hands of artists less profoundly impressed than was Donatello with a sense of the just limit of convention in sculpture, the importation of pictorial elements into bas-relief soon degenerated into confusion. Even the great Ghiberti marred the effect of many of his most graceful compositions by the introduction of perspective, and accessories copied too directly from nature. In many of the ornamental sculptures of the Certosa the fault is exaggerated until monuments, which should impress the spectator with grave admiration at their beauty and dignity, serve only to amuse him— resembling dolls' houses peopled by fairies, decked with garlands, hung with tablets, and fancifully overgrown with foliage, rather than serious works of Art commemorating the dead, or dedicated to sacred uses.

Another reproach which may with justice be addressed to many such monuments is the incongruity of the association of ideas connected with their purport, and those suggested by the ornaments displayed in their friezes, pilasters, panels, spandrils, and other enriched features. Tragic and comic masques, musical instruments, semi-Priapic terminals, antique altars, tripods, and vessels of libation, dancing *amorini*, and hybrid marine monsters and chimeras, harmonise but ill with monuments reared in consecrated edifices or dedicated to religious rites. This fault of the confusion of things sacred and profane may not, however, be altogether justly laid upon the shoulders of the *artists* of the Renaissance, whose works served but to reflect the dominant spirit of an age in which the revival of mythologic symbolism was but a protest against the hampering trammels of ascetic tradition erected into dogmatism under the rulers of the East, and endorsed by the Church during those centuries when its ascendancy over an ignorant and turbulent population was at its greatest height. The minds of even the most religious men were imbued with such incongruous associations in the fourteenth century; and it is not necessary to go further than the "Commedia" of Dante, which all the world of literature has designated as *the Divine Epic*, to recognise the tangled skeins of Gothic and classical inspiration with which the whole texture of contemporary literature was interwoven.

To the architect, the study of Italian Cinque-cento ornament in relief is of no less utility than it can possibly be to the sculptor, since in no style has ornament ever been better spaced out, or arranged to contrast more agreeably with the direction of the adjacent architectural lines by which it is bounded and kept in subordination. Rarely, if ever, is an ornament suitable for a horizontal position placed in a vertical one, or *vice versâ*; and rarely, if ever, are the proportions of the ornaments and the mouldings, or the styles and rails, by which regularity and symmetry are given to the whole, at variance with one another. In Plates LXXIV., LXXV., and LXXVI. *(pages 386–89)*, are collected a series of specimens, in the majority of which gracefulness of line, and a highly artificial, though apparently natural, distribution of the ornament upon its field, are the prevailing characteristics. The Lombardi, in their works at the Church of Sta. Maria dei Miracoli, Venice (Plate LXXIV., Figs. 1, 5, 7; Plate LXXVI., Fig. 2); Andrea Sansovino at Rome (Plate LXXVI., Fig. 9); and Domenico and Bernardino di Mantua, at Venice

PORTION OF A DOORWAY IN ONE
OF THE PALACES OF THE DORIAS
NEAR THE CHURCH OF SAN
MATTEO, GENOA

(Plate LXXIV., Figs. 8 and 9), attained the highest perfection in these respects. At a subsequent period to that in which they flourished the ornaments were generally wrought in more uniformly high relief, and the stems and tendrils were thickened, and not so uniformly tapered, the accidental growth and play of nature were less sedulously imitated, the field of the panel was more fully covered with enrichments, and its whole aspect made more bustling and less refined. The sculptor's work asserted itself in competition with the architect's: the latter in self-defence, and to keep the sculpture down, soon began to make his mouldings heavy: and a more ponderous style altogether crept into fashion. Of this tendency to *plethora* in ornament we already perceive indications in much of the Genoese work represented in Plate LXXV., Figs. 2–5, 8, 9, and 11; and in Plate LXXVI., Figs. 1, 3, 4, 5, and 7. Fig. 6 in the last-mentioned plate, from the celebrated Martinengo Tomb, at Brescia, also clearly exhibits this tendency to filling up.

In the art of painting, a movement took place concurrent with that we have thus briefly noticed in sculpture. Giotto, the pupil of Cimabue, threw off the shackles of Greek tradition, and gave his whole heart to nature. His ornament, like that of his master, consisted of a combination of painted mosaic work, interlacing bends, and free rendering of the acanthus. In his work at Assisi, Naples, Florence, and Padua, he has invariably shown a graceful apprehension of the balance essential to be maintained between mural pictures and mural ornaments, both in quantity, distribution, and relative colour. These right principles of balance were very generally

VERTICAL RUNNING ORNAMENT FROM THE CHURCH OF STA. MARIA DEI MIRACOLI, VENICE

understood and adopted during the fourteenth century; and Simone Memmi, Taddeo Bartolo, the Orcagnas, Pietro di Lorenzo, Spinello Aretino, and many others, were admitted masters of mural embellishment. That rare student of nature in the succeeding century, Benozzo Gozzoli, was a no less diligent student of antiquity, as may be recognised in the architectural backgrounds to his pictures in the Campo Santo, and in the noble arabesques which divide his pictures at San Gimignano. Andrea Mantegna, however, it was who moved painting as Donatello had moved sculpture, and that not in figures alone, but in every variety of ornament borrowed from the antique. The magnificent cartoons we are so fortunate as to possess of his at Hampton Court, even to their minutest decorative details, might have been drawn by an ancient Roman. Towards the close of the fifteenth century, the style, of polychromy took a fresh and marked turn, the peculiarities of which, in connexion with arabesque and grotesque ornament, we reserve for a subsequent notice.

Turning from Italy to France, which was the first of the European nations to light its torch at the fire of Renaissance Art, which had been kindled in Italy, we find that the warlike expeditions of Charles VIII. and Louis XII. infected the nobility of France with an admiration for the splendours of Art met with by them at Florence, Rome, and Milan. The first clear indication of the coming change might have been seen (for it was unfortunately destroyed in 1793) in the monument erected in 1499 to the memory of the first-named monarch, around which female figures, in gilt bronze, of the Virtues, were grouped completely in the Italian manner. In the same year, the latter sovereign invited the celebrated Fra Giocondo, architect, of Verona, friend and fellow-student of the elder Aldus, and first good editor of Vitruvius, to visit France. He remained there from 1499 to 1506, and designed for his royal master two bridges over the Seine, and probably many minor works which have now perished. The magnificent Château de Gaillon, begun by Cardinal d'Amboise in the year 1502, has been frequently ascribed to him, but, according to Emeric David and other French archaeologists, upon insufficient grounds. The internal evidence is entirely in favour of a French origin, and against Giocondo, who was more of an engineer and student than an ornamental artist. Moreover, intermingled with much that is very fairly classical, is so much Burgundian work, that it would be almost as unjust to Giocondo to ascribe it to him, as to France to deprive her of the credit of having produced, by a French artist, her first great Renaissance monument. The whole of the accounts which were published by M. Deville in 1850, set the question almost entirely at rest; for from them we learn that Guillaume Senault was architect and master-mason. It is, however, just possible that Giocondo may have been consulted by the Cardinal upon the general plan, and that Senault and his companions, for the most part French, may have carried out the details. The principal Italian by whom, if we may judge from the style, some of the most classical of the arabesques were wrought, was Bertrand de Meynal, who had been commissioned to carry from Genoa the beautiful Venetian fountain, so well known as the Vasque du Château de Gaillon, now in the Louvre, and from which (Plate LXXXI., *pages 398–99*, Figs. 27, 30, 34, 35) we have engraved some elegant ornaments. Colin Castille, who especially figures in the list of art-workmen as "tailleur à l'antique," may very possibly have been a Spaniard who had studied in Rome. In all essential particulars, the portions of Renaissance work not Burgundian in style are very pure, and differ scarcely at all from good Italian examples.

It was, however, in the monument of Louis XII., now at St. Denis, near Paris, and one of the richest of the sixteenth century, that symmetry of architectural disposition was for the first time united to masterly execution of detail in France. This beautiful work of art was executed between 1518 and 1530, under the orders of Francis I., by Jean Juste of Tours. Twelve semicircular arches inclose the bodies of the royal pair, represented naked; under every arch is placed an apostle; and at the four corners are four large statues of Justice, Strength, Prudence, and Wisdom: the whole being surmounted by statues of the King and Queen on their knees. The bas-reliefs represent the triumphal entry of Louis into Genoa, and the battle of Aguadel, where he signalised himself by his personal valour.

The monument of Louis XII. has been often ascribed to Trebatti (Paul Ponee), but it was finished before he came to France, as the following extract from the royal records proves. Francis I. addresses the Cardinal Duprat:—"Il est deu a Jehan Juste, mon *sculteur ordinaire*, porteur de ceste la somme de 400 escus, restans des 1200 que je lui avoie pardevant or donnez pour la menage et conduite de la ville de Tours au lieu de St. Denis en France, de la sculpture de marbre de feuz Roy Loys et Royne Anne, &c. Novembre 1531."

Not less worthy of study than the tomb of Louis XII., and executed at the same period, are the beautiful carvings in alto and basso relievo, which ornament the whole exterior of the choir of the Cathedral of Chartres; the subjects are taken from the lives of our Saviour and the Virgin, and from forty-one groups, fourteen of which are the work of Jean Texier, who commenced in 1514, after completing that part of the new clock-tower erected by him. These compositions are full of truth and beauty, the figures animated and natural, the drapery free and graceful, and the heads full of life; but the arabesque ornaments, which almost entirely cover the projecting parts of the pilasters, friezes, and mouldings of the base, are, perhaps, the most beautiful portions; they are very diminutive in size; the largest of the groups, which are those that cover the pilasters, being only eight or nine inches in breadth. Though so minute, the spirit of the carving, and variety of devices in these ornaments, are marvellous. Masses of foliage, branches of trees, birds, fountains, bundles of arms, satyrs, military ensigns, and tools belonging to various arts, are arranged with much taste. The F crowned—the monogram of Francis I.—is conspicuous in these arabesques, and the dates of the years 1525, 1527, and 1529, are traced upon the draperies.

The tomb which Anne of Brittany caused to be erected to the memory of her father and mother was finished and placed in the choir of the Carmelite Church at Nantes on the 1st of January, 1507. It is the masterpiece of an artist of great ability and *naïveté*—Michel Colombe. The ornamental details are peculiarly elegant. The monument to Cardinal d'Amboise, in the Cathedral at Rouen, was begun in the year 1515, under Roulant le Roux, master-mason of the Cathedral. No Italian appears to have assisted in its execution, and we may, therefore, fairly regard it as an expression of the vigour with which the Renaissance *virus* had indoctrinated the native artists.

It was in 1530 and 1531 that Francis I. invited Rosso and Primaticcio into France, and those distinguished artists were speedily followed by Nicola del' Abbate, Luca, Penni, Cellini, Trebatti, and Girolamo della Robbia.

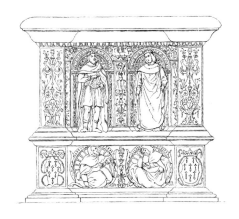

PORTIONS OF THE TOMB OF FRANCIS II.,
DUKE OF BRITTANY, AND HIS WIFE, MARGUERITE DE FOIX,
ERECTED BY ANNE OF BRITTANY IN THE CARMELITE CHURCH
AT NANTES, BY MICHEL COLOMBE, A.D. 1507

With their advent, and the foundation of the school at Fountainebleau, new elements were introduced into the French Renaissance, to which we shall subsequently advert.

It would exceed the limits of our present sketch to enter fully into the historical details connected with the art of wood-carving. It may suffice to point out that every ornamental feature available for stone, marble, or bronze, was rapidly transferred also to wood-work, and that at no period of the history of Industrial Art has the talent of the sculptor been more gracefully brought to bear upon the enrichment of sumptuous furniture. Our Plates, Nos. LXXXI. and LXXXII. *(pages 398–401)*, furnish brilliant evidence of the justice of our remarks on this head. The attentive student, however, as he goes over them, will be unable to avoid perceiving a gradual withdrawing from the original foliated ornament which formed the stock-in-trade of the early Renaissance artists. He will next notice a heaping up of various objects and "capricci," derived from the antique, accompanied by a fulness of projection and slight tendency to heaviness; and then, finally, he will recognise the general adoption of a particular set of forms differing from the Italian, and altogether national, such as the conventional volute incised with small square or oblong indentations (Plate LXXXI., Figs. 17 and 20), and the medallion heads (Plate LXXXI., Figs. 1 and 17).

The dawning rays of the coming revival of Art in France can scarcely be traced in the painted glass of the fifteenth century. The ornaments, canopies, foliage, and inscriptions, are generally *flamboyant* and angular in character, although freely and crisply made out, and the figures are influenced by the prevailing style of drawing. The glass, although producing a pleasing effect, is much thinner—especially the blue—than that of the thirteenth century. An immense number of windows were executed during this epoch, and specimens are to be found more or less perfect in almost every large church in France. St. Ouen, at Rouen, has some fine figures upon a white quarry ground in the clerestory windows; and good examples of the glass of the century will be found in St. Gervais at Paris, and Notre Dame at Chalons-sur-Marne.

Many improvements were introduced into the art at the epoch of the Renaissance. The first masters were employed to make cartoons; enamel was used to give depth to the colours without losing the richness, and much more white was employed. Many of the windows are very little more than grisailles, as those designed by Jean Cousin for the Sainte Chapelle at Vincennes; one of those representing the angel sounding the fourth trumpet is admirable, both in composition and drawing. The Cathedral of Auch also contains some exceedingly fine examples of the work of Arneaud Demole; Beauvais also possesses a great deal of the glass of this period, especially a very fine Jesse window, the work of Enguerand le Prince; the heads are grand, and the *poses* of the figures call to mind the works of Albert Dürer.

The grisailles, which ornamented the windows in the houses of the nobility, and even of the *bourgeoisie*, although small, were executed with an admirable delicacy, and in drawing and grouping leave little to be desired.

Toward the end of the sixteenth century the art began to decline, the numerous glass-painters found themselves without employment, and the celebrated Bernard de Palissy, who had been brought up to the trade, left it to engage in another presenting greater difficulties, but which eventually secured him the highest reputation. To him, however, we are indebted for the charming grisailles representing the story of Cupid and Psyche, from the designs of Raffaelle, which formerly decorated the Château of Ecouen, the residence of his great patron the Constable Montmorency.

Renaissance ornament penetrated into Germany at an early period, but was absorbed into the hearts of the people but slowly, until the spread of books and engravings quickened its general acceptation. From an early period there had been a steady current of artists leaving Germany and Flanders to study in the great Italian *ateliers*. Among them, men like Roger of Bruges, who spent much of his life in Italy, and died in 1464,—Hemskerk, and Albert Dürer, more especially influenced their countrymen. The latter, who in many of his engravings showed a perfect apprehension of the conditions of Italian design, leaning now to the Gothic manner of his master Wohlgemuth, and now to the Raffaellesque simplicity of Marc' Antonio. The spread of the engravings of the latter, however, in Germany, unquestionably conduced to the formation of the taste of men who, like Peter Vischer, first brought Italian plastic art into fashion in Germany. Even at its best the Renaissance of Germany is impure—her industrious affection for difficulties of the hand, rather than of the head, soon led her to crinkum-crankums; and strap-work, jewelled forms, and complicated monsters, rather animated than graceful, took the place of the refined elegance of the early Italian and French arabesques.

It may be well now to turn from the Fine to the Industrial Arts, and to trace the manifestation of the revival in the designs of contemporary manufactures. From the unchanging and unchangeable nature of vitreous and ceramic products, no historical evidence of style can be more complete and satisfactory than that which they afford, and hence we have devoted three entire Plates (Nos. LXXVIII., LXXIX., and LXXX., *pages 394–97*) to their illustration. The majority of the specimens thereon represented have been selected from the "majolica" of Italy, on which interesting ware and its ornamentation we proceed to offer a few remarks.

The art of glazing pottery appears to have been introduced into Spain and the Balearic Isles by the Moors, by whom it had long been known and used in the form of coloured tiles for the decoration of their buildings. The earthenware called "majolica" is believed to derive its name from the Island

ARABESQUE BY THEODOR DE BRY, ONE OF THE "PETITS MAITRES"
OF GERMANY (1598), IN IMITATION OF ITALIAN WORK, BUT INTRODUCING
STRAP-WORK, CARICATURE, AND JEWELLED FORMS

of Majorca, whence the manufacture of glazed pottery is supposed to have found its way into Central Italy; and this belief is strengthened by the fact of the earliest Italian ware being ornamented with geometrical patterns and trefoil-shaped "foliations" of Saracenic character (Plates LXXIX. and LXXX., *pages 395–97*, Figs. 30 and 13). It was first used by introducing coloured concave tiles among brickwork, and later in the form of encaustic flooring. The manufacture of this ware was extensively carried on between 1450 and 1700, in the towns of Nocera, Arezzo, Citta de Castillo, Forli, Faenza (whence comes *fayence*), Florence, Spello, Perugia, Deruta, Bologna, Rimini, Ferrara, Pesaro, Fermignano, Castel Durante, Gubbio, Urbino, and Ravenna, and also at many places in the Abruzzi; but Pesaro is admitted to be the first town in which it attained any celebrity. It was at first called "*mezza*," or "half" majolica, and was usually made in the form of thick clumsy plates, many of large size. They are of a dingy grey colour, and often have a dull yellow varnish at the back. The texture is coarse and gritty, but the golden and prismatic lustre is now and then seen, though they are more frequently of a pearly hue. This "half" majolica is believed by Passeri and others to have been made in the fifteenth century; and it was not till after that time that the manufacture of "fine" majolica almost entirely superseded it.

A mode of glazing pottery was also discovered by Lucca della Robbia, who was born at Florence in 1399. It is said that he used for this purpose a mixture of antimony, tin, and other mineral substances, applied as a varnish to the surface of the beautiful terra-cotta statues and bas-reliefs modelled by him. The secret of this varnish remained in the inventor's family till about 1550, when it was lost at the death of the last member of it. Attempts have been made at Florence to revive the manufacture of the Robbian ware, but with small success, owing to the great difficulties attending it. The subjects of the bas-reliefs of Della Robbia are chiefly religious, to which the pure glistening white of the figures is well adapted; the eyes are blackened to heighten the expression, and the white figures well relieved by the deep blue ground. Wreaths of flowers and fruits in their national tints were introduced by the followers of Della Robbia, by some of whom the costumes were coloured, whilst the flesh parts were allowed to remain unglazed. Passeri claims the discovery of this coloured glaze at a still earlier date for Pesaro, where the manufacture of earthenware was carried on in the fourteenth century; but though the art of combining it with colour may have been known at that early time, it had not attained much celebrity until 1462, when Matteo de Raniere of Cagli and Ventura di Maestro Simone dei Piccolomini of Siena established themselves at Pesaro, for the purpose of carrying on the manufacture of earthenware already existing there; and it is not improbable that their attention was attracted by the works of Della Robbia, who had been employed by Sigismond Pandolfo Malatesta at Rimini. Some confusion appears to have arisen with respect to the precise process invented by Della Robbia, and looked upon by himself and his family as the really valuable secret. We feel little doubt that it consisted rather in the tempering and firing of the clay to enable it to burn large masses truly and thoroughly than in the protecting glaze, about which there appears to have been very little novelty or necessity for concealment.

Prismatic lustre and a brilliant and transparent white glaze were the qualities chiefly sought for in the "fine" majolica and Gubbian ware; the metallic lustre was given by preparations of lead, silver, copper, and gold, and in this the Gubbian ware surpassed all others. The dazzling white glaze was obtained by a varnish made from tin, into which, when half-baked, the pottery was plunged; the designs were painted before this was dry, and, as it immediately absorbed the colours, it is not to be wondered at that we so frequently find inaccuracies in the drawings.

A plate of the early Pesaro ware in the Museum at the Hague bears a cipher, the letters of which appear to be "C. H. O. N." Another, mentioned by Pungileoni, has "G. A. T." interlaced, forming a mark. These instances are rare, as the artists of these plates seldom signed their works.

The subjects generally chosen were saints and historical events from Scripture; but the former were preferred, and continued in favour till the sixteenth century, when they were displaced by scenes from Ovid and Virgil, though designs from Scripture were still in use. The subject was generally briefly described with a reference to the text in blue letters at the back of the plate. The fashion of ornamenting the ware with the portraits of historical, classical, and living persons, with the names attached to each, was of rather later date than the sacred themes. All these subjects are painted in a flat, tame manner, with little attempt at shading, and are surrounded by a kind of rude Saracenic ornament, differing completely from the Raffaellesque arabesques, which, in the latter years of Guidobaldo's reign, were so much in fashion. The plates full of coloured fruits in relief were probably taken from the Robbian ware.

The decline of this manufacture caused by the Duke's impaired income and the want of interest in the manufacture felt by his successor, was hastened by the introduction of Oriental china and the increased use of plate in the higher and more wealthy classes; still, though historial subjects were laid aside, the majolica was ornamented with well-executed designs of birds, trophies, flowers, musical instruments, sea monsters, &c., but these became gradually more and more feeble in colouring and execution till, at last, their place was taken by engravings from Sadeler and other Flemings. From all these causes the manufacture fell rapidly to decay, in spite of the endeavours made to revive it by Cardinal Legate Stoppani.

The "fine" majolica of Pesaro attained its greatest perfection during the reign of Guidobaldo II., who held his court in that city, and greatly patronised its potteries. From that time, the majolica of Pesaro so closely resembled that of Urbino, that it is not possible to distinguish the manufacture of the two places from each other, the texture of the ware being alike, and the same artists being often employed in both potteries. As early as 1486 the Pesaro ware was considered so superior to all other Italian ware, that a protection was granted to it by the lord of Pesaro of that date, not only forbidding, under penalty of fine and confiscation, the importation of any kind of foreign pottery, but ordering that all foreign vases should be sent out of the state within eight days. This protection was confirmed, in 1532, by Francesco Maria I. In 1569, a patent for twenty-five years, with a penalty of 500 scudi for infringing it, was granted by Guidobaldo II. to Giacomo Lanfranco of Pesaro, for his inventions in the construction of vases wrought in relief, of great size and antique forms, and his application of gold to them. In addition to this, his father and himself were freed from all taxes and imposts.

From its variety and novelty, majolica was generally chosen by the lords of the Duchy for their presents to foreign princes. In 1478, Constanza Sforza sent to Sixtus IV. certain "vasa fictilia;" and in a letter from Lorenzo the Magnificent to Robert Malatesta, he returns thanks for a present of a similar kind. A service painted by Orazio Fontana from designs by Taddeo Zuccaro, was presented by Guidobaldo to Philip II. of Spain. A double service was also given by him to Charles V. The set of jars presented to the Treasury of Loreto by Francesco Maria II. were made by the order of Guidobaldo II., for the use of his own laboratory; some of them are ornamented with a portrait, or subject of some other description, and all are labelled with the name of a drug or mixture. The colours of these jars are blue, green, and yellow; about 380 of them still remain in the Treasury of Loreto. Passeri gives an interesting classification of ornamental pottery, with the terms made use of by the workmen to distinguish the various kinds of paintings used in ornamenting the plates, and also the sums paid to the artists by whom they were painted. He gives a curious extract from a manuscript in the handwriting of Piccolpasso, a "majolicaro" of the middle of the sixteenth century, who wrote upon his art; to understand which it is necessary to remember that the *bolognino* was equivalent to the ninth part, and the *gros* to the third part, of a paul (5$\frac{1}{6}$ pence); the livre was a third, and

the florin two thirds of a petit écu; and the petit écu, or écu ducal, two thirds of a Roman crown (now value four shillings and threepence one farthing).

Trophies.—This style of ornament consisted of ancient and modern arms, musical and mathematical instruments, and open books; they are generally painted in yellow cameo on a blue ground. These plates were chiefly sold in the province (Castel Durante) in which they were manufactured, one ducal crown a hundred being the sum paid to the painters of them. This style was much affected by the Cinque-centisti in marble and stone: witness the monument to Gian Galeazzo Visconti, in the Certosa, Pavia, and portions of the Genoese doorway we engrave.

Arabesques were ornaments consisting of a sort of cipher, loosely tied, and interlacing knots and bouquets. Work thus ornamented was sent to Venice and Genoa, and obtained one ducal florin the hundred.

Cerquate was a name given to the interlacing of oak-branches, painted in a deep yellow upon a blue ground; it was called the "Urbino painting," from the oak being one of the bearings of the ducal arms. This kind of decoration received fifteen gros the hundred; and when, in addition, the bottom of the plate was ornamented, by having some little story painted upon it, the artist received one petit écu.

Grotesques were the interlacing of winged male and female monsters, with their bodies terminated by foliations or branches. These fanciful decorations were generally painted in white cameo upon a blue ground; the payment for them being two écus the hundred, unless they were painted on commission from Venice, when the price was eight ducal livres.

Leaves.—This ornament consisted of a few branches of leaves, small in size, and sprinkled over the ground. Their price was three livres.

Flowers and Fruits.—These very pleasing groups were sent to Venice, and the artists received for them five livres the hundred. Another variety of the same style merely consisted in three or four large leaves, painted in one colour upon a different-coloured ground. Their price was half a florin the hundred.

Porcelain was the name of a style of work which consisted of the most delicate blue flowers, with small leaves and buds painted upon a white ground. This kind of work obtained two or more livres the hundred. It was, in all probability, an imitation of Portuguese importations.

Tratti were wide bands, knotted in different ways, with small branches issuing from them. Their price was also two livres the hundred.

Soprabianco was a painting in white upon a white-lead ground, with green or blue borders round the margin of the plate. These obtained a demi-écu the hundred.

Quartieri.—In this pattern the artist divided the bottom of the plate into six or eight rays, diverging from the centre to the circumference; each space was of a particular colour, upon which were painted bouquets of different tints. The painters received for this kind of ornament two livres the hundred.

Gruppi.—These were broad bands interwoven with small flowers. This pattern was larger than the "tratti;" and was sometimes embellished by a little picture in the centre of the plate: in that case the price of a demi-écu, but without it only two jules.

PORTIONS OF THE PILASTER OF A DOORWAY IN THE
PALACE AT GENOA, PRESENTED BY THE GENOESE TO ANDREA DORIA

Candelabri.—This ornament was an upright bouquet extending from one side of the plate to the other, the space on each side being filled up with scattered leaves and flowers. The price of the *candelabri* was two florins the hundred. The adjoining woodcut shows how common, how early, and how favourite a subject this was with the best artists of the Cinque-cento.

To dwell in detail upon the merits and particular works of artists, such as Maestro Giorgio Andreoli, Orazio Fontana, and Francesco Xanto of Rovigo, would be beyond the scope of this notice, and is the less necessary as Mr. Robinson, in his Catalogue of the Soulages Collection, has so recently thrown out some new and highly interesting speculations upon various difficult questions connected with the subject. Neither will it be desirable here to do more than point out the interesting modifications of ceramic design and practice carried out in France through the indomitable perseverence of Bernard de Palissy, master-potter to Francis I. In Plate LXXIX. *(pages 394–95),* Figs. 1 and 3, we have engraved several specimens of the decorations of his elegant ware, which occupy as to design, in reference to other monuments of the French Renaissance, much the same position that the design of the early majolica does to the monuments of the Italian revival. Although that style began to make its appearance in the works of the French jewellers in the reign of Louis XII., when the extensive patronage of the powerful Cardinal d'Amboise gave considerable impetus to the art, it was under Francis I., who invited to his Court the great master of the Renaissance—Cellini—that the jeweller's art reached its highest perfection. To rightly appreciate, however, the precise condition and nature of the precious metal-work, it is necessary to pass in rapid review the leading characteristics of the admirable school of enamellers, whose productions in the fifteenth century, and much more in the sixteenth, served to disseminate far and wide some of the most elegant ornaments which have ever been applied to metal-work.

LOWER PORTION SHOWING
THE SPRINGING OF SCROLL-
WORK OF A SMALL PILASTER,
BY THE LOMBARDI, IN THE
CHURCH OF STA. MARIA DEI
MIRACOLI, VENICE

About the end of the fourteenth century, the artists of Limoges found not only that the old champlevé enamels,—of which, in Plate LXXVII. *(pages 392–93)*, Figs. 1, 3, 4, 8, 29, 42, 43, 50, 53, 57, 61, we have given, for the sake of contrast, numerous examples,— had entirely gone out of fashion, but that almost every goldsmith either imported the translucid enamels from Italy, or executed them himself with more or less skill, according to his talents. In this state of things, instead of attempting competition, they invented a new manufacture, the processes of which belonged solely to the enameller, and enabled him to dispense entirely with the *burin* of the goldsmith. The first attempts were exceedingly rude, and very few of them now remain; but that the art progressed slowly is evident from the fact, that it is not until the middle of the fifteenth century that specimens are to be found in any quantity, or possessing any degree of merit. The process was this:—The design was traced with a sharp point upon an unpolished plate of copper, which was then covered with a thin coat of transparent enamel. The artist, after going over his tracing with a thick black line, filled in the intervals with the various colours, which were, for the most part, transparent, the black lines performing the office of the gold strips of the cloisonné work. The carnations presented the greatest difficulty, and were, first of all, covered over with the black colour, and the high lights and half-tints were then modelled upon that with opaque white, which occasionally received a few touches of light transparent red. The last operation was to appy the gilding, and to affix the imitations of precious stones,—almost the last trace of the Byzantine school, which had formerly exercised so much influence in Aquitaine.

The appearance of the finished works was very similar to that of a large and coarse translucid enamel,—a resemblance not unlikely to have been intentional, more especially as specimens of the latter were never made of any considerable size, and were therefore fit to supply the place of ivory in the construction of those small triptychs which were so necessary an appendage to the chambers and oratories of the rich in the middle ages. Accordingly, we find nearly all the early painted enamels are either in the form of triptychs or diptychs, or have originally formed parts of them; and a great number preserve their original brass frames, and are supposed by antiquaries to have been produced in the *atelier* of Monvearni, as the name or initials of that master are generally found upon them. As to the other artists, they followed, unfortunately, the but too common practice of most of the workmen of the middle ages, and, with the exceptions of Monvearni and P. E. Nicholat, or, as the inscriptions have been more correctly read, Penicaud, their names are buried in oblivion.

At the commencement of the sixteenth century the Renaissance had made great progress; and among other changes, a great taste for paintings in "camaieu," or "grisaille," had sprung up. The *ateliers* of Limoges at once adopted the new fashion, and what may be called the second series of painted enamels was the result. The process was very nearly the same as that employed with regard to the carnations of the earlier specimens, and consisted in, firstly, covering the whole plate of copper over with a black enamel, and then modelling the lights and half-tints with opaque white; those parts requiring to be coloured, such as the faces and the foliage, receiving glazes of their appropriate tints—touches of gold are almost always used to complete the picture; and occasionally, when more than ordinary brilliancy was wanted, a thin gold or silver leaf, called a "pallion," was applied upon the black ground, and the glaze afterwards superposed. All these processes are to be seen in the two pictures of Francis I. and Henry II., executed by Leonard Limousin, for the decoration of the Sainte Chapelle, but which have now been removed to the Museum of the Louvre. Limoges, indeed, owed no small debt of gratitude to the former monarch, who not only established a manufactory in the town, but made its director, Leonard, "peintre, émailleur, valet-de-chambre du Roi," giving him, at the same time, the appellation of "le Limousin," to distinguish him from the other and still more famous Leonardo da Vinci. And, indeed, the Limousin was no mean artist, whether we regard his copies of the early German and Italian masters, or the original portraits of the more celebrated of his contemporaries, such as those of the Duke of Guise, the Constable Montmorency, Catherine de

Medicis, and many others—executed, we must remember, in the most difficult material which has ever yet been employed for the purposes of art. The works of Leonardo extend from 1532 to 1574, and contemporaneously with him flourished a large school of artist-enamellers, many of whose works quite equalled, if they did not surpass, his own. Among them we may mention Pierre Raymond and the families of the Penicauds, and the Courteys, Jean and Susanna Court, and M. D. Pape. The eldest of the family of the Courteys, Pierre, was not only a good artist, but has the reputation of having made the largest-sized enamels which have ever been executed (nine of these are preserved in the Museum of the Hôtel de Cluny—the other three, M. Labarte informs us, are in England) for decorating the façade of the Château de Madrid, upon which building large sums were lavished by Francis I. and Henry II. We should observe that this last phase of Limoges enamelling was not confined, like its predecessor, to sacred subjects; but, on the contrary, the most distinguished artists did not disdain to design vases, caskets, basins, ewers, cups, salvers, and a variety of other articles of every-day life, which were afterwards entirely covered with the black enamel, and then decorated with medallions, &c. in the opaque white. At the commencement of the new manufacture, the subjects of most of the enamels were furnished from the prints of the German artists, such as Martin Schoen, Israel van Mecken, &c. These were afterwards supplanted by those of Marc' Antonio Raimondi and other Italians, which, in their turn, gave way about the middle of the sixteenth century to the works of Virgilius Solis, Theodore de Bry, Etienne de l'Aulne, and other of the *petits-maîtres*.

The production of the painted enamels was carried on with great activity at Limoges, during the whole of the fifteenth, sixteenth, and seventeenth centuries, and far into the eighteenth, when it finally expired. The last artists were the families of the Nouaillers and Laudins, whose best works are remarkable for the absence of the paillons, and a somewhat undecided style of drawing.

In conclusion, it remains for us only to invite the student to cultivate the beauties, as sedulously as he should eschew the extravagancies, of the Renaissance style. Where great liberty is afforded in Art no less than in Polity, great responsibility is incurred. In those styles in which the imagination of the designer can be checked only from within, he is especially bound to set a rein upon his fancy. Ornament let him have in abundance; but in its composition let him be modest and decorous, avoiding over-finery as he would nakedness. If he has no story to tell, let him be content with floriated forms and conventional elements in his enrichments, which please the eye without making any serious call upon the intellect; then, where he really wishes to arrest observation by the comparatively direct representation of material objects, he may be the more sure of attaining his purpose. In a style which, like the Renaissance, allows of, and indeed demands, the association of the Sister Arts, let the artist never lose sight of the unities and specialties of each. Keep them as a well-ordered family, on the closest and most harmonious relations, but never permit one to assume the prerogatives of another, or even to issue from its own, to invade its Sister's province. So ordered and maintained, those styles are noblest, richest, and best adapted to the complicated requirements of a highly artificial social system, in which, as in that of the Renaissance, Architecture, Painting, Sculpture, and the highest technical excellence in Industry, must unite before its essential and indispensable conditions of effect can be efficiently realised.

M. DIGBY WYATT.

BOOKS REFERRED TO FOR ILLUSTRATIONS. LITERARY AND PICTORIAL

ALCIATI (A.) *Emblemata D. A. Alciati, denuo ab ipso Autore recognita; ac, quœ desiderabantur, imaginibus locupletata. Accesserunt nona aliquot ab Autore Emblemata suis quoque eiconibus insignita.* Small 8vo. Lyons, 1551.

ANTONELLI (G.) *Collezione dei migliori Ornamenti antichi, sparsi nella città di Venezia, coll' aggiunta di alcuni frammenti di Gotica architettura e di varie invenzioni di un Giovane Alunno di questa I. R. Accademia.* Oblong 4to. Venezia, 1831.

BALTARD. *Paris et ses Monumens, mésurés, dessinés, et gravés, avec des Descriptions Historiques, par le Citoyen Amaury Duval: Louvre, St. Cloud, Fontainbleau, Château d'Ecouen, &c.* 2 vols. Large Folio. Paris, 1803–5.

C. BECKER AND J. VON HEFNER. *Kunstwerke und Geräthschaften des Mittelalters und der Renaissance.* 2 vols. 4to. Frankfurt, 1852.

BERGAMO (STEFANO DA). *Wood-Carvings from the Choir of the Monastery of San Pietro at Perugia, 1535. (Cinque-cento.)* Said to be from designs by Raffaelle.

BERNARD (A.) *Receuil d'Ornements de la Renaissance. Dessinés et gravés à l'eau-forte.* 4to. Paris, n. d.

CHAPUY. *Le Moyen - Age Pittoresque. Monumens et Fragmens d'Architecture, Meubles, Armes, Armures, et Objects de Curiosité X[e] au XVIIe Siècle. Dessiné d'après Nature par Chapuy, &c. Avec un Texte archéologique, descriptif, et historique, par M. Moret.* 5 vols. small Folio. Paris, 1838–40.

CLERGET ET GEORGE. *Collection portative d'Ornements de la Renaissance, recueillis et choisis par Ch. Ernest Clerget. Gravés sur cuivre d'après les originaux par C. E. Clerget et Mme. E. George.* 8vo. Paris, 1851.

D'AGINCOURT (J. B. L. G. S.) *Histoire de l'Art par ses Monumens, depuis sa Décadence au IVe Siècle, jusqu'à son Renouvellement au XVIe. Ouvrage enrichi de 525 planches.* 6 vols. Folio. Paris, 1823.

DENNISTOUN (J.) *Memoirs of the Dukes of Urbino, illustrating the Arms, Arts, and Literature of Italy from 1440 to 1630.* 3 vols. 8vo. London, 1851.

DEVILLE (A.) *Unedited Documents on the History of France. Comptes de Dépenses de la Construction du Château de Gaillon, publiés d'après les Registres Manuscrits des Trésoriers du Cardinal d'Amboise. With an Atlas of Plates.* 4to. Paris, 1850.

—— *Tombeaux de la Cathédrale de Rouen; avec douze planches, gravées.* 8vo. Rouen, 1837.

DURELLI (G. & F.) *La Certosa di Pavia, descritta ed illustrata con tavole, incise dai fratelli Gaetano e Francesco Durelli. 62 plates.* Folio. Milan, 1853.

DUSSIEUX (L.) *Essai sur l'Histoire de la Peinture sur Email.* 8vo. Paris, 1839.

GAILHABAUD (J.) *L'Architecture du Ve au XVIe Siècle et les Arts qui en dependent, le Sculpture, la Peinture Murale, la Peinture sur Verre, la Mosaïque, la Ferronnerie, &c., publiés d'après les Travaux inédits des principaux Architectes Français et Etrangers.* 4to. Paris, 1851, et seq.

GHIBERTI (LORENZO). *Le tre Porte del Battisterio di San Giovanni di Firenze.* 46 plates, engraved in outline by Lasinio, with description in French and Italian. Folio, half morocco. Firenze, 1821.

HOPFER. *Collection of Ornaments in the Grotesque Style, by Hopfer.*

IMBARD. *Tombeaux de Louis XII. et de François I., dessinés et gravés au trait, par E. F. Imbard, d'après des Marbres du Musée des Petits Augustins.* Small Folio. Paris, 1823.

JUBINAL (A.) *Récherches sur l'Usage et l'Origine des Tapisseries à Personnages, dites Historiées, dupuis l'Antiquité jusqu'au XVIe Siècle inclusivement.* 8vo. ph. Paris, 1840.

DE LABORDE (LE COMTE ALEXANDRE). *Les Monumens de la France, classés chronologiquement, et considérés sous le Rapport des Faits historiques et de l'Etude des Arts.* 2 vols. Folio. Paris, 1816–36.

DE LABORDE. *Notice des Emaux exposés dans les Galeries du Musée de Louvre. Première partie, Historie et Descriptions.* 8vo. Paris, 1852.

LABARTE (J.) *Description des Objects d'Art qui composent la Collection Debruge-Duménil, précédée d'une Introduction Historique.* 8vo. Paris, 1847.

LACROIX ET SERÉ. *Le Moyen Age et la Renaissance, Histoire et Description des Mœurs et Usages, du Commence et de l'Industrie, des Sciences, des Arts, des Littératures, et des Beaux Arts en Europe. Direction Littéraire de M. Paul Lacroix. Direction Artistique de M. Ferdinand Seré. Dessins fac-similes par M. A. Rivaud.* 5 vols. 4to. Paris, 1848–51.

LENOIR (ALEX.) *Atlas des Monumens des Arts libéraux, mécaniques, et industriels de la France, depuis les Gaulois jusqu'au règne de François I.* Folio. Paris, 1828.

—— *Musée des Monumens Français; ou, Description historique et chronologique des Statues en Marbre et en Bronze, Bas-reliefs et Tombeaux, des Hommes et des Femmes célèbres, pour servir à l'Histoire de France et à celle de l'Art. Ornée de gravures et augmentée d'une Dissertation sur les Costumes de chaque siècle.* 6 vols. 8vo. Paris, 1800–6.

MARRYAT (J.) *Collections towards a History of Pottery and Porcelain in the Fifteenth, Sixteenth, Seventeenth, and Eighteenth Centuries, with a Description of the Manufacture; a Glossary, and a List of Monograms. Illustrated with Coloured Plates and Woodcuts.* 8vo. London, 1850.

MORLEY (H.) *Palissy the Potter. The Life of Bernard Palissy of Saintes, his Labours and Discoveries in Art and Science, with an Outline of his Philosophical Doctrines, and a Translation of Illustrative Selections from his Works.* 2 vols. 8vo. London, 1852.

PASSERI (J. B.) *Histoire des Peintures sur Majoliques faites à Pèsari et dans les lieux circonvoisins, décrite par Giambattista Passeri (de Pésaro). Traduite de l'Italien et suivie d'un Appendice par Henri Delange.* 8vo. Paris, 1853.

QUERIERE (E. DE LA). *Essai sur les Girouettes, Epis, Crêtes, &c., des Anciens Combles et Pignons.* Numerous plates of Ancient Vanes and Terminations of Roofs. Paris, 1846.

RENAISSANCE. *La Fleur de la Science de Pourtraicture et Patrons de Broderie. Façon Arabicque et Ytalique. Cum Privilegio Regis.* 4to. Paris.

REYNARD (O.) *Ornemens des Anciens Maitres des XV., XVI., XVII. et XVIII. Siècles.* 30 plates, comprising copies of some of the most ancient and rare Prints of Ornaments, Alphabets, Silverwork. Folio. Paris, 1844.

SERÉ (F.) *Les Arts Somptuaires de V^e au XVIIe Siècle. Histoire du Costume et de l'Ameublement en Europe, et des Arts que en dependent.* Small 4to. Paris, 1853.

SOMMERARD (A. DU). *Les Arts au Moyen Age.* (Collection of the Hôtel de Cluny.) Text, 5 vols. 8vo.; Plates, 6 vols. Folio. Paris, 1838–46.

VERDIER ET CATTOIS. *Architecture Civile et Domestique, au Moyen Age et à la Renaissance.* 4to. Paris, 1852.

WARING AND MACQUOID. *Examples of Architectural Art in Italy and Spain, chiefly of the 13th and 16th Centuries.* Folio. London, 1850.

WILLEMIN (N. X.) *Monuments Français inédits, pour servir à l'Histoire des Arts, depuis le VIe Siècle jusqu'au commencement du XVIIe. Choix de Costumes civiles et militaires, d'Armes, Armures, Instruments de Musique, Meubles de toute espèce, et de Décorations intérieures et extérieures des Maisons, dessinés, gravés, et colorés d'après les originaux. Classés chronologiquement, et accompagnés d'un texte historique et descriptif, par André Pottier.* 6 vols. small Folio. Paris, 1806–39.

WYATT, M. DIGBY, AND J. B. WARING. *Hand-book to the Renaissance Court in the Crystal Palace, Sydenham.* London, 1854.

WYATT, M. DIGBY. *Metal Work and its Artistic Design.* London, 1851.

The introductions to the Renaissance and Italian sections in *The Grammar of Ornament* were prepared by Sir Matthew Digby Wyatt (1820–77). He came from a distinguished family of architects and participated in a number of prestigious building projects. In particular, he pioneered the Renaissance revival style, his finest work in this vein being the Durbar Court at the India Office in Whitehall (1867–68). He also tried his hand at more exotic forms, designing the oriental ironwork at London's Paddington station (1852–54) and an Islamic billiard room in Kensington Palace Gardens (1864). Wyatt served on the executive committee for the Great Exhibition, and collaborated closely with Jones on the subsequent displays at Sydenham.

1

2

3

4

5

6

7

PLATE LXXIV

1, 5, 7 Bas-reliefs from the Church of Sta. Maria dei Miracoli, Venice.
2 Bas-relief from the Scuola di San Marco, Venice.
3, 4 Bas-reliefs from the Church of San Michele in Murano, Venice.
6 Bas-relief forming the continuation upwards of Fig. 2.
8, 9 Bas-reliefs from the Scala dei Giganti, Venice.

8

9

Although it was not on the same scale as the classical or Gothic revivals, the Renaissance style did enjoy a return to favor in the nineteenth century. The first signs were apparent in 1802, when John Nash (1752–1835) designed the charming Italianate villa of Cronkhill. The chief exponent of the style, however, was Sir Charles Barry (1795–1860). He created two London clubs—the Travellers' (1830–32) and the Reform (1838–41) —in the guise of Renaissance palaces, and this led to similar work on a series of country houses. These included Trentham Hall in Staffordshire (1834–42) and Cliveden in Buckinghamshire (1850–51).

1

2

3

4

5

6

7

8

9

10

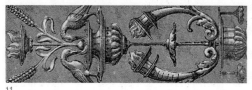

11

12

PLATE LXXV

1 From the first Ghiberti Gate of the Baptistery, Florence.
2, 8 From a Collection of Casts taken under the superintendence of Professor Varny, from the principal Cinque-cento Monuments of Genoa.
3, 4, 5, 9, 11 From Genoa.
6 From the Church of Santi Giovanni e Paolo, Venice.
10 From Venice.
12 From the Hôtel Bourgtheroulde, Rouen.

Most of the designs on these pages are taken from funerary sculptures. Commissioned by Pope Julius II, the lavishly carved tombs of Cardinals Sforza and Basso della Rovere (No. 9) are among the most celebrated works of Andrea Sansovino (*ca.* 1467–1529). More notable still, however, is Germain Pilon's sculpture of the *Three Graces* (1561–62, No. 8). This formed part of a monument containing the heart of King Henry II. Pilon (*ca.* 1525-90) was a Frenchman, but Wyatt elected to discuss his art in the next chapter *(see pages 430–31),* owing to the strong Italianate influences in his work.

1

3

2

4

5 6 7 8

9

10

PLATE LXXVI

1 Bas-relief from a Collection of Casts of the best Cinque-cento Ornaments of Genoa, taken under the superintendence of Professor Varny.
2 Bas-relief from the Church of Sta. Maria dei Miracoli, Venice.
3–5, 7 Bas-reliefs from Genoa.
6 Bas-relief from the Martinengo Tomb, Brescia.
8 Bas-relief from the Base of the "Trois Graces" of Germain Pilon in the Louvre.
9 Bas-relief by Andrea Sansovino, from the Church of Sta. Maria del Popolo, Rome.
10 Bas-relief from the Hôtel Bourgtheroulde, Rouen.

Jones and Wyatt were able to include a very wide selection of artworks in this chapter because of changing perceptions about the Renaissance. It had traditionally been viewed as a revival in the field of arts and letters, but in the mid-nineteenth century it was broadened to describe an entire historical period. The most influential study came from the Swiss historian Jacob Burckhardt (1818–97), whose book, *The Civilization of the Renaissance in Italy* (1860), proved a milestone in this field.

PLATE LXXVII

1–3 Ornaments enamelled on Copper in the early Limoges Champlevé style, Hôtel Cluny Museum, Paris.

4–8 Ditto, of a later period.

9 Ornaments from the background of a Picture, Hôtel Cluny.

10, 11 Enamels on Gold Ground, from the Louvre.

12 Silver Inlay in Ivory, of the Sixteenth Century, Hôtel Cluny.

13 From a Casket, Hôtel Cluny.

14 From a Powder-horn in Iron of the Sixteenth Century, Hôtel Cluny.

15–17 Similar objects in Boxwood, Hôtel Cluny.

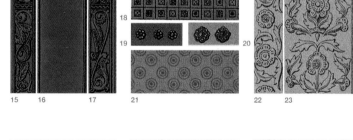

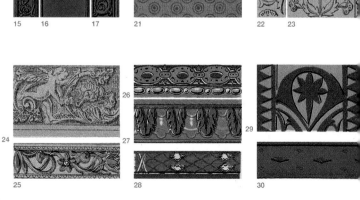

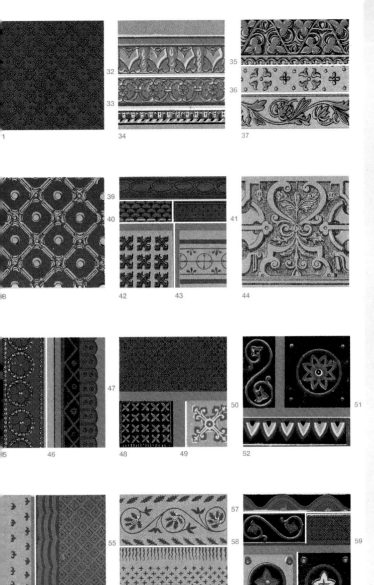

PLATE LXXVII

18–20 From Sixteenth-century Limoges Enamels, Hôtel Cluny.
21 From ditto, Louvre.
22, 23 From Pottery of the Sixteenth Century, Louvre.
24 Portion of an Ebony Cabinet of the Sixteenth Century, Hôtel Cluny.
25 Inlaid Ornament on a Dagger Sheath, Sixteenth Century, Hôtel Cluny.
26–28 Enamels on Gold Ground, Sixteenth Century, Louvre.
29 Limoges Champlevé Enamel on Copper, Hôtel Cluny.
30 Painted Ornaments, Hôtel Cluny.
31 From the Armour of Henri III., Louvre.
32–34 From Goldsmiths' Work of the Sixteenth Century, Louvre.
35–37 From Metal Work, Louvre.
38 From the Armour of François II., Louvre.
39–41 Repoussé Ornaments in Copper, Hôtel Cluny.
42, 43 Limoges Champlevé Enamel, Hôtel Cluny.
44 A Metal Plate, Louvre.
45, 46 From a Picture in Limoges Painted Enamel, Sixteenth Century, Hôtel Cluny.
47 Ornament in Copper, from the above.
48 Ivory Inlay in Ebony, from the above.
49 Painted Ornament, from the above.
50–53 Limoges Champlevé Enamel, from the above.
54–56 From Accessories to Pictures, from the above.
57–61 Limoges Champlevé Enamel.

Majolica was the most popular form of Italian pottery. Originating in Spain, it was imported into Italy via Majorca. Early examples had a pronounced Spanish character, but by the late fifteenth century the technique had been absorbed into Italian culture so thoroughly that majolica was used as a generic term for most native forms of lustered earthenware. The style was widely copied in the nineteenth century. Herbert Minton (1793–1858) displayed his version of majolica at the Great Exhibition of 1851, and a similar line was marketed by Wedgwood in 1860. The designs also proved popular in the US, where variants of Italian majolica were produced.

PLATE LXXVIII

Ornaments taken from Specimens of Hispano-Arabic, French, and Italian Earthenware, preserved in the South Kensington Museum, and principally from the Majolican Wares of Pesaro, Gubbio, Urbino, Castel Durante, and other Italian towns of the Fifteenth, Sixteenth, and Seventeenth Centuries.

1

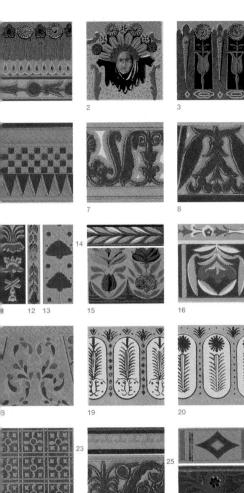

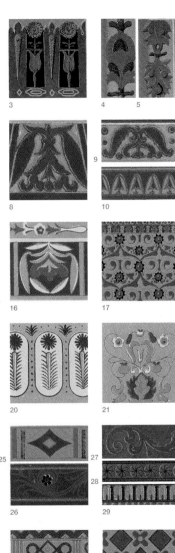

PLATE LXXIX

1–3 Ornaments from the *faience*, or Enamelled Earthenware, of Bernard de Palissy, in the Hôtel Cluny.

4–10 From Specimens of Majolica, in the Hôtel Cluny.

11–13 From *faience* of the Fifteenth Century, in the Hôtel Cluny.

14–18, 21 From *faience* of the Sixteenth Century, in the Louvre.

19, 20 From Porcelain of the Seventeenth Century, in the Louvre.

22–30, 33 From Earthenware, French, Spanish, and Italian, in the Hôtel Cluny.

31, 32 From the German Pottery, *en grès*, with Painted Glaze of the Sixteenth Century, in the Hôtel Cluny.

34 From the Louvre.

RENAISSANCE

The use of the word "faience" as a generic term for glazed earthenware was more common in Jones's day. It derives from the Italian town of Faenza, which was a major center for ceramics throughout the fifteenth and sixteenth centuries. The decoration of Renaissance pottery had a significant impact on Victorian design. Its influence can be seen in a number of prestigious building plans, most notably at London's Victoria and Albert Museum. Here, some of the earliest courts and galleries were designed by Godfrey Sykes (1824–66), an avid supporter of the Renaissance revival. He used a wide variety of materials, including terra cotta, majolica, and mosaic.

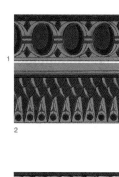

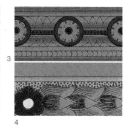

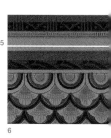

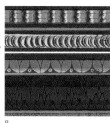

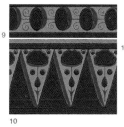

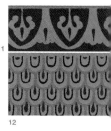

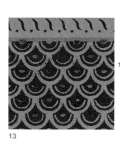

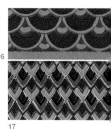

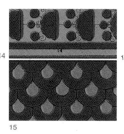

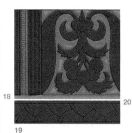

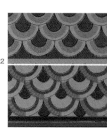

25

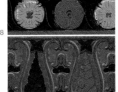

26

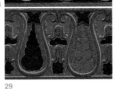

28

27

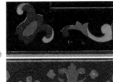

31

29

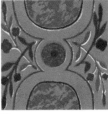

32

33

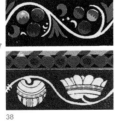

37

34 35 36

38

39

41

42

PLATE LXXX

1, 2 Ornaments from *faience*.
3–6 Ornaments from *faience* of the Sixteenth Century.
7–10 Ornaments from *faience* of the Seventeenth Century.
11, 12 From *faience* with Metallic Lustre.
13 From a Vase in Venetian Glass of the Sixteenth Century.
14–21 From *faience* of the Sixteenth Century.
22, 23 From *faience* of an Earlier Date.
24–27 From *Grès Flamand*, or Earthenware.
28–32 From *faience* of the Sixteenth Century.
33 From a Carved-wood Panel of the Seventeenth Century.
34–38 From Enamelled Earthenware.
39–42 From Silk Embroidery on Velvet.

N.B.—The whole of the Specimens on this Plate have been derived from the Hôtel Cluny, Paris.

RENAISSANCE

🅐 Built in 1485–98, the Hôtel de Cluny is one of the finest pre-Revolutionary structures in Paris. It was created as the official residence of the abbots of Cluny (an important Benedictine monastery). In essence, the *hôtel* was constructed in the late Gothic style, but some of its ornamental details proved suitable for inclusion in this chapter. By Jones's day the place had already lost its religious links and was operating as a museum. Today, as the Musée Cluny, it is devoted to the art and culture of the Middle Ages. Its most famous exhibit is the sixteenth-century tapestry of *The Lady and the Unicorn.*

PLATE LXXXI

1 From a Sideboard carved in wood, dated 1554, in the Hôtel-Cluny.
2 Wood Panels of the Sixteenth Century, in the Hôtel Cluny.
3 From an Oak Chair-back, in the Hôtel Cluny.
4–6 From Carved-wood Stalls of the Fifteenth Century, in the Hôtel Cluny.
7, 8, 9, 11, 25, 26, 36, 38 From Furniture, in the Hôtel Cluny.

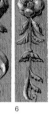

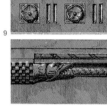

23

23

24

PLATE LXXXI

10 End of a Beam of the end of the Fifteenth Century, in the Hôtel Cluny.

12, 13, 20, 21, 37, 40 From Furniture of the Sixteenth Century, in the Hôtel Cluny.

14, 15 From Furniture of the Fifteenth Century, in the Hôtel Cluny.

16 From a Sideboard, in the Hôtel Cluny.

17 Shutter Panels of the end of the Fifteenth Century, in the Hôtel Cluny.

18 Carved Ornament from the Louvre.

19 From a Boxwood Comb, in the Hôtel Cluny.

22 Stone Balustrading, from the Château d'Anet.

23 Stone Carving from the Louvre.

24 From a Chimneypiece, in the Hôtel Cluny.

27–30 Carving in Marble from the celebrated Basin in the Fountain of the Château Gaillon, now in the Louvre.

31, 32 Stone Carving, Seventeenth Century, in the Louvre.

33 Wood Carving, from the Hôtel Cluny.

34, 35 From the Fountain of the Château Gaillon, Louvre.

39 From the Stock of an Arquebus of the Sixteenth Century, in the Hôtel Cluny.

26

27

28

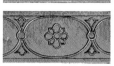

29

31

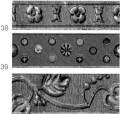

32

33

35

36

37

38

39

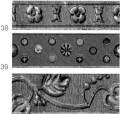

40

The merits of the Renaissance revival style aroused a good deal of controversy in Victorian times. It was promoted by some organizations, among them London's School of Design (now the Royal College of Art), and by journals such as *L'Art et L'Industrie*. In other quarters, however, the style provoked considerable hostility. One of its fiercest detractors was the critic John Ruskin (1819–1900). His views were shared by some members of the Pre-Raphaelite circle. As their name suggests, they advocated a return to the simpler and more truthful values of the age that preceded Raphael (1483–1520)—then regarded as the quintessential Renaissance artist.

1

2

3

4

5

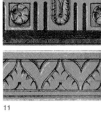

6

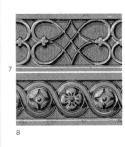

7

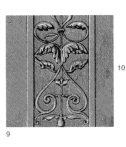

8

9

10

11

12

13

14

15

16

18

19

PLATE LXXXII

1–9 Carved Ornament from Oak Furniture of the Sixteenth Century, in the Hôtel Cluny.

10, 11, 19, 34 From the Bed of François I., in the Hôtel Cluny.

12, 13, 14, 32, 33 From Oak Furniture of the Sixteenth Century, in the Hôtel Cluny.

15–17 From a Sideboard of the Fifteenth Century.

18 From an Oak Sideboard, dated 1524, in the Hôtel Cluny.

20–29 From Furniture of the Sixteenth Century, in the Hôtel Cluny.

30, 31 Panels of Shutters of the end of the Fifteenth Century, in the Hôtel Cluny.

21

23

22

24

26

27

28

29

31

32

33

34

CHAPTER XVIII

ELIZABETHAN ORNAMENT

Prior to describing the characteristics of what is commonly termed the Elizabethan style, it will be well to trace briefly the rise and progress of the revival of the Antique in England to its final triumph over the late Gothic style in the sixteenth century. The first introduction of the Revival into England dates from the year 1518, when Torrigiano was employed by Henry VIII. to design a monument in memory of Henry VII., which still exists in Westminster Abbey, and which is almost a pure example of the Italian school at that period. In the same style, and of about the same date, is the monument of the Countess of Richmond at Westminster; Torrigiano designed this also, and, very shortly afterwards, went to Spain, leaving, however, behind him several Italians attached to the service of Henry, by whom a taste for the same style could not be otherwise than propagated. Amongst the names preserved to us at this time are Girolamo da Trevigi, employed as an architect and engineer, Bartolomeo Penni, and Antony

Toto (del' Nunziata), painters, and the well-known Florentine sculptor, Benedetto da Rovezzano: to these may be added, though at a later period, John of Padua, who appears to have been more extensively employed than any of the others, and, amongst other important works, designed old Somerset House in 1549. But it was not a purely Italian influence which aided in the development of the new style in this country; and already we find the names of Gerard Hornebande, or Horebout, of Ghent, Lucas Cornelis, John Brown, and Andrew Wright, serjeant-painters to the king. In the year 1524 the celebrated Holbein came to England, and to him and John of Padua is mainly due the naturalization of the new style in this country, modified by the individual genius and German education of the one, and the local models and reminiscences of the other, by whom many features of the earlier Venetian school of the Revival were reproduced, with great modifications, however, in this country. Holbein died in 1554, but John of Padua survived him many years, and designed the noble mansion of Longleat about the year 1570. On the occasion of the funeral of Edward VI. A.D. 1553, we find in the rule for the procession (*Archœol.* vol. xii. 1796) the names of Antony Toto (before mentioned), Nicholas Lyzarde, painters, and Nicholas Modena, carver; all the other names of master-masons, &c., being English. Somewhat later, during the reign of Elizabeth, we find only two Italian names, Federigo Zucchero (whose house at Florence, said to have been designed by himself, would rather serve to show that the English style of architecture had influenced him, than *vice versâ*), and Pietro Ubaldini, painter of illuminated books.

It is from Holland that, at this period, when the Elizabethan style may be justly said to have been formed, we must look for the greater number of artists: Lucas de Heere of Ghent, Cornelius Ketel of Gouda, Marc Garrard of Bruges, H. C. Vroom of Haarlem, painters; Richard Stevens, a Hollander, who executed the Sussex monument in Boreham church, Suffolk; and Theodore Haveus of Cleves, who was architect of the four gates, Humilitatis, Vertutis, Honoris, et Sapientiæ, at Caius College, Cambridge, and, moreover, designed and executed the monument of Dr. Caius about the year 1573. Besides these we approach now a goodly array of English names, the most remarkable being the architects,—Robert and Bernard Adams, the Smithsons, Bradshaw, Harrison, Holte, Thorpe, and Shute (the latter, author of the first scientific work on Architecture in English, A.D. 1563), Hilliard the goldsmith and jeweller, and Isaac Oliver, the portrait-painter. Most of the above-named architects were employed also during the early part of the seventeenth century, at which time the knowledge of the new style was still more extended by Sir Henry Wotton's "Elements of Architecture."* Bernard Jansen and Gerard Chrismas, both natives of Holland, were much in vogue during the reign of James I. and Charles I., and to them is due the façade of Northumberland House, Strand.

Before the close of James I.'s reign—*i.e.* in 1619—the name of Inigo Jones brings us very nearly to the complete downfall of the Elizabethan style, on the occasion of the rebuilding of Whitehall Palace; an example

---

* The works of Lomazzo and De Lorme are said to have been translated into English during the reign of Elizabeth, but I have never met with copies of them.

which could hardly fail of producing a complete revolution in Art. The Palladian style of the sixteenth century had been, moreover, introduced even before this by Sir Horatio Pallavicini, in his house (now destroyed) at Little Shelford, Cambridgeshire; and although Nicholas Stone and his son, architects and sculptors, appears to have continued the old style, especially in sepulchral monuments, it was displaced speedily for the more pure, but less picturesque fashion of the best Italian schools.

Thus, taking the date of Torrigiano's work at Westminster, 1519, and that of the commencement of Whitehall by Inigo Jones in 1619, we may include most of the works of art during that century as within the so-called Elizabethan period.

In the foregoing list of artists we perceive a fluctuating mixture of Italian, Dutch, and English names. In the first period, or during the reign of Henry VIII., the Italian names are clearly dominant, and amongst them we are justified in placing Holbein himself, since his ornamental works in metal, &c.—for example, the goblet designed by him for Jane Seymour, and a dagger and sword, probably executed for the king—exhibit a purity and gracefulness of style worthy of Cellini himself. The arabesques painted by him in the large picture of Henry VIII. and his family at Hampton Court, though more grotesque and heavy, are still close imitations of cinque-cento models; and the ceiling of the Royal Chapel of St. James's Palace, designed by him in 1540, is quite in the style of many rich examples at Venice and Mantua.

During the reign of Elizabeth we meet with a great preponderance of Dutch names, for this country was bound both by political and religious sympathy with Holland; and although the greater number are described as painters only, yet we must remember how closely all the Arts were connected in those days, painters being frequently employed to design models for ornament, both painted and carved, and even for architecture; and in the accessories of their own pictures was found frequent scope for ornamental design,—as, for example, may be seen in the portrait of Queen Mary, painted by Lucas de Heere, having panelled compartments of geometrical interlaced forms, filled up with jewelled foliage. During the early part of Queen Elizabeth's reign we are, then, justified in concluding that a very important influence must have been exercised on English Art through the medium of the Protestant States of the Low Countries, and of Germany also.[†] It was during this period, also, that Heidelberg Castle was principally built (1556–1559); and it would not appear unlikely that it may have had an effect on English Art when we remember that the Princess Elizabeth, daughter of James I., held court here as Queen of Bohemia, at the beginning of the seventeenth century.

At the latter part of Elizabeth's reign, and during that of James I., English artists are numerous, and appear, with the exception of Jansen and Chrismas, to have the field to themselves; consequently it is at this period that we expect to find a more decidedly native school. And, in fact, it is now that we meet with the names of English designers connected with such

[†] The remarkable monument of Sir Francis Vere (time, James I.) at Westminster, is almost identical in design with that of Englebert of Nassau, in the cathedral of Breda (sixteenth century).

buildings (and with their concomitant decoration) as Audley End, Holland House, Woollaton, Knowle, and Burleigh.

Thus we may expect to meet with the purest Italian ornament in the works of the artists of Henry VIII.'s reign; and this will be found to be the case, not only on the subjects we have already mentioned, but in the examples given in Plate LXXXIII. *(pages 414–15)*, Nos. 1 and 4. During Elizabeth's reign we perceive but a slight imitation of Italian models, and a complete adoption of the style of ornament practised by the decorative artists of Germany and the Netherlands. In the reign of James I. we find the same style continued by English artists, but generally in a larger manner, as at Nos. 6 and 10, Plate LXXXIV. *(pages 416–17)*, from Aston Hall, built at the latter part of his reign. There is little, then, that can be justly termed original in the character of the ornament of this period, and it is simply a modification of foreign models. Even at the close of the fifteenth century may be seen the germs of the open scroll-work in many decorative works in Italy, such as stained glass and illuminated books. The beautifully executed ornamental borders, &c. of Giulio Clovio (1498–1578), pupil of Giulio Romano, present in many parts all the character of Elizabethan scroll, band, nail-head, and festoon-work: the same may be remarked of the stained-glass windows of the Laurentian Library, Florence, by Giovanni da Udine (1487–1561); and still more noticeable is it in the frontispieces of Serlio's great work on Architecture, published in Paris in 1515. As regards another main feature in Elizabethan ornament, viz. the complicated and fanciful interlaced bands, we must seek its origin in the numerous and excellent designs of the class of engravers known as the "petits-maîtres" of Germany and the Netherlands, and more particularly those of Aldegrever, Virgilius Solis of Nuremberg, Daniel Hopfer of Augsburg, and Theodore de Bry, who sent forth to the world a great number of engraved ornamental designs during the sixteenth century. Nor should we forget to mention, at the close of this century, the very fanciful and thoroughly Elizabethan compositions, architectural and ornamental, of W. Dieterlin, which Vertue asserts were used by Chrismas in his designs for the façade of Northumberland House. These were the principal sources from which the so-called Elizabethan style of ornament was mainly founded; and we may here remark, that whilst it is evident that decoration ought, and indeed in some cases must, vary in its character, according to the different subjects and materials on which it is applied, and whilst the Italian masters, recognising this æsthetical fact, did in most instances carefully abstain from carrying the pictorial style into sculptured and architectural works, confining it to its just limits, such as illuminated books, engravings, Damascene metal-work, and other purely ornamental subjects,—so, on the other hand, the artists employed in England during the period of which we treat carried the pictorial style of ornament into every branch of Art, and reproduced even on their buildings the unfettered fancies of the decorative artists as they received them through the medium of the engraver.

As regards the characteristics of Elizabethan ornament, they may be described as consisting chiefly of a grotesque and complicated variety of pierced scroll-work, with curled edges; interlaced bands, sometimes on a geometrical pattern, but generally flowing and capricious, as seen, for example, on No. 10, Plate LXXXIII. *(pages 414–15)*, and Nos. 24 and 26, Plate LXXXIV. *(pages 416–17)*; strap and nail-head bands; curved and broken outlines; festoons, fruit and drapery, interspersed with roughly-executed figures of human beings; grotesque monsters and animals, with here and there large and flowing designs of natural branch and leaf ornament, as shown in No. 3, Plate LXXXIII., a noble example of which still exists also on the great gallery ceiling at Burton Agnes, in Yorkshire; rustications of ball and diamond work, panelled compartments often filled with foliage or coats-of-arms; grotesque arch-stones and brackets are freely used; and the carving, whether in stone or wood, is marked by great boldness and effect, though roughly executed. Unlike the earliest examples of the Revival on the Continent, especially in France and Spain, these ornaments are not applied to Gothic forms; but the groundwork or architectural mass is essentially Italian in its nature (except in the case of windows): consisting of a rough application of the orders of architecture one over another, external walls with cornice and balustrade, and internal walls bounded with frieze and cornice, with flat or covered ceilings; even the gable ends, with their convex and concave outlines, so common in the style, were founded on models of the early Renaissance school at Venice.

The coloured patterns of diaper work—on wood, on the dresses of the monumental statues, and on tapestries,—show in most cases more justness and purity of design than the carved work: the colours, moreover, being rich and strongly marked. A great quantity of this kind of work, especially the arras with which walls and furniture were constantly decorated, no doubt came from the looms of Flanders, and in some cases from Italy, since the first native factory of the kind was established at Mortlake in the year 1619.

Nos. 5, 7, 8, and 16, Plate LXXXV. *(pages 418–19)*, are the most Italian in their character of the examples given; No. 8 being stated, indeed, to be the design of an Italian artist. Nos. 3, 15, and 17, also of a good Italian character, being taken from portraits of the time of Elizabeth and James I., are probably the work of Dutch or Italian artists. Nos. 1, 6, 9, 10 and 14, though in the Italian taste, are marked by much originality; whilst Nos. 11 and 18 are in the ordinary Elizabethan style. Fine examples of coloured ornament are still preserved in the pall belonging to the Ironmongers' Company, date 1515, the ground of which is gold, with a rich and flowing purple pattern; similar in every respect to the painted antependiums of several altars at Santo Spirito, Florence (fifteenth century), and probably of Italian manufacture.

At St. Mary's Church, Oxford, is preserved a rich pulpit hanging of gold ground with a blue pattern; and at Hardwicke Hall, Derbyshire, is a fine piece of tapestry of a yellow silk ground, with a crimson and gold thread pattern. But, perhaps, the most beautiful specimen of this kind of work is in the possession of the Saddlers' Company, a gold pattern on a crimson velvet pall,[§] made in the early part of the sixteenth century. Although in

[§] For these, see Shaw's very beautiful work on the "Arts of the Middle Ages."

those we have referred to, and in the examples given in Plate LXXXV. *(pages 418–19),* two colours only are principally relied on for effect, yet in other subjects every variety of colour is freely used; gilding, however, being generally predominant over colour—a taste probably derived from Spain, where the discovery of gold in the New World led to an extravagant use of it as a means of decoration in the reigns of Charles V. and Philip II. An example of this style may be seen in the magnificent chimneypiece, with elaborate gilt carving combined with black marble, now preserved in the Governor's room at the Charterhouse.

By the middle of the seventeenth century the more marked characteristics of the style had completely died out, and we lose sight of that richness, variety, and picturesqueness; which, although deficient in good guiding principles, and liable to fall into straggling confusion, could not fail to impress the beholder with a certain impression of nobility and grandeur.

J. B. WARING.

October, 1856.

BOOKS REFERRED TO

H. SHAW. *Dresses and Decorations of the Middle Ages.*

—— *The Decorative Arts of the Middle Ages.*

—— *Details of Elizabethan Architecture.*

C. J. RICHARDSON. *Studies of Ornamental Design.*

—— *Architectural Remains of the Reigns of Elizabeth and James I.*

—— *Studies from Old English Mansions.*

JOSEPH NASH. *The Mansions of England in the Olden Times.*

S. C. HALL. *The Baronial Halls of England.*

JOSEPH GWILT. *Encyclopœdia of Architecture.*

HORACE WALPOLE. *Anecdotes of Painting in England.*

Archœlogia, vol. xii. (1796).

The Builder (several Articles by C. J. RICHARDSON), 1846.

DALLAWAY. *Anecdotes of the Arts in England.*

CLAYTON. *The Ancient Timber Edifices of England.*

BRITTON. *Architectural Antiquities of Great Britain.*

ELIZABETHAN

There was a revival of interest in Elizabethan architecture in the early decades of the nineteenth century, largely as an expression of patriotic sentiment. This was emphasized in 1835 when the organizers of the competition for the new Houses of Parliament specified that the design should be in the "Gothic or Elizabethan style." This attitude was reinforced after the accession of Queen Victoria in 1837, when pundits were eager to find echoes of the reign of "Good Queen Bess." Significantly this coincided with major studies of the style by C. J. Richardson in 1837 and John Shaw in 1839.

1   2   3

4   5   6   7

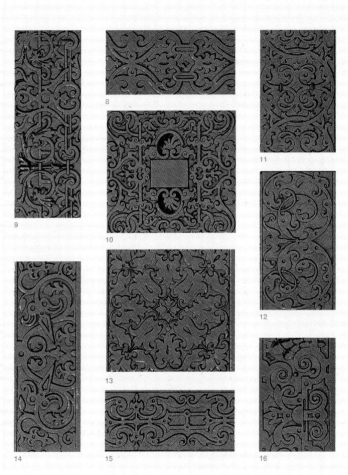

PLATE LXXXIII

1 Frieze, from Goodrich Court, Herefordshire. Time of Henry VIII. or Elizabeth. Flemish Workmanship.

2 Wood Carving over a Doorway to a House near Norwich. Elizabeth.

3, 7 Wood Carving from Burton Agnes in Yorkshire. James I.

4 The centre portion of the Ornament in a Stone Chimneypiece, formerly in the Royal Palace, Westminster, now in the Robing Room of the Judges' Court of Queen's Bench.

5 Stone Carving from an old House, Bristol. James I.

6 Ornaments in a Church Pew, Wiltshire. Elizabeth.

8, 10, 13 Wood Carving, from Montacute, in Somersetshire. Elizabeth.

9 Wood Carving, from a Chimneypiece, Old Palace, Bromley, near Bow. James I.

11 Wood Carving, from the Hall of Trinity College, Cambridge.

12, 15 Carving in Stone from the Tomb at Westminster Abbey. James I.

14 Wood Carving, from a Pew, Pavenham Church, Bedfordshire. James I.

16 Stone Carving, from Crewe Hall. James I.

ELIZABETHAN

⁂ This chapter includes many examples of strapwork, one of the most common elements of Elizabethan decoration. It gained its name because of the resemblance to curling straps of leather. In Tudor times the motif was used in two very different fields—printing and architecture. Engravers of the period used it to decorate the borders or title cartouches of illustrations, which featured in early printed books. In architecture strapwork was often employed on ornamental parapets or in the decoration of table tombs. The ultimate source of the motif is uncertain, but it was popularized in the West by the mannerist artists who were working at Fontainebleau during the 1530s.

PLATE LXXXIV

1 Painted Ornament, Staircase, Holland House, Kensington. James I.
2 Stone Ornament from one of the Tombs at Westminster. Elizabeth.
3 From an Old Chair. Elizabeth.

18

7   19

0   21   22

24

3

5   26   27   28

PLATE LXXXIV

4, 18, 26 Stone Diapers, from Crewe Hall, Cheshire. James I.

5, 12 From Burton Agnes. The last of late date pub. Charles II.

6 Wood Carving, Aston Hall, Warwickshire. Late James I.

7 Wood Carving, Holland House.

8 Ditto, ditto.

9 Stone Ornament, Burton Agnes, Yorkshire. James I.

10 Wood Diaper, Aston Hall. James I.

11 Wood Diaper, Old Palace, Enfield. Elizabeth.

13, 28 Wood Ornaments, from the Pewing, Pavenham Church, Bedfordshire. James I.

14, 25 Ornaments from Burton Agnes, Yorkshire. James I.

15, 23 Wood Ornaments, in Peter Paul Pindar's House, Bishopsgate. James I.

16, 17 Wood Ornament, from Burton Agnes, Yorkshire. James I.

19 From a Tomb, Aston Church. James I.

20 From a Cabinet. James I. French Workmanship.

21 Ornament on a Bethesdan Marble Chimneypiece, Little Charlton House, Kent.

22 From a Tomb, Westminster Abbey. James I.

24 Wood Carving, from the Staircase, Aston Hall, Warwickshire. Late James I.

27 Plaster Enrichment to a Panel Ceiling at Cromwell Hall, Highgate. Charles II.

417

🎕 Embroidery and tapestry were two of the chief art forms that William Morris and his colleagues sought to revive when they embarked on their venture as designers. Britain had once enjoyed a great reputation in this field. In its day, the type of embroidery known as *opus anglicanum* ("English work") was the envy of Europe. Morris hoped to revive these glories when he and his friends decorated his Red House at Bexleyheath in the early 1860s. For this, they produced a number of embroidered wall hangings, using authentic, historical techniques. The results were shown at the International Exhibition of 1862 and helped to cement the reputation of Morris's firm.

1

2

3

4

5

6

7

8

10

11

2

13

14

15

6

17

18

PLATE LXXXV

1, 9, 14 Diapers from Burton Agnes, Yorkshire.
2 Wood Diaper, from the Hall of Trinity College, Cambridge.
3, 4, 15, 17 Patterns from Dresses, Old Portraits. Elizabeth or James I.
5 Pattern from Drapery in a Tomb at Westminster. Elizabeth.
6 Wood Diaper, from an old House at Enfield. James I.
7 From a Damask Cover to a Chair at Knowle, in Kent. James I.
8 Appliqué Needlework. James I. or Charles I. By an Italian Artist.
10 Plaster Diaper, from an old House near Tottenham Church. Elizabeth.
11, 18 Wood Diaper, from the Hall of Trinity College, Cambridge. Late James I.
12 From Drapery in a Tomb at Westminster. Elizabeth.
13 Needlework Tapestry. Elizabeth. From the collection of Mr. Mackinlay. The ground, light green; the subject in light yellow, blue, or green; the outline, yellow silk cord.
16 Appliqué Needlework. James I. or Charles I. In the collection of Mr. Mackinlay. The ground in dark red; the ornament in yellow silk; outline, yellow silk cord.

CHAPTER XIX

ITALIAN ORNAMENT

S hortly after the commencement of the sixteenth century, that movement toward the restoration of the antique which we have recognised in Italy as fragmentary and imperfect during the fifteenth, became systematised, and consequently invigorated, mainly through the means of popularisation afforded by the arts of printing and engraving. Through them translations of Vitruvius and Alberti, copiously illustrated and ably commented upon, were speedily in the possession of every designer of eminence in the country, and without its limits also; while, before the close of the century, the treatises of Serlio, Palladio, Vignola, and Rusconi, presented permanent records of the zeal with which the monuments of antiquity had been studied. But inasmuch as the requirements of the Italian Social system of the sixteenth century differed from those of the Imperial ages of Rome, so of a necessity the nature of the monuments created to supply those wants materially differed. In the Renaissance styles of the fifteenth century the artist's attention had been

mainly directed to the imitation of ancient ornament; in the sixteenth, however, it was principally the restoration of ancient proportions, both of the five orders and of architectural symmetry generally, that engaged the designer's attention; pure ornament having been to a great extent neglected in its details, and considered only in its mass as a decorative adjunct to architecture. Those arts which during the fifteenth century had been so frequently united in the persons of the *maestri*, under whom great monuments had been carried into execution, in the sixteenth became individualised. The genius of such intellectual giants as Raffaelle and Michael Angelo could alone maintain the triple attributes of painters, architects, and sculptors, in due relative sub-ordination; when, in after times, men such as Bernini and Pietro da Cortona attempted similar combinations, the result was little else than general confusion and failure. As the rules of Art became more complex, academies arose in which the division-of-labour system was introduced. The consequences, with certain rare and notable exceptions, were obvious; architects thought of little else but plans, sections, and elevations, in which the setting out of columns, arches, pilasters, entablatures, &c., was all in all; painters worked more in their studios, and less in the buildings, their works were to adorn; forgetting altogether general decorative effect, and looking only to anatomical precision, powerful chiar'oscuro, masterly composition, and breadth of tone and handling. Sculptors of a high class deserted ornamental carving and gave their attention, almost exclusively, to isolated statues and groups, or monuments in which general effects of beauty were made subservient to the development of the plastic features alone. Ornament was left in a great degree to accident or caprice in its design, and to second-rate artists in its execution. Favourable specimens of such ornaments may be seen in our woodcuts. The painted arabesques of the Italian style, and the *stucchi* with which they were occasionally accompanied, form so remarkable an exception to the above, that it will be well to reserve them for special notice. Although the architecture which Raffaelle has left to us in the Pandolfini Palace at Florence, and the Caffarelli, late Stoppani, at Rome, is excellent; it is in his connexion with the

VERTICAL
ORNAMENT FROM
GENOA

subject of arabesque that his celebrity as an ornamentist consists, and we shall not therefore further allude to him here. Neither shall we dwell upon the works of Baldassare Peruzzi, interesting though they be, since, so far as ornament was concerned, they approached so closely to the antique as to offer no striking individuality. Bramante, too, is to be regarded rather as a Renaissance artist than in any other light. It is to the great Florentine, whose fervid genius, impatient of restraint, broke away from tradition, that we must look for that germ of self-willed originality that infected all his contemporaries in every department of art, and engendered a license which, it is vain to deny, ultimately, and in feebler hands than his, resulted in a departure from taste and refinement in every branch of art.

Michael Angelo was born in 1474 of the noble Florentine family of the Buonarrotti, descendants of the Counts of Canossa: he was a pupil of Domenico Ghirlandaio; and having early distinguished himself by his talent for sculpture, he was invited to study in the school founded for its culture by Lorenzo de Medici. On the banishment of the Medici family from Florence in 1494, Michael Angelo retired to Bologna, where he worked at the tomb of St. Dominic; after some little time he returned to Florence, and, before he was twenty-three years of age, he had executed the celebrated "Cupid," which was the cause of his being invited to Rome, and also his "Bacchus." At Rome, amongst many other works by him, is the "Pieta" sculptured by order of Cardinal d'Amboise, and now in St. Peter's. The gigantic statue of "David," at Florence, was his next great performance; and at twenty-nine years of age he returned to Rome, summoned by Julius II. for the purpose of erecting his mausoleum; for this building the "Moses" at San Pietro in Vincoli, and the "Slaves" in the Louvre, were originally destined, but it was completed on a smaller scale than was at first intended. The painting of the Sistine Chapel was the next work undertaken by him, and one of his greatest, whether we regard the sublimity of the performance, or the influence which it exercised on contemporary art, as well as on that of after-times. In 1541 he completed his vast fresco of the "Last Judgment," painted for Pope Paul III. The remainder of his long life was chiefly devoted to the construction of St. Peter's, on which work he was employed at the time of his death, in 1564, and for which he refused all remuneration.

In everything executed during the long life of Michael Angelo the desire for novelty seems to have divided his attention from the study of excellence alone. His daring innovations in ornament are no less striking than in other departments of design. His large broken pediments and mouldings, his sweeping consoles and scrolls, his direct imitation (saving an alloy of exaggeration) of Nature in some of his enrichments, and the amount of plain face he uniformly preserved in his architectural compositions, brought new elements into the field, which were greedily snapped up by men of less inventive power than he himself possessed. The style of the Roman school of design was altogether changed through Michael Angelo; and Giacomo della Porta, Domenico Fontana, Bartolomeo Ammanati, Carlo Maderno, and, last not least, Vignola himself, so far as ornament was concerned, adopted, with a few of his beauties, many of his defects, the greatest being exaggeration of manner. At Florence, Baccio Bandinelli and Benvenuto Cellini were among his ardent admirers and imitators. Happily Venice escaped the contagion in a great degree,—or, at least, resisted its influence longer than almost any other part of Italy. This immunity was due, in a great degree, to the counteracting influence of a genius less hardy than that of Michael Angelo, but far more refined, and scarcely less universal. We allude, of course, to the greatest of the two Sansovinos—Giacopo.

This noble artist was born at Florence, of an ancient family, in the year 1477. Having at an early age displayed a remarkable predisposition for Art, he was placed by his mother with Andrea Contucci of Monte Sansovino (of whom we have briefly spoken in Chapter XVII.), then working at Florence, who, says Vasari, "soon perceived that the young man promised to become very eminent." Their attachment speedily assumed such a character that, being regarded almost as father and son, Jacopo was no longer called "de' Tatti," but "di Sansovino;" and as he was then named so is he called now, and ever will be. Having distinguished himself by his abilities at Florence, and being considered a young man of great genius and excellent character, he was taken to Rome by Giuliano da San Gallo, architect to Pope Julius II. At Rome he attracted the notice of Bramante, and made a large copy in wax of the "Laocoon" (under Bramante's direction), in competition with other artists, among whom was Alonzo Berruguete, the celebrated Spanish architect. Sansovino's was adjudged to be the best, and a cast was taken of it in bronze, which finally coming into the possession of the Cardinal de Lorraine, was taken by him into France in the year 1534. San Gallo falling ill was obliged to leave Rome, and Bramante, therefore, found a dwelling for Jacopo in the same house with Pietro Perugino, who was then painting a ceiling for Pope Julius in the Torre Borgia, and who was so pleased with Jacopo's ability that he caused him to prepare many models in wax for his use. He also became acquainted with Luca Signorelli, Bramantino di Milano, Pincturicchio, Cesare Cesariano, famous for his Commentaries on Vitruvius; and was finally presented to and employed by the Pope (Julius). He was in a fair way of advancement, when a serious illness caused him to return to his native city. Here he recovered, and successfully competed with Bandinelli and others for a large marble figure. He was in continual employment at this time, and among other works he executed for Giovanni Bartolini the beautiful "Bacchus," now in the Gallery degli Uffizii at Florence.

In the year 1514, great preparations being made at Florence for the entry of Leo X., Jacopo was employed in making various designs for triumphal arches and statues, with which the Pontiff was so much pleased, that Jacopo Salviati took his friend Sansovino to kiss the feet of the Pope, by whom he was received very kindly. His Holiness immediately gave him an order to make a design for the façade of San Lorenzo at Florence, which would seem to have given so much satisfaction, that Michael Angelo, who was to compete with him for the control of its construction, would appear to have outwitted Sansovino, and effectually prevented his success; for, says Vasari, "Michael Angelo was determined to keep all for himself." Not disheartened, however, he continued in Rome, and was employed both in sculpture and architecture, and gained the great honour of being the successful competitor for the Church of St. John of the Florentines, against Raffaelle, Antonio da Sangallo, and Balthazar Peruzzi. Whilst superintending the commencement of the works he fell, and was so severely hurt that he left the city. Various causes led to the suspension of the works until the pontificate of Clement, when Jacopo returned and recommenced it. From that period he was engaged in every work of importance at Rome, until, on the 6th of May, 1527, that city was taken and sacked by the French.

Jacopo sought refuge in Venice, intending to visit France, where the King had offered him employment. The Doge, Andrea Gritti, however, persuaded him to remain, and to undertake the restoration of the cupolas of St. Mark's. This work he performed so satisfactorily, that he was appointed Proto-Maestro to the Republic, assigned a house, and provided with a stipend. The duties of this office he performed with such sagacity and diligence, that by various improvements and alterations of the city he materially added to the income of the State. Amongst his finest works here—and, indeed, among the finest examples of Italian Art anywhere—are to be noted, the Libreria Vecchia, the Zecca or Mint, the Palaces Cornaro and Moro, the Loggia round the Campanile of St. Mark, the Church of San Georgio dei Greci, the Statues of the Giant's Staircase, the monument of Francesco Veniero, and the bronze gates of the Sacristy. His character as depicted by Vasari (edit. Bohn, vol. v. p. 426) is eminently agreeable, sagacious, amiable, courageous, and active. He appears to have been generally honoured, and had a large school of pupils, amongst whom may be mentioned Tribolo and Solosmeo Danese, Cattaneo Girolamo of Ferrara, Jacopo Colonna of Venice, Luco Lancia of Naples, Bartolomeo Ammanati, Jacopo de Medici of Brescia, and Alessandro Vittoria of Trent. He died on the 2d of November, 1570, aged ninety-three; "and (as Vasari tells us) notwithstanding that the years of his life had come to an end in the pure course of nature, yet all Venice lamented his loss." It is mainly to the happy influence exerted by Sansovino that the School of Venice is indebted for its celebrity in ornamental bronze-work.

Turning from Italy to France, we resume the thread of national progress, interrupted by the introduction into the service of Francis I. (*circa* A.D. 1530) of those Italian artists who formed what is familiarly known as the "School of Fontainebleau." The leading and most popular member of that fraternity was Primaticcio, a master whose style of drawing was founded upon the Michael-Angelesque system of proportion, somewhat attenuated in limb, and moulded into a somewhat more artificial and serpentine line of grace. The manner of arranging and defining drapery peculiar to the Fontainebleau masters exerted a singular influence upon the native artists, and that not only in the corresponding department of art, but in ornament generally. The peculiar crinkled folds of the garments, disposed not as they would obviously fall if left to themselves, but as they would best fill up voids in composition, induced a general levity in the treatment of similar elements, and led to that peculiarly *fluttering* style which may be recognised in the works of all those artists who reflected and reproduced the prevalent mode of the day. Among the most remarkable of these, and, moreover, a man of singular originality of intellect, stands conspicuous the renowned Jean Goujon, who was born in France early in the sixteenth century. His principal works are (for, happily, they have for the most part survived to our days) the "Fontaine des Innocents," at Paris (1550); the gallery of the "Salle des Cent Suisses," now "des Caryatides," supported by four colossal female figures, which are considered among his best works. The celebrated Diana of Poitiers, called "Diane Chasseresse," a small and very beautiful bas-relief of the same subject, his wooden doors to the Church of St. Maclou at Rouen, his carvings of the Court of the Louvre, and his "Christ at the Tomb," in the Museum of the Louvre. Goujon partook warmly of the enthusiasm the recovery of the writings of Vitruvius excited universally, and contributed an essay in respect to them in Martin's translation. He was unfortunately shot during the massacre of St. Bartholomew, whilst working on a scaffold at the Louvre, in 1572. An artist who had imbibed even more of the Italian spirit of the School of Fontainebleau than did Jean Goujon, narrowly escaped sharing his fate. Barthélemy Prieur was only saved from immolation by the protection of the Constable Montmorency, whose monumental effigy he was ultimately destined to place upon its pedestal. Contemporary with Goujon and Prieur was Jean Cousin, the most ardent disciple of the Michael-Angelesque form. He is principally known as the sculptor of the noble statue of Admiral Chabot, and, as we have stated (Chapter XVII.), by his designs for stained glass. Prominent, however, among the artistic band of the period was Germain Pilon, who was born at Loué, near Mans. The statues at the Convent of Soulesmes are among his earliest works. About the year 1550 his father sent him to Paris, and in 1557 his monument to Guillaume Langei du Bellay was placed in the Cathedral of Mans. About the same time he executed the monument of Henry II. and Catherine de Medici, in the Church of St. Denis, near Paris, from a design by Philibert de Lorme. One of his best works was the monument to the Chancellor de Birague.

The beautiful and well-known group of the "Three Graces," cut out of one solid block of marble, was intended to support an urn containing the hearts of Henry II. and Catherine de Medici; it is now in the Louvre. In order to give an idea of the ornamental style of Pilon, we have engraved the base of this monument. See Plate LXXVI. *(pages 390–91)*, Fig. 8. The statues and bas-reliefs on the monument of Francis I. are by Pilon and Pierre Bontemps. After 1590 no works of his are known, and Kugler gives it as the date of his death.

The length of limb and artificial grace peculiar to the school of Fontainebleau was pushed to the farthest point of extravagance by Francavilla, or Pierre Francheville, of Cambray (born 1548), who introduced into France the even greater wiriness of the style of John of Bologna, whose pupil he had been during many years. The general characteristics of the style of ornament prevalent during the first half of the seventeenth century, and which served as an induction into what is generally known as Louis XIV. work, cannot be better studied than in the apartments of Marie de Medici, executed for her in the Palace of the Luxembourg, Paris, about 1620.

This manner was succeeded by that of Le Pautre, an artist of great cleverness and fertility. Our woodcut *(overleaf)* gives an idea of his style.

Leaving for awhile the subject of *sculptured* Italian and French Ornament, it may be well to advert to that of *painted*; the more especially as for a short time, during which a great degree of zeal for the preservation of old Roman vestiges of polychromatic decoration was exercised, a very high and remarkable degree of perfection and beauty was attained. It is ever to be borne in mind that a very wide difference existed between the

PANEL FOR A CEILING, FROM A DESIGN BY LE PAUTRE

painted and carved arabesques of the ancients. The latter during the period of the Early Renaissance were almost entirely neglected, whilst the former were imitated with great success, as may be seen from the interesting pilaster panels, designed by Baccio Pintelli for the Church of Sant' Agostino at Rome, and which form the subject of our woodcuts on page 435.

The study of ancient Rome and Greek sculptures was naturally followed by that of the antique decorations in marble and stone, which throughout Italy abounded so profusely, and which every day's excavation brought to light,—such, for instance, as perfect remains or shattered fragments of ornamental vases, altars, friezes, pilasters, &c., groups or single figures, busts or heads, in medallions or on architectural backgrounds; fruit, flowers, foliage, and animals, intermixed with tablets of various forms, bearing allegorical inscriptions. An infinite variety of such gems of beauty offered themselves to the notice of the artists of that period who visited Rome for the express purpose of making drawings of such remains; and in transferring the subject so sketched to the modern arabesques, it was scarcely possible that the early artists should avoid also transferring to their paintings somewhat of the formal character inseparable from the sculptured and material character of the objects from which their original drawings had been made.

Such circumstances may go far to explain the differences we cannot fail to recognise between the imitation and the object imitated, in many of the first attempts to reproduce the painted decorations of the Romans of Imperial times. Among such diligent students, none was more conspicuous than was Pietro Perugino during his residence in Rome at the latter part of the fifteenth century. How fully and to what good purpose he accumulated studies of ancient ornament was shown by the immediate commission he received from his fellow-townsmen to decorate the vaults of their Exchange, or "Sala di Cambio," with frescoes, in which the ancient style and certain antique subjects should be vividly reproduced. This beautiful work of art, for such it proved to be, was executed soon after his return to Perugia from Rome; and manifests how deeply he must have drunk at the classic fountain of antique Art. It is, without doubt, the first complete reproduction of the "grotesques" of the ancients, and is singularly interesting, not only as establishing the claim of Pietro to be regarded as the first great and accurate reviver of this graceful style of decoration, but as having been the "trial-piece" on which so many "'prentice hands" were exercised, whose efforts subsequently carried it to the highest perfection.

The principal scholars of Perugino, whose labours there is little doubt materially aided in the elaboration of these graceful fancies, were Raffaelle, then aged sixteen or seventeen; Francesco Ubertini, better known as Bacchiacca; and Pinturicchio. And it is curious to trace the influence of the success of this their first attempt upon the after career of each of the three. It led immediately to the employment of Raffaelle and Pinturicchio, in conjunction, in the decoration of the celebrated Library at Sienna, and subsequently, to the cultivation of such studies on the part of the former as induced his composition of the inimitable arabesques of the Loggie of the Vatican, &c. &c.; and on that of the latter artist to the execution of the ceilings of the choir of Sta. Maria del Popolo, and those of the Apartamenti Borgia, &c., at Rome. Bacchiacca became so completely enamoured of the style, that his whole life was devoted to painting animals, flowers, &c., in "grotesque" decoration; and he ultimately became famous throughout Italy as a perfect master of that variety of design.

In freedom and cleverness of drawing, in harmony of colour, in brilliancy of touch, in nice balance of the "pieni" and "vuoti," and in close imitation of the paintings of the ancient Romans, this specimen is one of the most successful that has ever been executed, although, in delicacy of finish and refined study, it can scarcely be expected to equal the subsequent productions of Giovanni da Udine and Morto da Feltro.

During the stay of Raffaelle in Rome, under the pontificate of Leo X., he was commissioned by that pontiff to decorate an arcade, which had been constructed during the reign of his predecessor, Julius II., by Bramante, whose daughter Raffaelle married.

It was determined, that while the theme of the necessary decorations should be sacred, their style and manner of execution should rival the finest remains of ancient painting which had been discovered at Rome up to that period. The general designs appear to have been made by Raffaelle himself, and the details to have been carried out by a chosen band of assistants, who unquestionably entered with wonderful zeal into the realisation of the great work. It was by their hands, controlled by the exquisite taste of the great Urbinese, that those celebrated "loggie," which have ever since their execution been a theme of admiration for all artists, were created. We have given a careful selection, showing the principal ornamental motives comprised in them in Plate LXXXVI *(pages 460–61)*.

These arabesques cannot fairly be compared with the ancient, as the former were executed by the greatest masters of the age, and are applied to the decoration of an edifice of the highest magnificence

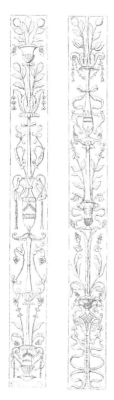

ARABESQUES DESIGNED
BY BACCIO PINTELLI FOR
THE CHURCH OF SANT'
AGOSTINO, ROME

and importance, whilst the latter were the productions of a less distinguished period of Art, and those now in existence ornament buildings of a class relatively far less important to Imperial magnificence than the Vatican was to Papal. The comparison might be fairer if we could but recall the faded glories of the Palace of the Cæsars, or the "Golden House" of Nero.

"The ancient arabesques have, in almost every instance, all their parts kept upon a reduced scale, in order to favour the apparent extent of the locality they decorate; in addition to which they generally manifest a predominating general proportion between their several parts. They never present such striking differences in scale between the principal subjects as we find in the arabesques of Raffaelle, the component parts of which are sometimes as unreasonably large as they sometimes are unreasonably small. The greater is often placed beside and above the less, thereby emphaticising the dissonances, and being the more offensive by a deficiency in symmetry, as well as in the very choice of the motives for decoration. Thus, close to the richest arabesques, presenting, on a very small scale, elegant and minute combinations of flowers, fruit, animals, human figures, and views of temples, landscapes, &c., we find calices of flowers putting forth twisted stalks, leaves, and blossoms—all which, with reference to the adjoining and first-described arabesques, are of colossal proportion; thereby not only injuring the accompanying decorations, but also destroying the grandeur of the whole architectural design. Lastly, on examining the choice of subjects with respect to the association of ideas indicated thereby, and the decorations in the symbols and allegories employed to convey them, we find that the works of the ancients, who reverted to no other source than their mythology, appear to great advantage, in point of unity of idea, when compared with the prevailing intermixture in the Loggie of that imaginary world with the symbols of Christianity." Such are among the general conclusions to which that profound student of ancient polychromy, M. Hittorff, has arrived, and it is impossible not to concur in their propriety; while condemning, however, such faults of *ensemble*, we must not lose sight of the exquisite graces of detail wrought out in their execution by Raffaelle and his scholars. "Proceeding from the Vatican to the Villa Madama, we find, immediately on entering its halls, that divisions create a less confusing general effect. In all the principal decorations there is a better regulated proportion, and greater symmetry; and in the magnificent roofs, notwithstanding the multiplicity of their ornaments, a more gratifying and calming influence is exerted upon us. Here, where all the principal subjects represent scenes from the mythology of the ancients, we find a pervading unity conceived more in the spirit of the ancients. If we adopt the general opinion and look upon this beautiful work as a second undertaking conceived by Raffaelle in the spirit of the Loggie, and executed entirely by Giulio Romano and Giovanni da Udine, we see how the favourite pupils of the incomparable master succeeded in avoiding faults against good taste, which he and his contemporaries cannot fail to have recognised in his former work, favourably as it was received by the popular voice, not only of courtiers, but of artists." Unlike the arabesques of the Vatican, which are executed, for the most part, upon white ground, those of this delicious suburban retreat are, for the most part, worked out upon variously coloured grounds—a habit to which Giulio Romano appears to have been more partial than either Raffaelle or Giovanni da Udine.

The villa itself was built by Romano and his fellow-labourer for Pope Clement VII., when Cardinal Giulio de Medici, the first designs having been given by Raffaelle. The work was still incomplete when it was partially destroyed by Cardinal Pompeo Colonna, to revenge himself upon Clement VII., who had burnt fourteen of his castles in the Campagna of Rome. The villa is now rapidly going to decay; but the grandeur of the three arches still remaining is sufficient to show that the design was worthy of Raffaelle; and that it was his is proved beyond a doubt, by a letter to Francesco Maria,

DETAIL OF A PORTION OF A STUCCO CEILING IN
THE PALAZZO MATTEI DI GIOVE, ROME, BY CARLO MADERNO

Duke of Urbino, written by Castiglione, as well as by some drawings, which, together with the letter, are still in existence.

The Villa Madama was purchased after the confiscation of the Medicis property, in 1537, by Margaret, daughter of Charles V., and widow of Duke Alexander de Medici, and from her title of Madama the villa takes its name. The building was partially restored, though never completed, and Margaret resided there on her marriage with Ottavio Farnese. The crown of Naples afterwards became possessed of it, with the rest of the Farnese property, through a marriage with that family.

So large a number of arabesque decorations were executed by the pupils and followers of Raffaelle, and so great was the skill acquired by them in this art, that it is now difficult to ascertain to whom we owe the beautiful arabesques which still decorate many of the palaces and country-houses in the neighbourhood of Rome. After the premature death of Raffaelle, the bond that had united the brotherhood which had gathered around his person was snapped, and those who had so ably worked with him spread themselves in various directions throughout Italy, carrying with them the experience and knowledge they had acquired in the conduct of the great undertakings placed under his charge. Thus sown broadcast over the land were the elements of painted arabesque decoration. In proportion, however, as the artists, by whom subsequent works were undertaken, removed from the classic influences of Rome, their styles became more pictorial, and less purely decorative; and in the seventeenth century the arabesque manner became almost entirely merged in such florid decorations as suited the extravagant ideas of architectural magnificence nourished by the Jesuits. In the days of Bernini, and at a later period in those of Borromini, the Stuccatore triumphed in every species of flourish, while in the scanty openings left between the fluttering wings and draperies of angels and saints suspended in vaults and cupolas in mid-air, the decorative painter was allowed to place little else than the perspective tricks of the Padre Pozzo and his school.

Before leaving the subject of arabesque altogether, it may be well to trace a few anomalies in its varied local aspects. As may reasonably be inferred, the presence of ancient remains has almost invariably affected the local style of ornament in those spots where they have most abounded. Thus at Rome the school of arabesque ornament most nearly approached the antique, while in cities such as Mantua, Pavia, and Genoa, other and distinct types and influences may be traced. The Mantuan system of ornamentation, for instance, may be distinctly subdivided into the school of nature and that of conventional vigour approaching caricature, imported by Giulio Romano, and a reflex of the favourite Paganism of Rome. In the deserted chambers of the Palazzo Ducale are fast fading into nothingness the graceful frescoes, of which we have presented numerous specimens in Plates LXXXVII. and LXXXVIII. *(pages 464–66)*; executed for the most part upon a white ground. Leaves, flowers, and tendrils, frequently wind round a central reed, as at Figs. 6 and 9, Plate LXXXVII.; and in such cases Nature appears as the directly inspiring deity. In other instances, as in Figs. 1, 2, 3, 4, 5, and 7, of the same plate, a simple style of convention is followed, in which the hand of the artist sweeps out as wayward fancy prompts an ever-recurring, yet rarely monotonous, series of scrolls and curves; the leading points of which are generally accentuated by calices, and the dominant lines of which are adorned, and from time to time interrupted, by foliage of parasitic growth.

A marked difference of style in the decoration of the same building is inaugurated in the specimens (Figs. 1, 2, 4, and 5) we have collected in Plate LXXXVIII. In them the artist has withdrawn himself farther from nature, retaining at the same time an even more pictorial mode of representation than in the earlier and purer examples. Far be it from us to assert that beauty of the highest and most architectonic character may not be obtained in ornament entirely conventional in conception; but certain it is, that to be agreeable such ornament should be expressed in a simple and flat style of treatment, both as regards light, shade, and colour. In direct proportion as the elements of which an ornament is composed have been taken with more or less divergence from the ordinary aspect of nature, so should the mode be varied in which that ornament should be portrayed. Thus, in the more refined arabesques of Plate LXXXVII., in which the forms of growing plants have been freely sketched from the garden and field, an amount of delicate modelling and indication of accidental effect is admissible, which in the representation of the more absolutely conventional elements of the specimens given in Plate LXXXVIII., strikes us as somewhat officious and feeble. Already in the bustle of line, the fluttering ribbons, and vague jewelled forms of No. 5, and in the monotonous masques and foolscaps of No. 1 (Plate LXXXIX., *page 467*), may be traced that tendency to caricature which disfigured so much that the genius of Romano threw off with masterly power, but unfortunately with too great fecundity. So long, as at the Villa Madama, and in other of his Roman works, his exuberance was controlled by association with artists of purer taste than himself, there is little with which to reproach him; but when he subsequently emerged into the "Gran Signore" at Mantua, his vanity fairly intoxicated him, and with much that was beautiful he blended not a little that was ridiculous.

The specimens of his arabesques, which we have collected in Plate LXXXVII. *(pages 464–65)*, illustrate at once his ability and his weakness as an ornamentist. Unable to divest himself of his recollections of the antique, and at the same time too egotistic to be content with its careful reproduction, the motives he borrowed from it assume an aspect of unquiet rarely to be recognised in the remains of classic antiquity. The motives he derived from Nature are equally maltreated, since he gathered flowers from her bosom only to crush them in his rude grasp. There are yet, however, a daring in his fancy, and a rare sweep and certainty in his handling, which must secure for him an honourable niche in the Temple of Art. Like "Van who wanted grace, yet never wanted wit," it is on the score of taste that he who in his time was one of its chief arbiters most frequently fails. This fallibility is stamped upon several of the ornaments we have engraved in Plate LXXXIX. *(page 467)*, which are taken principally from the Palazzo del Te, at Mantua. Thus, in No. 2, a scroll ornament freely dashed out is entirely spoilt by the ludicrous object from which it springs. Again, in No. 4, the ridiculous masques seem sneering at the graceful forms which surround them; and in No. 3, nature and the antique are alike maltreated. No. 6 in the same plate "points a" severe "moral". Servile, where an ornament should be most free in the disposition of its main lines; and free, where deference to some received type of form ceases to be servile, in the accessory elements of which it is composed, his running scroll, which is adapted from one of the commonest patterns of antiquity, betrays at once Giulio's feebleness of imagination, and his want of taste.

TYPOGRAPHIC ORNAMENT FROM ONE OF THE
PRODUCTIONS OF THE EARLY PARISIAN PRESS
(STEPHANS' GREEK TESTAMENT)

The peculiar influence of local associations upon styles of ornament, which we have already noticed in the case of arabesques, may be traced with equal facility in the best typographic and xylographic illustrations of the early printers. Thus, in the ornaments, Figs. 2, 3, 5, 7, 8–14, 24, Plate XC. *(pages 468–69)*, taken from the celebrated "Etymologion Magnum," printed at Venice in the year 1499, the forms of the ornament, and the almost even distribution of the "pieni" and "vuoti," have been evidently based on the style of those Oriental or Byzantine fragments in which Venice was so pre-eminently rich. Many of the Aldine initial letters in the last-named plate appear as though they might have been engraved by the very same hands that ploughed out the damascene patterns in the metal-work of the period.

ORNAMENTS DESIGNED FOR
MARQUETRY BY FAY, IN THE STYLE OF LOUIS SEIZE

The Tuscan Bible of 1538 presents us with endless conventional renderings of the ordinary Cinque-cento sculpture, which abounded in the churches of Florence. Nor are the specimens of the Parisian press less worthy of the veneration of the virtuoso.

In the productions of the Stephans (Fig. 19, from the celebrated Greek Testament), of Colinæus, his pupil (Fig. 4), of Macé Bonhomme of Lyons, in 1558, Theodore Rihel of Frankfort, in 1574, Jacques de Liesveldt of Antwerp, in 1554, Jean Palier and Regnault Chauldière of Paris, may be found many agreeable and interesting illustrations of local

PANELS DESIGNED BY FAY,
IN THE STYLE OF LOUIS SEIZE

differences in ornamental detail of a semi-antique character.

Returning to Italy, and to its purer style, before briefly proceeding to trace the "first causes" of the general decline of revived Classical Art, we propose glancing at one or two branches of industry it would be unfair to altogether pass over. The first and most interesting of them is that of Venetian Glass— a commodity which helped to spread the fame of Venice far and wide over the habitable globe.

The taking of Constantinope by the Turks, in 1453, drove the skilled Greek workmen thence to Italy; and at that period the glass-manufacturers of Venice learned from the exiled Greeks their modes of enriching their productions by colouring, gilding, and enamelling. In the early part of the sixteenth century, the Venetians appear to have invented the art of introducing threads of coloured and opaque white *(latticinio)* glass into the substance of the articles they manufactured, forming a beautiful and enduring enrichment, suitable, from the lightness of its character, to the delicate forms of the objects to which it was applied. The secret of this art was most jealously guarded by the State; and the severest penalties were enacted against any workmen who should divulge it, or exercise their craft in any other country. On the other hand, the masters of the glass-houses at Murano received great privileges, and even the workmen were not classed with ordinary artisans. In 1602 a gold coin was struck at Murano, with the avowed object of handing down to posterity the names of those who established the first glass-houses on the island; and from it we learn that they were the following: Muro, Leguso, Motta, Bigaglia, Miotti, Briati Gazzabin, Vistosi, and Ballarin. For about two centuries the Venetians contrived to retain their valuable secret, and monopolised the glass trade of Europe; but at the commencement of the eighteenth century, the taste for heavy cut glass began to prevail, and the trade was dispersed to Bohemia, France, and England.

Many very splendid works in the precious metals were executed at this period. A very large amount of these is supposed to have been melted down, in Italy, about the date of the sack of Rome; and in France to pay the ransom of Francis I.; and much more was, no doubt, re-fashioned in aftertimes; but the Cabinet of the Grand Duke of Tuscany at Florence, and the Museum of the Louvre at Paris, still contain fine collections of jewelled and enamelled cups and other objects, which sufficiently attest the skill and taste of the goldsmiths and jewellers of the sixteenth century. One of the richest jewels which the fashion of the period introduced, and which continued to be used for a considerable time, was the "enseigne," a species of medal generally worn in the hats of the nobles and in the head-dress of the ladies. The custom of giving presents on all important occasions furnished constant employment to the jewellers of both countries, and in the vicinity of the courts, even during the most troubled periods. The restoration of peace in Italy, by the conventions of Château Cambresis, and in France at the accession of Henry IV., caused an increased demand for the goldsmiths' productions; and subsequently the magnificence of the Cardinals Richelieu and Mazarin paved the way for the

ARABESQUE BY THEODORE DE BRY,
ONE OF THE "PETITS-MAÎTRES"

age of "Louis le Grand" in France, for whom numerous fine works of art were executed by the Parisian goldsmith, Claude Ballin, who, together with Labarre, Vincent, Petit, Julian Desfontaines, and others, worked in the Louvre. One of the objects which greatly employed the ingenuity of the jeweller at this period was the "aigrette," which was generally worn by the nobility. From this time the style of the French jewellery rapidly declined, perfection of workmanship in metal-work having been transferred to bronze and brass, in which last alloy the chasings of the celebrated Gouthier, in the days of Louis XVI., were above all praise. Of designs for such work we engrave two pleasing specimens of the Parisian burin. The wiriness and frivolity of this class of ornament were redeemed by its faultless execution.

The details of the art, and its popularity, were not without their influence upon general design; for since the delicate draughtsmen and engravers of the day were much employed by the goldsmiths in working out their designs and patterns, it followed, as no unnatural consequence, that many of the forms peculiar to jewellers' work were introduced into decorations designed for altogether different purposes. This was especially the case in Germany, and more particularly in Saxony, where a great deal of a mixed style of Renaissance and bastard Italian, with strap and ribbon-work, cartouches, and intricate complications of architectural members, was executed for the Electors. The engraving we present of a decoration composed by Theodore de Bry affords no bad illustration of the way in which motives expressly adapted for enamelling in the style of Cellini were thrown together, to make up the ordinary grotesque of the day. It is by no means in the works of Theodore de Bry alone that such solecisms are to be found; for in the French etchings of Etienne de Laulne, Gilles l'Egaré, and others, the same features are presented.

Engravers and designers of this class were also much employed, both in Germany and France, in providing models for the damascene work, which was long popular in both these countries, as well as in Italy.

It is remarkable, that although we find that the Crusaders bought Oriental arms at Damascus, and sometimes brought the more elaborate articles to Europe, as in the case of the "Vase de Vincennes," no attempts should have been made to imitate the manufacture until the middle of the fifteenth century, when we find it in use in Italy for decorating the plate-armour, which was then adopted in that country. It is most probable that the art was first introduced by the great trading cities, such as Venice, Pisa, and Genoa, from the East, and was afterwards taken up as a more permanent decoration for armour than parcel-gilding by the artists of Milan, which city was then to Europe what Damascus had been to the East, viz. the great emporium for the best arms and armour. So exclusively, indeed, was the art, in the first instance, employed upon weapons, that to the very last the Italian writers designate it under the title of "lavoro all' azzimina." At the beginning of the sixteenth century the art began to be exercised out of Italy; and it is by no means improbable that it was taught to the workmen of France and Spain by those travelling artists whom the good taste, or possibly the vanity, of the kings of those countries attached to their courts. Probably the finest existing specimen of damascening is the armour of Francis I., now in the Cabinet de Médailles, at Paris. Both this and the shield in Her Majesty's possession at Windsor have been attributed to the famous Cellini; but on comparing them with any of his known works, the drawing of the figures indicates rather an Augsburg artist than the broad style which Cellini had acquired from his study of the works of Michael Angelo.

From that time down to the middle of the seventeenth century a great number of arms were decorated with damascening, of which the Louvre, the Cabinet de Médailles, and the Musée d'Artillerie, contain numerous fine specimens; and the names of Michael Angelo, Negroli, the Piccinini, and Cursinet, may be mentioned as excelling in damascene work, as well as in the art of the armourer generally.

In our own country the process does not appear to have been much exercised; parcel-gilding, engraving, blacking, and russeting, being well received as substitutes; and the few specimens we possess were probably imported, or captured in our foreign wars, as in the case of the splendid suits of armour brought to England by the Earl of Pembroke after the battle of St. Quentin.

As it has been our pleasant task to record how French Ornamental Art was regenerated by imitation of Italian models in the sixteenth century, so it now becomes our less agreeable duty to note how deleterious an influence was exercised in the seventeenth from the same procedure. There can be no doubt that two highly-gifted, but overrated, Italian artists,

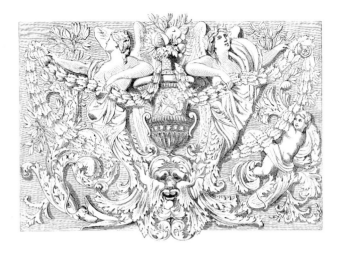

ORNAMENTAL COMPOSITION, FROM A DESIGN BY LE PAUTRE

set during their lives upon pinnacles which made them the "observed of all observers," effected an immense amount of mischief to French Art. These artists were Lorenzo Bernini and Francesco Borromini. The former was the son of a Florentine sculptor, and was born in 1598. He evinced an unusually precocious talent for sculpture; and whilst yet a youth was fully employed, not only as a sculptor, but as an architect. He resided almost entirely at Rome, where he designed the fountain of the Barcaccia in the Piazza di Spagna, the celebrated Triton in the Piazza Barberini, and the large fountains of the Piazza Navona; the College de Propaganda Fide; the great hall and façade of the Barberini Palace, facing the Strada Felice; a campanile to St. Peter's (afterwards taken down); the Ludovico Palace, on the Monte Citorio; the celebrated Piazza of St. Peter's; and the great staircase from St. Peter's to the Vatican, besides numerous other works. Busts by Bernini were eagerly sought after by the sovereigns and nobles of Europe; so much so, that when he was sixty-eight years of age, Louis XIV., who was unused to be refused anything, and much less to be forced to beg, was actually obliged to write supplicatory letters to the Pope, and to Bernini, requesting the sculptor's presence at Paris. During his residence there, though he did but little, he is said to have received five golden louis a-day, and at his departure fifty thousand crowns, with an annual pension of two thousand crowns, and one of five hundred for his sons, who accompanied him. On his return to Rome he made an equestrian statue in honour of Louis, which is now at Versailles. Besides his works in architecture, sculpture, and bronze, he appears to have had a decided mechanical turn; and, moreover, to have painted as many as five hundred pictures in the Case Barberini and Chigi. He died in the year 1680.

Francesco Borromini was born near Como, in the year 1599. Apprenticed at an early age to Carlo Maderno, he speedily became both a brilliant carver and architect. On Maderno's death he succeeded to the charge of the works at St. Peter's under Bernini, with whom he very shortly quarrelled. From his fervid imagination and rare facility as a draughtsman and designer, he soon obtained ample employment; and in his capricious vagaries, every tendency to extravagance that Bernini's style possessed Borromini contrived to caricature. Until near his death, in 1667, he continued sedulously occupied in subverting all known principles of order

FRIEZE ORNAMENT, LOUIS SEIZE, BY FAY

and symmetry, not only to his own enrichment, but to the admiration of the leaders of fashion of the day. The anomalies he introduced into design, the disproportionate mouldings, broken, contrasted, and re-entering curves, interrupted and crooked lines and surfaces, became the *mode* of the day, and all Europe was speedily busy in devising similar enormities. In France the fever raged speedily, and the popular style, in place of the quaint but picturesque forms to be seen in the engravings of Du Cerceau, 1576— substituted the more elaborate, but less agreeable ones to be found in Marot, 1727—and Mariette, 1726–7. Borromini's works, which were published in the year 1725—and Bibiena's, which were not much purer, and which were given to the world in 1740—had a large circulation, and tended to confirm the public taste in facility and elaboration *versus* simplicity and beauty. Despite this debasing influence, many of the French artists of the time, both of Louis XIV. and XV., in the midst of their extravagance, made many beautiful ornamental designs, showing in them a sense of capricious beauty of line rarely surpassed. In some of Le Pautre's designs (reign of

PANEL SUITABLE FOR
REISNER MARQUETRY, DESIGNED BY FAY

Louis XIV.), this quality may be recognised, as well as in many of the interior decorations given in Blondel's works published during the reign of Louis XV.

De Neufforge is, however, the master of the ceremonies in this latter court of revels, and does sufficiently graceful fooling in the 900 plates comprised in his great body of Ornament. To dwell upon individuals among the mass of clever ornamental designers, draughtsmen, and engravers, to whom the Grand Monarque and the brilliant court of his successor gave good pay and plenty of work, would be out of place here. There is one, however, Jean Berain, who cannot be passed over, seeing that he held the special appointment of "Dessinateur des Menus Plaisirs du Roi" (Louis XIV.), and that to him we are indebted for the best designs which will render the name of Buhl famous so long as a taste for beautiful furniture exists. He contributed materially to the decoration of the Galerie d'Apollon of the Louvre, and of the State apartments in the Tuileries, as is elegantly testified in a work published

FRIEZE STYLE,
LOUIS SEIZE, BY FAY

in the year 1710. Another large collection of his admirably sportive designs was engraved by Daigremont, Scotin, and others. With the advent of Louis XV. to the throne, in 1715, the manner of designing grew far more "rococo" and "barocque" than it had been during the greatest part of his predecessor's reign. In spite of the fine talents and good example set by the architect Soufflot in his works, the twisted and foliated scrolls and shells of the former grew into the "rocaille" and grotto-work of the latter; degenerating at last into all the eccentricities of "Chinoiserie." From this style of approaching inanition, ornament revived under Louis XVI. to an elegant though liney style, corresponding in some degree to that introduced into this country by Robert Adams, principally in his buildings in the Adelphi. The genius of three very able men exercised a beneficial influence over industrial design at a period shortly preceding the Revolution—Reisner, the cabinet-maker, celebrated for his exquisite marquetry; Gouthier, brass-chaser to Marie Antoinette; and

Demontreuil, carver in wood to the royal family. During the Revolution Chaos reigned, and out of it came order in the shape of an utter abjuration of the "colifichets" of the Monarchy in favour of the Republican severity of a David. As the Republic, however, ripened into the Empire, the "mode" from stern Republican grew magnificent Imperialist. The best artists were liberally employed by Napoleon I., and the talent of Percier, Fontaine, Normand, Fragonard, Prudhon, and Cavelier, developed in its highest perfection the graceful and learned, but stiff and cold, "style de l'Empire." With the Restoration the antique went out of fashion, and confusion again ensued. The native ability of the country, however, aided by judicious and liberally conducted educational institutions, soon revived the public interest, and an enthusiasm for rivals of a somewhat archæological nature supervened. The monuments of the middle ages and of the Renaissance were cared for, sought for, restored, and imitated on all hands; and out of the manifold studies so made, styles of eclectic character, but approaching originality, are rapidly forming themselves throughout the country.

France is, it must be confessed, at the present time, master of the field in the distribution and execution of ornament of almost every class; but so rapid and hopeful is the progress now taking place in this country, that it is by no means impossible that an historian writing some few years hence may, happily, be enabled to place the Allies, as they should be, upon a footing of equality.

M. DIGBY WYATT.

BOOKS REFERRED TO FOR ILLUSTRATIONS. LITERARY AND PICTORIAL

ADAMS (E.) *The Polychromatic Ornament of Italy.* 4to. London, n.d.

ALBERTI (L. B.) *De Re Ædificatoria Opus.* Florent. 1485, in folio.

ALBERTOLLI. *Ornamenti diversi inventati, &c., da.* Milano, in folio.

D'ANDROUET DU CERCEAU. *Livre d'Architecture.* Paris, 1559, in folio.

D'AVILER. *Cours d'Architecture, par.* Paris, 1756, in 4to.

BIBIENA. *Architettura di.* Augustæ, 1740, in folio.

BORROMINI (F.) *Opus Architectonicum.* Romæ, 1725, in folio.

CLOCHAR (P.) *Monuments et Tombeaux mésurés et dessinés en Italie, par. 40 Plans and Views of the most remarkable Monuments in Italy.* Paris, 1815.

DEDAUX. *Chambre de Marie de Médicis au Palais du Luxembourg; ou, Recueil d'Arabesques, Peintures, et Ornements qui la décorent.* Folio, Paris, 1838.

DIEDO E ZANOTTO. *Sepulchral Monuments of Venice. I Monumenti cospicui di Venezia, illustrati dal Cav. Antonio Diedo e da Francesco Zanotto.* Folio, Milan, 1839.

DOPPELMAYR (J. G.) *Mathematicians and Artists of Nuremberg, &c. Historische Nachricht von den Nurnbergischen Mathematicis und Künstlern, &c.* Folio, Nürnberg. 1730.

GOZZINI (V.) *Monumens Sépulcraux de la Toscane, dessinés par Vincent Gozzini, et gravés par Jerôme Scotto. Nouvelle Edition, augmentée de vingt-neuf planches, avec leur Descriptions.* 4to. Florence, 1821.

GRUNER (L.) *Description of the Plates of Fresco Decorations and Stuccoes of Churches and Palaces in Italy during the Fifteenth and Sixteenth Centuries. With an Essay by J. J. Hittorff on the Arabesques of the Ancients compared with those of Raffaelle and his School. New edition, largely augmented by numerous plates, plain and coloured.* 4to. London, 1854.

—— *Fresco Decorations and Stuccoes of Churches and Palaces in Italy during the Fifteenth and Sixteenth Centuries, with descriptions by Lewis Gruner, K.A. New edition, augmented by numerous plates, plain and coloured.* Folio, London, 1854.

—— *Specimens of Ornamental Art selected from the best Models of the Classical Epochs. Illustrated by 80 plates, with descriptive text, by Emil Braun. (By Authority.)* Folio, London, 1850.

MAGAZZARI (G.) *The most select Ornaments of Bologna. Raccolta de' piu scelti Ornati sparsi per la Città di Bologna, desegnati ed incisi da Giovanni Magazzari.* Oblong 4to. Bologna, 1827.

DE NEUFFORGE. *Recueil élémentaire d'Architecture, par.* Paris (1757). 8 vols. in folio.

PAIN'S *British Paladio.* London, 1797, in folio.

PALLADIO. *Architettura di.* Venet. 1570, in folio.

PASSAVANT (J. D.) *Rafael von Urbino und sein Vater Giovanni Santi. In zwei Theilen mit vierzehn Abbildungen.* 2 vols. 8vo. 1 vol. folio, Leipzig, 1839.

PERCIER ET FONTAINE. *Recueil de Décorations intérieures, par.* Paris, 1812, in folio.

PERRAULT. *Ordonnance des cinq Espèces de Colonnes, selon les Anciens, par.* Paris, 1683, in folio.

PHILIBERT DE LORME. *Œuvres d'architecture de.* Paris, 1626, in folio.

PIRANESI (FR.) *Différentes Manières d'orner les Cheminées, &c., par.* Rome, 1768, in folio. And other works.

PONCE (N.) *Description des Bains de Tite.* 40 plates, folio.

RAPHAEL. *Life of Raphael, by Quatremère de Quincy.* 8vo. Paris, 1835.

Recueil d'Arabesques, contenant les Loges du Vatican d'après Raphael, et grand nombre d'autres Compositions du même genre dans le Style antique, d'après Normand, Queverdo, Boucher, &c. 114 platres, imperial folio. Paris, 1802.

RUSCONI (G. ANT.) *Dell' Architettura, lib. X., da.* Venez. 1593, in folio.

SCAMOZZI. *Idea dell' Architettura da,* Venez. 1615. 2 vols. in folio.

SERLIO (SEB.) *Tutte le Opere d'Architettura di.* Venet. 1584, in 4to.

—— *Libri cinque d'Architettura di.* Venet. 1551, in folio.

Terme de Tito. A series of 61 engravings of the paintings, ceilings, arabesque decorations, &c., of the Baths of Titus, engraved by Carloni. 2 vols. in 1, atlas folio, oblong, Rome, n. d.

TOSI AND BECCHIO. *Altars, Tabernacles, and Sepulchral Monuments of the Fourteenth and Fifteenth Centuries, existing at Rome.* Published under the patronage of the celebrated Academy of St. Luke, by MM. Tosi and Becchio. Descriptions in Italian, English, and French, by Mrs. Spry Bartlett. Folio, Lagny, 1853.

VIGNOLA. *Regola dei cinque Ordini d'Architettura, da.* In folio.

VOLPATO ED OTTAVIANO. *Loggie del Raffaele nel Vaticano, &c.* Roma, 1782.

* ZAHN (W.) *Ornamente aller Klassischen Kunst-Epochen nach den originalen in ihren eigenthümlichen farben dargestellt.* Oblong folio, Berlin, 1849.

ZOBI (ANT.) *Notizie Storiche sull' Origine e Progressi dei Lavori di Commesso in Pietre Dure che si esequiscono nell' I. e R. Stabilimento di Firenze.* Second Edition, with additions and corrections by the author. 4to. Florence, 1853.

* From this interesting work the materials for Plates LXXVII., LXXVIII., LXXIX., have been derived.

———————•:•———————

The meaning of the term "arabesque" has altered slightly over the centuries. Originally it was used to describe foliage and scrollwork patterns, arranged in an "Arabic" or Moorish manner. Then, as today, it specifically excluded human and animal motifs. In Jones's time, however, the word was employed more loosely. It also encompassed "grotesque" ornament *(see pages 433–34)*, some examples of which are included here (Nos. 7, 8, 9). The inspiration for this type of fanciful decoration, characterized by interweavings of flowers, fruit, masks, vases, human figures, and chimerical monsters, came from a series of ancient wall paintings discovered in Rome and excavated in the 1480s. The name reflects the fact that they were found in subterranean structures resembling grottoes.

1

2

3

4

5

6

PLATE LXXXVI

7

8

9

1–9 A series of Arabesques, painted in Fresco by Giovanni da Udine, Perino del Vaga, Giulio Romano, Polidoro da Carravaggio, Francesco Penni, Vincenzio da San Gimignano, Pellegrino da Modena, Bartolomeo da Bagnacavallo, and possibly other artists, from designs by Raffaelle, selected from the decorations of the *Loggie*, or central open Arcade of the Vatican, Rome.

No artist did more to ensure the popularity of "grotesque" imagery *(see page 460)* than Raphael (1483–1520), one of the most successful Renaissance artists. He designed and supervised the execution of a dazzling series of grotesques at two major sites, the Loggie in the Vatican (1517–19), and Cardinal Giulio de' Medici's Villa Madama (*ca.* 1516). These proved enormously influential. They were circulated as engravings and widely copied by other artists. Indeed, for a time "Raphaelesques" became an alternative name for grotesques. Even in the nineteenth century Raphael was still regarded as the supreme exponent of the style. In the *Recueil d'Arabesques* (1802), Raphael's designs were presented alongside those of modern artists as exemplars of the genre.

14

10

11

12

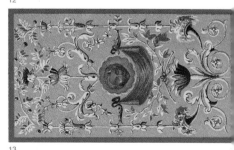

13

15

16

17

18

9

20

23

24

PLATE LXXXVI*

10–24 A series of Arabesques, painted in Fresco by Giovanni da Udine, Perino del Vaga, Giulio Romano, Polidoro da Carravaggio, Francesco Penni, Vincenzio da San Gimignano, Pellegrino da Modena, Bartolomeo da Bagnacavallo, and possibly other artists, from designs by Raffaelle, selected from the decorations of the *Loggie,* or central open Arcade of the Vatican, Rome.

Arabesques and grotesques *(see pages 460, 462)* did not play a very significant role in Victorian design. Instead, their heyday came in the eighteenth century, when they formed an essential ingredient of the rococo style. This trend was started by Jean Bérain (1640–1711), who developed an elegant and playful form of grotesque, omitting its slightly sinister monsters. His lead was followed by Claude Audran (1658–1734), Claude Gillot (1673–1722), and the greatest of all rococo artists, Jean-Antoine Watteau (1684–1721). In the nineteenth century arabesques were occasionally employed by some Renaissance revival designers, most notably Godfrey Sykes (1824–66) and Marc Solon (1835–1913).

1

2

3

4

PLATE LXXXVII

1–9 A series of Arabesques, painted in Fresco on a white ground, in the Palazzo Ducale at Mantua.

After Raphael, the most celebrated Italian exponent of the arabesque was the mannerist artist Giulio Romano (1499–1546). He undoubtedly acquired his taste for this style of decoration during his apprenticeship in Raphael's studio. In 1524 he moved to Mantua, where he created his greatest masterpiece, the Palazzo del Tè (1527–35) for Federigo Gonzaga (1519–40). Giulio was both the architect and decorator of this remarkable summer house. Inside, its most striking feature was a series of frescoes devoted to the stories of Cupid, Psyche, and the rebel giants. These were divided into separate compartments by flowing bands of painted arabesques *(see page 460)*.

PLATE LXXXVIII

1–5 A series of Arabesques, painted in Fresco on partially-coloured grounds, for the most part in the Palazzo Ducale at Mantua.

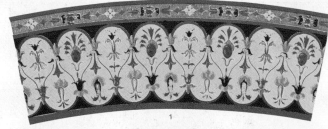

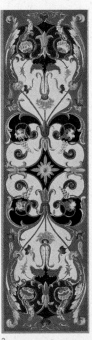

1

2

PLATE LXXXIX

1–6 A series of
Arabesques, painted in
Fresco on fully-coloured
grounds, in the Palazzo del
Te, at Mantua, from Designs
by Giulio Romano.

3

5

4

6

Victorian scholars and designers displayed the same sort of fascination for early printed books as they did for the glories of medieval manuscripts. These pages contain samples of work by some of the most illustrious names in the field, among them Aldus Manutius the Elder and the Younger, Lucantonio Giunta, and various members of the Stephanus (or Estienne) family. With their ornamental borders and decorated initials, these works mimicked the style of earlier illuminators and, in turn, were emulated by some nineteenth-century publishers. The most notable of these was William Morris *(see pages 334, 418)*, who founded the Kelmscott Press in 1891, hoping to recapture the spirit of the industry's pioneers.

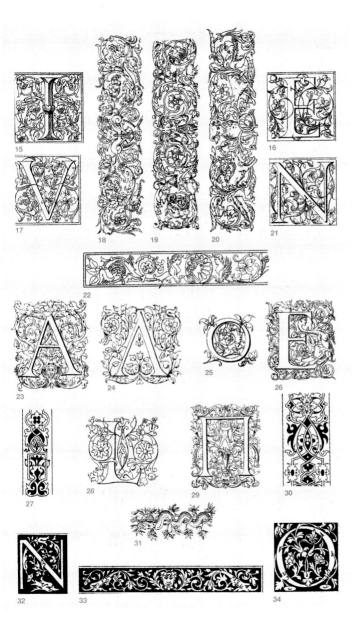

PLATE XC

1–34 A series of Specimens of Typographic Embellishments of the Sixteenth Century in Italy and France; selected from works published by the Aldines, the Giuntas, the Stephans, and other celebrated Printers.

CHAPTER XX

LEAVES AND FLOWERS
FROM NATURE

W e have endeavoured to show in the preceding chapters, that in the best periods of art all ornament was rather based upon an observation of the principles which regulate the arrangement of form in nature, than on an attempt to imitate the absolute forms of those works; and that whenever this limit was exceeded in any art, it was one of the strongest symptoms of decline: true art consisting in idealising, and not copying, the forms of nature.

We think it desirable to insist rather strongly on this point, as, in the present uncertain state in which we are, there seems a general disposition arising to reproduce, as faithfully as may be possible, natural form as works of ornament. The world has become weary of the external repetition of the same conventional forms which have been borrowed from styles which have passed away, and therefore can excite in us but little sympathy. There has risen, we say, a universal cry of "Go back to nature, as the ancients did;" we should be amongst the first to echo that cry, but it will depend much on what we go to seek, how far we may succeed. If we go to nature as the Egyptians and the Greeks went, we may hope; but if we go there like the Chinese, or even as the Gothic artists of the fourteenth and fifteenth centuries, we should gain but little. We have already, in the floral carpets, floral papers, and floral carvings of the present day, sufficient evidence to show that no art can be produced by such means; and that the more closely nature is copied, the farther we are removed from producing a work of art.

Although ornament is most properly only an accessory to architecture, and should never be allowed to usurp the place of structural features, or to overload or to disguise them, it is in all cases the very soul of an architectural monument.

By the ornament of a building we can judge more truly of the creative power which the artist has brought to bear upon the work. The general proportions of the building may be good, the mouldings may be more or less accurately copied from the most approved models; but the very instant that ornament is attempted, we see how far the architect is at the same time the artist. It is the best measure of the care and refinement bestowed upon the work. To put ornament in the right place is not easy; to render that ornament at the same time a superadded beauty and an expression of the intention of the whole work, is still more difficult.

Unfortunately, it has been too much the practice in our time to abandon to hands most unfitted for the task the adornment of the structural features of buildings, and more especially their interior decorations.

The fatal facility of manufacturing ornament which the revived use of the acanthus leaf has given, has tended very much to this result, and deadened the creative instinct in artists' minds. What could so readily be done by another, they have left that other to do; and so far have abdicated their high position of the architect, the head and chief.

How, then, is this universal desire for progress to be satisfied—how is any new style of ornament to be invented or developed? Some will probably say, A new style of architecture must first be found, and we should be beginning at the wrong end to commence with ornament.

We do not think so. We have already shown that the desire for works of ornament is co-existent with the earliest attempts of civilisation of every people; and that architecture adopts ornament, does not create it.

The Corinthian order of architecture is said to have been suggested by an acanthus leaf found growing round an earthen pot; but the acanthus leaf existed as an ornament long before, or, at all events, the principle of its growth was observed in the conventional ornaments. It was the peculiar application of this leaf to the formation of the capital of a column which was the sudden invention that created the Corinthian order.

The principle of the foliation, and even the general form of the leaves, which predominate in the architecture of the thirteenth century, existed long before in the illuminated MSS.; and derived as they were, most probably, from the East, have given an almost Eastern character to early English ornament. The architects of the thirteenth century were, therefore, very familiar with this system of ornamentation; and we cannot doubt, that one cause of the adoption so universally of this style during the thirteenth century arose from the great familiarity with its leading forms which already existed.

The floral style, in direct imitation of nature, which succeeded, was also preceded by the same style in works of ornament. The facility of painting flowers in direct imitation of nature in the pages of a missal, induced an attempt to rival them in stone in the buildings of the time.

The architectural ornament of the Elizabethan period is mostly a reproduction of the works of the loom, the painter, and the engraver. In any borrowed style, more especially, this would be so. The artists in the Elizabethan period were necessarily much more familiar with the paintings, hangings, furniture, metal-work, and other articles of luxury, which England received from the Continent, than they would be with the architectural monuments; and it is this familiarity with the ornamentation of the period, but imperfect knowledge of the architecture, which led to the development of those peculiarities which distinguish Elizabethan architecture from the purer architecture of the Revival.

We therefore think we are justified in the belief, that a new style of ornament may be produced independently of a new style of architecture; and, moreover, that it would be one of the readiest means of arriving at a new style: for instance, if we could only arrive at the invention of a new termination to a means of support, one of the most difficult points would be accomplished.

The chief features of a building which form a style are, first, the means of support; secondly, the means of spanning space between the supports; and, thirdly, the formation of the roof. It is the decoration of these structural features which gives the characteristics of style, and they all follow so naturally one from the other, that the invention of one will command the rest.

It would appear, at first sight, that the means of varying these structural features had been exhausted, and that we have nothing left but to use either the one or the other of the systems which have already run their course.

If we reject the use of the column and horizontal beam of the Greeks and Egyptians, the round arch of the Romans, the pointed arch and vault of the Middle Ages, and the domes of the Mohammedans, it will be asked—What is left? We shall perhaps be told that all the means of covering space have already been exhausted, and that it were vain to look for other forms. But could not this have been said in all time? Could the Egyptian have ever imagined that any other mode of spanning space would ever be found than his huge blocks of stone? Could the Mediæval architect have ever dreamed that his airy vaults could be surpassed, and that gulfs could be crossed by hollow tubes of iron? Let us not despair; the world has not seen, most assuredly, the last of the architectural systems. If we are now passing through an age of copying, and architecture with us exhibits a want of vitality, the world has passed through similar periods before. From the present chaos there will arise, undoubtedly, (it may not be in our time), an architecture which shall be worthy of the high advance which man has made in every other direction towards the possession of the tree of knowledge.

To return to our subject,—How is any new style of art or new style of ornament to be formed, or even attempted to be formed? In the first place, we have little hope that we are destined to see more than the commencement of a change; the architectural profession is at the present time too much under the influence of past education on the one hand, and too much influenced by an ill-informed public on the other: but the rising generation in both classes are born under happier auspices, and it is to them we must look for hope in the future. It is for their use that we have gathered together this collection of the works of the past; not that they should be slavishly copied, but that artists should, by an attentive examination of the principles which pervade all the works of the past, and which have excited universal admiration, be led to the creation of new forms equally beautiful. We believe that if a student in the arts, earnest in his search after knowledge, will only lay aside all temptation to indolence, will examine for himself the works of the past, compare them with the works of nature, bend his mind to a thorough appreciation of the principles which reign in each, he cannot fail to be himself a creator, and to individualise new forms, instead of reproducing the forms of the past. We think it impossible that a student fully impressed with the law of the universal fitness of things in nature, with the wonderful variety of form, yet all arranged around some few fixed laws, the proportionate distribution of areas, the tangential curvatures of lines, and the radiation from a parent stem, whatever type he may borrow from Nature, if he will dismiss from his mind the desire to imitate it, but will only seek to follow still the path which it so plainly shows him, we doubt not that new forms of beauty will more readily arise under his hand, than can ever follow from a continuation in the prevailing fashion of resting only on the works of the past for present inspiration. It will require but a few minds to give the first impulse: the way once pointed out, others will follow, readily improving, refining upon each other's efforts, till another culminating point of Art shall be again reached, to subside into decline and disorder. For the present, however, we are far enough removed from either stage.

We have been desirous to aid this movement to the extent of our power; and in the ten plates of leaves and flowers which accompany this chapter, we have gathered together many of those natural types which we thought best calculated to awaken a recognition of the natural laws which prevail in the distribution of form. But, indeed, these laws will be found to be so universal that they are as well seen in one leaf as in a thousand. The single example of the chestnut leaf, Plate XCI. *(page 480)*, contains the whole of the laws which are to be found in Nature; no art can rival the perfect grace of its form, the perfect proportional distribution of the areas, the radiation from the parent stem, the tangential curvatures of the lines, or the even distribution of the surface decoration. We may gather this from a single leaf. But if we further study the law of their growth, we may see in an assemblage of leaves of the vine or the ivy, that the same law which prevails in the formation of the single leaf prevails also in the assemblage of leaves. As in the chestnut leaf, Plate XCI., the area of each lobe diminishes in equal proportion as it approaches the stem, so in any combination of leaves each leaf is everywhere in harmony with the group; as in one leaf the areas are so perfectly distributed that the repose of the eye is maintained, it is equally so in the group; we never find a disproportionate leaf interfering to destroy the repose of the group. This universal law of equilibrium is everywhere apparent in Plates XCVIII., XCIX., C *(pages 487–89)*. The same laws prevail in the distribution of lines on the surface of flowers; not a line upon the surfaces but tends more surely to develop the form,—not a line which could be removed, and leave the form more perfect, and this, why? Because the beauty arises naturally from the law of the growth of each plant. The life-blood,—the sap, as it leaves the stem, takes the readiest way of reaching the confines of the surface, however varied that surface may be; the greater the distance it has to travel, or the weight it has to support, the thicker will be its substance. (See Convolvulus, XCVIII., XCIX.)

On Plate XCVIII. we have shown several varieties of flowers, in plan and elevation, from which it will be seen that the basis of all form is geometry, the impulse which forms the surface, starting from the centre with equal force, necessarily stops at equal distances; the result is symmetry and regularity.

Who, then, will dare say that there is nothing left for us but to copy the five or seven-lobed flowers of the thirteenth century; the Honeysuckle of the Greeks or the Acanthus of the Romans,—that this alone can produce art? Is Nature so tied? See how various the forms, and how unvarying the principles. We feel persuaded that there is yet a future open to us; we have but to arouse from our slumbers. The Creator has not made all things beautiful, that we should thus set a limit to our admiration; on the contrary, as all His works are offered for our enjoyment, so are they offered for our study. They are there to awaken a natural instinct implanted in us,—a desire to emulate in the works of our hands the order, the symmetry, the grace, the fitness, which the Creator has sown broadcast over the earth.

In this chapter Jones had some assistance from Christopher Dresser (1834–1904), a young man who would later become one of the great names of Victorian design. By the age of 20 he was already lecturing on botany, and one of his earliest publications was the influential study of *Botany as Adapted to the Arts and Art Manufactures* (1857–58). Dresser's philosophy of design owed much to A. W. N. Pugin and Jones; indeed, he gave a lecture on the latter at Jones's Memorial Exhibition (1874). His own work was remarkably versatile, including designs for porcelain, furniture, glass, textiles, and cast iron. In later years he became noted for his interest in oriental art, producing a major survey of *Japan, its Architecture, Art and Art Manufactures* (1882).

PLATE XCI

1 Horse-chestnut Leaves. Traced from Natural Leaves.

1

PLATE XCII

Flowers were often employed as symbolic elements in ornamental patterns. Ivy (*right*, Nos. 1–5), for example, was widely used in Christian manuscripts. Its trailing form made it an ideal component for decorative borders and large initials. At the same time its status as an evergreen plant meant that it could also represent the hope of eternal life, as promised in the Christian scriptures. Similarly the fig leaf (*far right*, No. 3) was an emblem of Buddha, featuring prominently in oriental decoration, while the laurel (*far right*, No. 5) was sacred to Apollo— through his role as the leader of the Muses it became a conventional symbol for literary and artistic achievement.

PLATE XCIII

1 Ivy Palmata.
2, 3, 4, and 5 Common Ivy.
Traced from Natural Leaves.

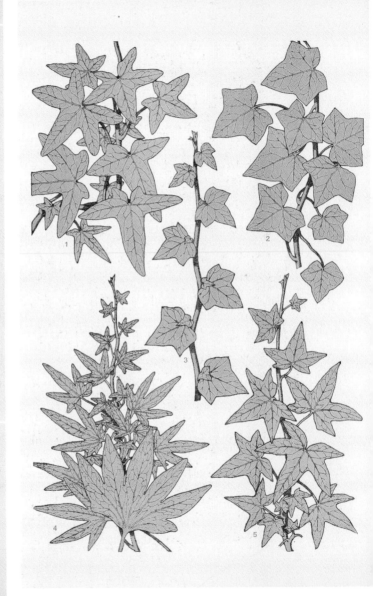

PLATE XCIV

1 White Oak.
2 Scarlet Oak.
3 Fig-tree.
4 White Bryony.
5 Laurel.
6 Maple.
7 Bay-tree.
Traced from Natural Leaves.

🎋 The subject of floral decoration was highly topical in the design world of the nineteenth century. It had been brought to the fore by A. W. N. Pugin's final book, *Floriated Ornament*, which was published in 1849. In this important study the author endeavored to show how plant forms had inspired the great architectural achievements of the Middle Ages. He also believed that they had a major part to play in modern design, arguing that "by disposing natural leaves and flowers in geometrical forms, the most exquisite combinations are produced . . . " Pugin's book was enthusiastically received and no doubt influenced the work of Jones, Christopher Dresser *(see page 480)*, and William Morris *(see pages 334, 418, 468)*.

PLATE XCV

1 Vine.
2 Holly.
3 Oak.
4 Turkey Oak.
5 Laburnum.
Traced from Natural Leaves.

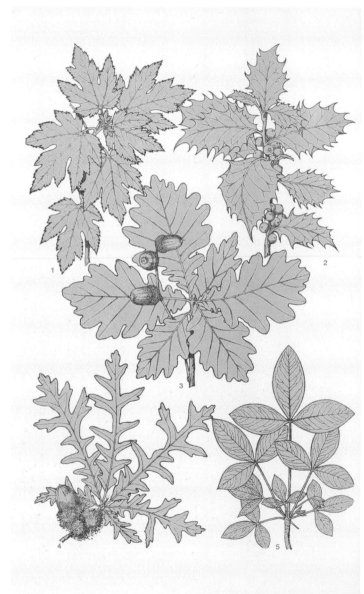

PLATE XCVI

1 Wild Rose.
2 Ivy.
3 Blackberry.
Traced from Natural Leaves.

Christopher Dresser's colorful study of flowers *(far right)* stands out from the other illustrations in this section. It is designed to show the underlying geometry of botanical specimens, which A. W. N. Pugin had previously noted, but it also resembles the host of flower prints that were produced during this period. The immediate stimulus for these came from the growing fashion for conservatories in Victorian homes. Gardening became a popular pursuit for the middle classes, encouraged by numerous illustrated books on the subject. One of the most successful figures in this field was Jane Loudun (1807–58), who became a household name with books such as *The Ladies' Flower Garden of Ornamental Annuals* (1842).

PLATE XCVII

Hawthorn, Yew, Ivy, and Strawberry-tree. Traced from Nature.

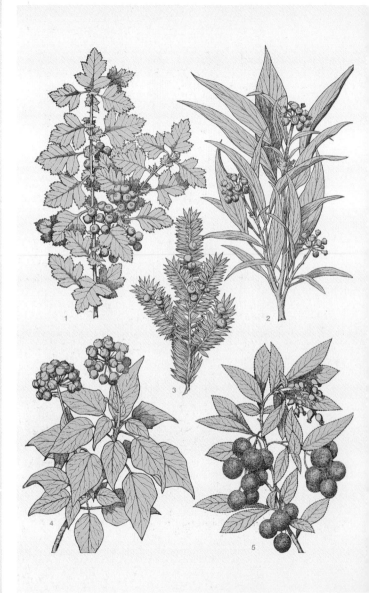

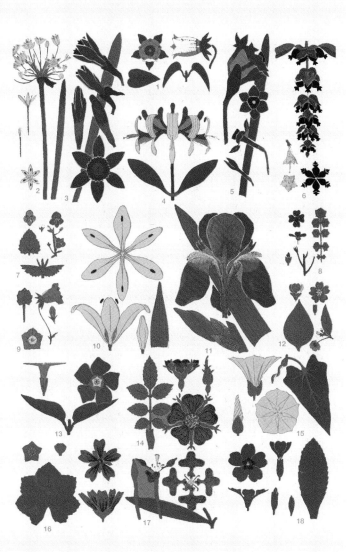

PLATE XCVIII

Plans and Elevations of Flowers.

1 Glossocomia clematidea.
2 Onion.
3 Daffodil.
4 Honeysuckle.
5 Narcissus.
6 Leycesteria formosa.
7 Speedwell.
8 Ladies' Smock.
9 Harebell.
10 White Lily.
11 Isis.
12 Mouse-ear.
13 Periwinkle.
14 Dog-Rose.
15 Convolvulus.
16 Mallow.
17 Clarkia.
18 Primrose.

Jones's appeal for a systematic use of floral ornament would eventually bear fruit in the work of William Morris (1834–96). Widely acknowledged as one of the founding fathers of the Arts and Crafts Movement, this prolific artist revolutionized Victorian design, after setting up the firm of Morris, Marshall, Faulkner & Co. in 1861. Under its auspices he produced designs for a wide range of goods, including carpets, tapestries, wallpaper, and tiles. Many of these consisted of simple, repeated patterns, composed of flowing arrangements of stylized flowers and plants. Honeysuckle (*right*, No. 1) was one of Morris's favorite motifs, featuring prominently in wallpapers, chintzes, and the celebrated *Woodpecker Tapestry* (1885).

PLATE XCIX

1 Honeysuckle.
2 Convolvulus.

PLATE C

1 Passion Flowers.

Owen Jones:

A CHRONOLOGY

1809   Born in Thames Street, London.

1825   Becomes a pupil of Lewis Vulliamy.

1830   Visits Paris, Rome, and Venice.

1833   Journeys to Alexandria, Cairo, Thebes, and Constantinople.

1834   Initial stay at Granada.

1836   Publishes the first part of *Plans, Elevations, Sections, and Details of the Alhambra* (completed 1845).

1837   Further stay at the Alhambra.

1841   Decorates the interior of Christ Church, Streatham.

1842   Produces *Designs for Mosaic and Tessellated Pavements*.

1843   Provides illustrations for *Views on the Nile* and designs for *Encaustic Tiles*.

1845   Designs two Moorish-style houses in Kensington Palace Gardens, London.

1849   Publication of *The Illuminated Books of the Middle Ages*.

1850   Appointed joint architect of the Great Exhibition; decorates the apse of Vulliamy's All Saints, Ennismore Gardens, London.

1851   The Great Exhibition opens in Hyde Park.

1852   Appointed director of Decorations for the new Crystal Palace exhibition; teaches at the Department of Science and Art in the South Kensington Museum.

1854   Exhibition opens at the Crystal Palace, now relocated in Sydenham.

1856   Publication of *The Grammar of Ornament*.

1857   Receives a gold medal from the Royal Institute of British Architects.

1858   Architect of St. James's Hall, London (demolished).

1862   Awarded a medal at the Paris International Exhibition.

1863   Decorates the home of George Eliot.

1867   Produces *Examples of Chinese Ornament*.

1871   Advises George Eliot on the cover of her novel, *Middlemarch*.

1873   Receives a medal at the Vienna Exhibition.

1874   Dies at his home in Argyll Place, Regent Street, London. Buried in Kensal Green cemetery.

Index to the Commentaries and Introduction

INDEX TO OWEN JONES'S TEXT